GUIDE FOR THE BEDEVILLED

GUIDE FOR THE BEDEVILLED

BEN HECHT

MILA PRESS
Jerusalem, 1996

Library of Congress Catalog Card Number 96-077363

A Guide for the Bedevilled by Ben Hecht

ISBN: 0-9646886-2-X

MILAH Press
POB 267
New London, NH 03257

MILAH Publications
POB 2765
Jerusalem, Israel 91027

Printed in Israel

A NOTE TO READERS

We live in an information age. There is too much information to assimilate. To form an intelligent opinion on any given issue, out of the confusion of conflicting presentations, is difficult to say the least. Every once in a while, however, in the midst of it all, there comes along a really special book.

This book has the ring of authenticity - it provides a depth of understanding and insight that one did not have before reading the book. Sometimes it is a comforting book. And sometimes it is frightening to read, such as a book which shares the tragic ineffectiveness and even evil which lurks in an establishment as it turns its back on mass murder. Always however such a book opens up to us the possibility of real growth.

There is no clearer description that I can give you of the kind of book that I am thinking about. I hope you know what I mean.

It is those "really special" books which we want to make available to you through Milah Press.

We of course know that we may not always see eye to eye on what constitutes a "really special" book. That's okay. I suspect that we will find enough common language to enjoy reading together. For us, Milah Press is one way to participate in making the world a better place. We are honored to have you as our partners.

RABBI MORDECHAI GAFNI, Director and Scholar-in-residence
MILAH
JERUSALEM

INTRODUCTION TO THE SECOND EDITION

If Ben Hecht had been in the crowd thrilling to the "new clothes" of the king in Hans Christian Anderson's famous fable, it would not have fallen to a young child to cry out: "The king has no clothes on!" Hecht was constitutionally unable to dissimulate.

Fifty years after the end of World War II, some historians still try to convince us that the Jews of the 1930s and 1940s did not know what was going on, simply could not believe that the land of Goethe could murder millions of Jews. Ben Hecht *knew* and *said so*, because, unlike most of the Jewish leaders around him, he could not cry out anything other than the obvious fact that the Germans were murderers and were killing the Jews of Europe.

Hecht was writing his *Guide for the Bedevilled* in 1943. He wrote of the murder of over 3,000,000 Jews and tried to help others see and understand the horrible reality that confronted them. He recounted the long history of German cruelty and cited Nietzsche's contempt for the backwardness, vulgarity, and brutality of his fellow Germans.

Nietzsche died in 1900 and knew no Nazis. And it was pre-Nazi Germans that Hecht personally saw mercilessly killing over 2,000 German political prisoners in 1921. Perched high in a tree outside Moabit prison, he peered at the bloody spectacle through powerful binoculars. And he wrote about it. His account was printed in newspapers all over the world. The account is here, in his *Guide for the Bedevilled*. Hecht saw naked the German murderers and called them what they were.

Ben Hecht would have liked Professor Daniel Jonah Goldhagen. Goldhagen, who recently published *Hitler and His Willing Executioners,* gives the lie to those who believe that academicians cannot do unbiased research and report their findings in clear, undisguised prose. Note the similarities in the following paragraphs, the first from Hecht's book, published in 1944 and the second from Goldhagen's book, published fity-two years later, in 1996:

> "The Germans sat at desks and held conferences, discussing the most economical way to murder Jews. The Germans at those desks were not fantastic Germans. They were usual Germans....At these desks were all the German students and leaders and polite citizens whom we will see again when, as tourists, we visit the streets of conquered Berlin." (Hecht, *Guide for the Bedevilled,* p. 142).

> "The first task in restoring the perpetrators to the center of our understanding of the Holocaust is to restore to them their identities, grammatically by using not the passive but the active voice in order to ensure that they, the actors, are not absent from their own deeds (as in, "five hundred Jews were killed in city X on date Y"), and by eschewing convenient, yet often inappropriate and obfuscating labels, like "Nazis" and "SS men," and calling them what they were, "Germans." The most appropriate, indeed the only appropriate *general* proper name for the Germans who perpetrated the Holocaust is "Germans." (Goldhagen, *Hitler and His Willing Executioners,* pp. 5-6).

Goldhagen's meticulous research and unvarnished reporting of his conclusions have been met with dismay by some, including Professor Yehuda Bauer, considered by many as the "dean" of Holocaust historians. Hecht knew well the Professor Bauers of his day. Of them he wrote: "The villain who halts our pens is also called by the name Good Taste. Virtue is to an ugly woman what good taste is to a stupid man - a false riches. Writers who are too timorous, too vacuous, too thin-hearted, to set to paper anything but the dullest of matters...are obviously not people to tackle the Germans."

Ben Hecht was arguably the most succesful and influential writer in the history of Hollywood. But his influence reached far beyond that Tinseltown. The famous industrialist, Bernard Baruch, was dispatched by President Roosevelt to quiet Hecht's widely read protests against American silence and inaction *vis-a-vis* the murder of European Jewry. On May 9, 1943, over 40,000 people saw his Madison Square Guarden production "We Will Never Die." When the dramatization moved on to Washington, several Supreme Court justices and Roosevelt administration members were in the audience.

To mine the riches of this book, many will want to read it more than one time or two. It is a rare glimpse into the mind of a great writer, a brilliant observer of human nature, an honest man.

In writing of his mission to "remember these Germans," Hecht wrote: "I shall keep their name in a lime kiln of my own until I am dead. And I shall bear witness after I am dead - if there are any ears to listen."

Hecht died in 1962. *Guide for the Bedevilled* has been out of print for many years. Milah Press has reprinted it to help Ben Hecht bear witness after his death, if there are any eyes to read. The dedication and preface which follow are the same as appeared in the 1944 edition.

DAVID MORRISON

DEDICATION AND PREFACE

To Jenny, Aged 3 Days

Old Woman, were you ever like my daughter, newly born?
Old man, did such contentment ever star your brow?
What a difference appears to all the world when I look on my daughter, newly born.
Where is the world gone that has lost her face?
I marvel that statesmen once had hands so small and spirits so divine.
I marvel that warriors came all to being with a helpless, trusting gurgle much like hers.
I marvel that all the crude, half-mad, half-evil cry of men with things embattled - began thus,
Began with soft enthusiasm for nothing but the air and light;
Began with graceful look at things unknown,
Began with clear eyes and with tiny, clownish innocence believing in the warmth of God.
All the soldiers dying were like her,
All the angry and tormented ones,
All the fools and scoundrels and all the ogres of unreason
Were like her -
With face no larger than a heart,
Began like her, no more ruffled than the dew tiptoeing on the grass.
Where did the robbery take place?
Where was she stolen from the world, and all the world left without an elfin bugle blowing,
Without a breath of Eden stirring except on my daughter's face - newly born?

A Guide for the Bedevilled

I DECIDE TO WRITE A BOOK

I was lunching with a famous lady, a lady a little lacking in wit but full of very high-sounding ideas. If you were in doubt concerning the meanings of freedom and liberty you could ask this lady and receive the most lyrical of answers. I can best describe her by confessing that she was more famous than intelligent - which is one of the hazards of democracy.

In New York you can pick out easily the people of fame. They look and walk like pall bearers. Perhaps this is because they are carrying truth and beauty to their graves. Or perhaps it is because they are merely stiffened with their press notices and as conscious of their fame as if it were a paraffin injected into their veins.

Whenever I met this lady with whom I was lunching, I wondered if Joan of Arc or Semiramis, the one-breasted queen of the Amazons, had been as full of visible importance. I doubt it, for the importance of spiritual and royal leaders is a small thing beside the strut of those who wear the paper crowns of ideas.

This lady and I have known each other for some years and our meetings have been always of an amiable nature. We admired each other but, having ideas more or less alike, there was never much we could talk about. There is nothing as dull as an intellectual ally - after a certain age.

Our lunch this time was a bit duller than usual. We gossiped aimlessly for an hour on the stupidity of the movies, the stupidity of the theater, and the stupidity of literature - from which it can be seen that we were avoiding any topics of importance. We moved into the library, rather elegantly, to have our coffee.

Here my hostess fell silent and took to regarding me with a rolling and pregnant eye. Her fine brow became full of furrows and, by this and other signs, I knew she was deep in thought, or possibly working around to asking some favor of me.

"I would like you to tell me something, very frankly," she said, finally. "Do you mind talking about Jews?"

"It is one of my favorite topics," I answered, lying gallantly - for at that time, a year ago, it was a topic with which I had hardly more than flirted.

"I am very glad," she said. "Jews are often a little skittish about the subject."

"You don't have to be too tactful," I said. "Jewishness is not a venereal disease."

"I was sure you'd feel just that way," she said, "because, after all, you are not the kind of a Jew who thinks that any discussion of Jews is intended as a personal slight."

"No, I am not that kind of Jew," I said soothingly.

But I was socially a little surprised. It had never occurred to me that my friend regarded me as a Jew of any kind. I sat up. Here was the little slap that pinks the face of the American Jew. He fancies himself a social, spiritual, and literary ally - an individual colored only by his ideas and achievements - and presto! he hears his true name called over a coffee cup. My hostess was looking at something special - not quite a dinosaur, but a Jew. Her eyes were a trifle defiant and her cheeks flushed. I was aware that after many years of intellectual kinship, a divorce had taken place. We were no longer two Americans in a library, as alike as the stripes on our flag. We were a pair of unrelated and mysterious coffee drinkers.

I beamed at the lady, for it was an important moment in my life - the first in which I had ever been addressed as a Jew - and thus called upon to be one.

"What do you want to know about Jews?" I asked.

"A great deal," she said, "a very great deal."

"My information is a little limited," I said. "Renan is a better authority. There is also a magnificent modern scholar named Klausner. He lives in Palestine."

"That's the whole trouble!" she cried. "Scholars, historians! They can tell us nothing about Jews. But *you* can. Because you are the greatest sort of authority - the thinking Jew. The Jew who knows himself."

The compliment confused me and I was silent.

"I would like to know," she went on, "how *you* explain the unpopularity of the Jews. I mean, what do you think it is about the Jew that makes him so constant a victim? What is it in him that attracts so much anger and arouses people everywhere?"

The question embarrassed me. It had too much eagerness in it. It did not seem to ask for an answer so much as to make an unanswerable statement - that the Jews were to blame for their unpopularity. I had the impression that my hostess was accusing me of withholding vital information from the world. She seemed to be asking me, as a Jew, to break down and confess something that would clear up the murder of the three million Jews of Europe and also throw a light on the true secret of anti-Semitism everywhere.

"Don't you see that only a Jew can speak on this subject," she said, "because he is actually inside it? Not outside it."

The picture came to me of an angry policeman badgering a corpse for explanations of the crime committed against it. I am not a corpse, nor do I even feel myself a victim. Nor do I bear the marks of blows that have laid low other Jews. I was not in the picture - but it was there.

"The Jews complain," she spoke on, "they suffer dreadfully. And they accuse. But they never stop to reason or to explain or to figure the thing out and tell the world what they, and only they, know."

The picture of my hostess became clearer. She was a policeman intent on solving a crime by arresting the corpse.

"You are asking for introspection from Amos Lasky," I said."

"Who is Amos Laskey?" she demanded.

"Amos is a gentleman who was mugged last week," I said. "He was returning home from a card party and five hoodlums beat him up and took his winnings away. He died in Bellevue Hospital this morning, leaving a wife and three children."

"Nothing of the sort," she said. "Jews are not Amos-victims. They are - how shall I put it? - collaborative victims, a thing they refuse to see. I am asking them only to help clear up a situation that has become too wretched, too horrible to go on in the dark. And I am asking you to use your mind."

She continued to stride and speak, and I did as she requested. I used my mind, but in silence. For my thoughts had a greater fascination for me than they might for her. I thought, as she flung her humanitarian phrases about the library - a library filled with the noblest minds of the modern centuries - that my hostess was suffering from a malady become as common in the world as the head cold. She had picked up some anti-Semitism germs. There was yet no fever, but the sneeze was there. This lady, who had stood for years on the side of the angels, was giving voice to attitudes a trifle short of divine. It was a melancholy thing to hear. I wondered where the germs had come from and how this lapse had happened.

Perhaps her querulous feeling about Jews was based only on the fact that the Jews were complaining so much against their extermination. Cries for help are always irksome to the preoccupied humanitarian. Or perhaps she was preparing herself to forgive the Germans, now that they were losing the war. She had a hatred of Nazism, but she had always insisted that the German people were a fine folk and that they were more the victims of Nazism that even its enemies. I can see this argument but I do not understand it. It is like arguing: who commits the murder? - the man who fires the gun or the gun that shoots? The man who fires is obviously a murderer but obviously, too, the gun that shoots is no feather duster. In fact, without his weapon obligingly at hand, the murderer is harmless.

"The Germans," cried my hostess, as if reading my thoughts, "are not a race of killers, fiends, of a special and different sort of sub-human beings. You cannot say that as a man of intelligence."

"Yes, I can," I said.

"No, you are speaking now only as a Jew," my hostess pointed out triumphantly. "You are emotional and one-sided. I'm rather surprised."

The certainty grew in me that she was engaged in a political war within herself. She was doing her best to shift the blame of the millions of murdered Jews from the fine Germans to the dubious Jews themselves; not all the blame, but enough to remove murder as a political issue. This would require considerable legerdemain, but I had no doubts she would succeed. Anti-Semitism is an easy trick even for the most amateur of villains. It is more than a trick. It is an oasis in which saints can disport themselves lecherously, a little ward of lunacy in which philosophers can relax, and a prescription for the cure of acne, frost bite, ulcers, and many other diseases. My hostess, who was saint, philosopher, and invalid - along with her many other callings - would find, before she was done, much riches in anti-Semitism.

The telephone, much as it does on stage, ended our scene. My hostess had appointments with Liberty and Freedom in a number of places. We shook hands gingerly.

"I would like to discuss the matter more fully with you," she said.

"You mean about what's wrong with the Jews?" I said.

"Not wrong," she smiled. "It is not a matter of right and wrong. It is a matter of aloof psychological inquiry."

"It is that," I agreed.

"We might do something together on the subject that would be of great help," she said.

I thought this over as I walked away. I decided I would do something about the subject, but without the further help of my hostess. She had assisted me enough. I decided I would write a book and try to put in it the little of what I knew about Jews and the great deal that I knew about their enemies. No such urgent decision had ever commanded me before.

IT IS A VERY DIFFICULT BOOK

When I wrote a daily column recently for a newspaper in New York I composed occasional articles about Jews and ventured once or twice a month into the discussion of anti-Semitism. This was always a literary gesture comparable to sticking your head in a lion's mouth.

Each article I wrote resulted in a great deal of mail arriving at my desk. More than half the communications were from Jews. They were usually indignant with me for having misstated the case, betrayed the Jews, and added my wretched talents to their misfortunes. Many berated me for writing about Jews at all and offered (a little hysterically) the theory that the solution of the Jewish problem lay in not calling anybody's attention to it. These critics told me that they themselves were Americans and not Jews and that Jew-consciousness was a spiritual ghetto into which they refused to be driven. And shame on me for driving them! I answered as best as I could that it was seemingly a spiritual ghetto out of which they refused to be rescued; for it is obvious to me that the fear of being Jews is about the only thing that distinguishes Jews adversely. It is a fear that lessens all their valor, that makes the proudest of them look foolish, and the most intelligent of them sound mysteriously like liars. I have seen this fear protruding like a large patch in the striped pants of the most elegant and important Jews - and making them seem always a little comically dressed at their lordliest functions.

Another part of my correspondence was from readers who had a loud, but anonymous, distaste for Jews. They filled my mail with attacks on me and "my kind" that lacked syntax, logic, and signature, but were as full of hate as the jog trot of a lynching mob.

There were also readers who forwarded me religious brochures and assured me that if I read them and became a Christian my troubles would be over. These advices usually came from the far West.

Of favorable communications, there were a small, but pleasing, number. Though a minority, the spirit of these seemed to outweigh all the caterwaulings that filled the other envelopes. It was not toward my ideas that these expressed favor as much as it was for their own egos that they raised a shout. They were stormy, unafraid Jews - illiterate youths, businessmen, scholars. They were people full of a health and gayety that was as refreshing as a wind from the sea. The heavy hand of anti-Semitism had swung vainly at their middles. They dodged as gracefully and powerfully as that little ring general who was Ruby Goldstein, and known in fight circles as the Galloping Ghost. They were as gay as Americans, and never as nervous as Jews. It is for these I write. But it is all the others, I hope, who will read me.

All in all, from the responses to my previous writing about Jews, I learned one thing - that the subject is a moody one, and that a writer seeking to endear himself had better avoid it. The warning has failed to instruct me. For the decision that came to me was an urgent one. I have a mission to write about Jews. I have a mission, also, to write about anti-Semites. And this, too, elates me more that any task to which I ever have set myself.

There are several difficulties that worry me as I start. One of them is important. It is the look and sound of my country. I doubt if there was ever a brighter land than mine. I have hailed it eagerly since I was old enough to see to the top of its buildings. I have enjoyed it and prospered in it. Its history makes the finest page of print I know. For it is a history of honorable intentions, of human goals and not Arcs de Triomphe. To write of its underworld of irration and bigotry is a depressing business. And if I succeed in making the USA - home of the free - seem only a breeding ground for anti-Semites, I will be doing as glum a disservice as was ever done a land.

I make a distinction in my mind. It is not of my country I write. The USA, as it speaks its disordered and exuberant say on the world stage, is a healthy orator. I applaud. If my orator has at moments a bilious look in his eye, it will pass. It will not survive the roaring of his lungs. And if he pauses to gargle in public, I am willing to bide my time until he recovers his manners. He is an orator who finishes always to applause.

Such I conceive my country to be and I do not write of it - any more than the astronomer writes of angels when he records the fall of meteors. They are from the heavens, but are no part of them. I write of these excrescences that tumble wantonly and dangerously out of our democratic skies. I write, not of my country's amiability, which is as wide as its prairies, but of the cinders and refuse falling on it.

I write not of its intellect, but of its intellectual slums where the anti-Semites cluster, of its dawning cynicism and its war-sickened nerves that are the wrangling parents of anti-Semitism.

I write of fools, pip-squeaks, social impostors, spiritual harelips, tormented homosexuals, lonely sadists, intellectual bankrupts; of unctuous gossip-mongers for whom speech is a form of masturbation; of bile peddlers, and invalids whose teeth ache, whose bladders drip and whose hearts are a sackful of worms; of religious zanies who woo God by spitting in His eye, and anti-religious zanies who fill the dark of their heads with ugly screams; of cunning rabble-rousers lusting for a nickel's worth of power, and of the dough-headed rabble ever ready with its false coin and its sickly cheers; I write of all that mincing and bepimpled, clapper-tongued and swivel-brained tribe of lame ducks who make up the ranks of the anti-Semites. They are a cinder in my orator's eye. Perhaps I can help him fish it out.

My other difficulties are chiefly those of authorship. I have experienced these before - for there is no villain as troublesome as the untouched sheet of white paper - but this is the first time I have troubled a reader with them. The grunts of composition are not for his ears. But this is an odd enterprise. I am not writing a book that is already in my head. I am investigating publicly, exposing my mind spontaneously to the reader, and I am a little alarmed at the disorder in store for him. For the investigation of anti-Semitism is not a hunt for a collar button. It is a look everywhere. It is a study of history such as never has been made, and a life course in all the sciences. It makes a mock of scholarship and there are no boundaries to enclose the pursuit.

Since I cannot, however I prod myself, hope to look everywhere or come out of this bout against twenty-eight hundred years of unreason with too reasonable an air, I shall peer only where it pleases me and hit only where I see a fetching target.

You can be sure that no work of scholarship will result. You can be sure, also, that I shall blunder into contradictions that a child of four (let alone a critic) will be able to spot in a twinkling (and what a lot of fun this is for such critical fishermen, to whom the ocean is famous for its yield of minnows). And you can be sure that I shall come out from various phases of the scrimmage with no more evidence of victory to offer than a black eye. During all this darting about, the continuity of my effort may seem somewhat absent. I may seem to be running backward, or to have stopped moving entirely, or to have vanished with a squeak down a rat hole. But the continuity, movement and sapience will all be there. They will lie in my dedication to my mission. However jumpy my parables and autobiographical discourses may become, behind them all will remain the double mission I have mentioned - to write of Jews with love and of their enemies with something else.

I hope that the gladness I feel in this missionary work will sustain my readers through any tortuous passages, and that it will serve to cement all my flights, rambles, stumbles and creepings into the autobiography of an idea.

THE GLIMMERINGS OF A PREMISE

I will begin by stating a fact not to be argued with. Such facts are rare, even in science. But the Jews have one to offer.

The Jew can be charged with the longest-standing crime in history. He has been able for two thousand years to turn his neighbor into a jackass. In many lands and for long periods of time this has been practically his only accomplishment.

The long tale of anti-Semitism is the account of hysterias evoked by the Jew, and evoked not so much by his antics nor his qualities as by the simple black magic of his name. Otherwise worthy peoples given to fine mottoes have, on beholding the Jew in their midst, fallen into brutality and irration.

There are many explanations of the unpopularity of the Jew. Much less attention has been given to the psychology of his host of ill-wishers.

When we write of the Jewish problem we usually write about Jews. This is like describing a building in terms of its nails. The Jews are the nails that hold the structure of anti-Semitism together, and, true enough, without new Jews being constantly nailed into its props and beams, cellars and steeples, the hobgoblin edifice would fall apart.

I shall not limit my investigation to this ancient and immemorial keg of nails.

THE OBVIOUS VERSUS X

We writers seldom say that the anti-Semite is the eternal booby beating the drums of unreason. If we do make such statements, they are made chiefly by poets talking to themselves or by philosophers (not many of them) who speak a language only of whispers.

There are a hundred thousand reasons for this, two of which occur to me now. The Jew is a fully dramatized figure. The veriest ninny of a writer can present you with an arresting puppet labeled "Jew." He requires no research and less lucubration. The Jew waits in the wings, fully caparisoned and completely dialogued. Any bumpkin can whistle him on stage.

This is one reason the Jew is easy to write about. The other reason is even more active. The enemy of the Jew is not easy to write about. You cannot whistle him on stage. You must coax him on with the languages of all the sciences. For a look at the enemy of the Jew you need history, psychiatry, biology, economics, and a sense of despair. He is too big a character, this enemy. His name is the Mind of Man and its deplorable Underworld.

I am neither wise, witty, nor despairing enough to bring this enemy on stage. But I promise you the stage will not remain empty - and that you will see more on it than a Jew dying.

THE CROWN OF ILLOGICAL THORNS

The explanations of the Jew's unpopularity began long ago with the battle cry that he was responsible for the killing of Christ. The explanations reach another climax in our day with the charge that he is responsible for the invention of Christ.

There is also the charge that the Jew is a creature interested only in the amassing of money; and next the charge that he is responsible for a system of economics (Socialism, Communism) that seeks to undermine the whole principle of money-making. Next is the charge that he is ill-bred and brings social stigma into the neighborhoods in which he takes residence; and alongside this comes the charge that he is concerned too much with the arts and higher professions and is inclined to pre-empt these from under noses straighter and more deserving than his own.

There is the charge that the Jew is an international soul who cannot give full allegiance to the country in which he lives; and beside it stands the charge that the Jew is not deserving of full citizenship rights regardless of any allegiance or devotion he may have shown for his country. There is the charge that the Jew is an unmartial creature and even a cowardly one whose timidity holds back the military ascendancy of a land; and with this, the charge that the Jew is a dangerous fellow who conspires to drag the world into wars for his own secret ends.

He stands, our Jew, before the many courts of gossip, charged with crimes so contradictory and characteristics so diverse, that it is apparent - and has been always apparent - that the only criminal involved is the accuser.

Being a member of the human family, the Jew is most certainly guilty of being, on occasion, a little less than god-like. It is not difficult to discover Jews who are greedy, timid, bellicose, cunning, blatant, fogheaded, boorish, Utopia-ridden, bigoted, and even intolerant. There are Jewish millionaires, Jewish bomb-throwers, Jewish oafs, and Jewish geniuses a-plenty in the world. I have met Babbitt, Bill Sykes, Tartuffe, Uriah Heap, Munchausen, and False Tarquin under a yarmulka.

The crime of the accuser lies, not in miscalling the qualities of the Jew, but in identifying them as Jewish. He is an accuser who obviously selects a few facets of human nature at the moment repugnant to him and labels them Jewish. They are as much his own as the Jew's. In fact, when he turns anti-Semitic, they become more his own than the Jew's.

It was greed for Jewish gold that led the early French kings to expel the Jews from their realm, and the accusation was that the Jewish temperament belittled the glory of France by its obsession with money. It was a perversion of the faith they professed that inspired the Jesuits to burn the Jews of Spain on the grounds that the Jews perverted the meaning of God and Justice. It is the sick dream of social purity that inspires the Germans of 1943 to rid the world of Jews via the route of massacre, and here we have a people befouling its nest with mass murder and startling brutalities under the delusion that they are removing an uncleanliness.

SHAKE WELL BEFORE USING

The anti-Semite is an invalid who will not go to the doctor. He goes only to the Jew. The Jew is his patent medicine guaranteed to cure him. If he is weak, the Jew will make him strong. If he is stupid, he has only to swallow a few Jews and become brilliant. If he is suffering from being unknown, he can find fame out of Jews. They are a magic indispensable to fools.

That he wrestles with the Jew much as an ape might assault his own unlovely image behind a mirror, that he proves his charge of greed by unleashing criminally his own greeds, his charge of cowardice by becoming himself a coward, that he proves the charge of social undesirability by becoming himself as socially desirable as a chimpanzee - that he makes of anti-Semitism a clownish paradox - is known even to anti-Semites when they rest from their labors. It is known to men of probity the year round.

You would imagine a thing so known as the absurdities of anti-Semitism would eventually disappear from the human scene - as did the fear of witches and the fancy that the world was flat. The hatred of Jews has in it, however, a vitality that rises not out of the Jew, but out of his enemy.

The human being relinquishes his follies slowly, like an infant clinging to his rattle. They are as necessary to him as the pap of reason and the breast of enlightenment. Science has snatched away his flat world, his werewolves, his alchemist's wand, his conclave of angels on the point of a needle. But he hangs on to the Jew. It would almost seem that the more enlightened he becomes, the more avidly he clings to this ancient rattle. It is not his last one, but it is a particularly endearing and magic rattle. When he shakes it, he rolls his eyes, gurgles happily, and triumphs blissfully over reason. This all men love to do - to triumph over reason. For, as reasonable creatures, they are small and edited figures. As fools, there is no limit to their greatness.

It is one of the misfortunes of the Jew that he not only inspires drunkenness of this kind. He is also the butt of the hangover. He is resented as a cause of folly - when the folly is spent. He stands, then, as a sort of sinister proof of human idiocy. And his unpopularity is doubled. We humans have always reserved our finest ferocities for those who sought to prove us stupid or fallible.

A MORNING'S CORRESPONDENCE

I receive a letter in the mail today. The envelope is stamped Hollywood, Cal. The letter inside is a piece of lined paper folded once. When I open it, the letter is easier to read than most. Across the page in large red crayon letters are scrawled the words, "Kill All The Jews."

How bold and defiant this idea looks in red crayon! Yet how cringing is the writer. He is not on the envelope, nor on the sheet of paper. He is as invisible as bacteria. I look at the communication and wonder that anyone so violent as this writer should be content to remain so anonymous.

The letter grins back at my wonder. There is one calling in which greatness and anonymity are buddies - murder. The sheet of paper I hold is not a letter, but a crime. The red crayon is blood spilling. The large bold letters are made by a hand that wielded a knife. And the missing signature is not cowardice. It is the murderer triumphantly leaving the scene of his crime without dropping a clue.

This little Jew-killer with the red artist's crayon walks the streets of Hollywood full of gloat this morning. He committed the perfect crime. With his red crayon he slew me. He sees me opening the letter, staring at the red words as if they were the point of a dripping dagger. Then the dagger words sink into my heart and I topple to the floor.

And in this game of murder played by me and this little Jew-killer, there is another joy - for him. It is the joy of the unended crime. I am not actually dead. I did not actually topple to the floor. Thus he relives the arrival of his letter on a more realistic level. What happened, he thinks, was that I merely sank into a chair, overcome with terror. I know now there is a man in Hollywood out to kill all the Jews. How clever he was, my little murderer beams, not to have signed his name. For had he signed his name, I would know who he was and be afraid only of him. Now I do not know who he is - so I am afraid of everybody. I sit frightened, thinking he may be this man or that man, that face in the crowd, that smile on the corner. My fears enlarge him. He is everybody. He can go around feeling himself a mob.

He has enjoyed my death and my terror. Now there is a third pleasure for him. He enjoys my rage. I most certainly will want to have him arrested. He has really committed a crime - not the mystic crime of murder, but of using the mails to threaten. At this point my little Nemesis chuckles with sheer delight. The Jews are all-powerful, he thinks, but with all their power, they cannot lay their hands on him. He has baffled all the Jews. He has outwitted them. And the police, too. And all society. He is a brainy fellow, and he glitters with satisfaction. When he comes home tonight from the movie studio in which he works with his artist's crayon - a studio likely run by a Jew - he will be kittenish with his wife and give his son an extra quarter and order ice cream for dessert. But tomorrow morning when he wakes up, all these pleasures will be gone. He will remember I am still alive, still flourishing. He will lie thinking that I probably tore his letter up and threw it in the wastebasket and called him some derogatory name. His anger against me will seem a powerless thing. His whole crime will seem to him silly, misdirected, footling. He will growl, feel a pain in his stomach and go to work with the scowl of an embittered and defeated man.

I answer the letter of my little Jew-killer:

"Tormented little man who finds relaxation in murder fantasies, the Jews will not cure you. Look around you with your glittering eyes - there are three million Jews already murdered in Europe - and do you feel any better? Millions more will die in the lime kilns and gas chambers operated by your friends, the Germans, and will you then be any better off? No. Your little stomach ulcer will burn as miserably as when all the Jews were alive. A little hot Roman candle will continue to go off in your head. Your taxes will be just as high, your libido just as low. Dear sir, do not misunderstand me. I do not ask you to stop killing all the Jews with your little red crayon, because that would be foolish of me. We both know whom you would start killing then - yourself. And, though I think it a much more sensible way for you to be rid of your troubles, you are not exactly a creature of sense - and my good advice would be wasted on you. Still, if a sensible mood should ever take hold of you and send you to the attic with a strong piece of rope - before you hang yourself - write me again. I shall be pleased to hear from you - yet not too pleased. For I, too, know how cruel a place the world is."

AN ANTI-SEMITE OF MORE CHARM

Not all anti-Semites write in red crayon. Many of them write in fine ink, Monsieur Voltaire, for instance. Monsieur Voltaire does not come in my mail. He stands on my bookshelf with all his electric sentences alive between covers. That sparkling grin! I know it well. I almost grin back. "Down with the wretched little Jews," Monsieur Voltaire cries, and I stop grinning.

The red crayon letter is in the wastebasket. Monsieur Voltaire is open on my desk. He is much more articulate than my correspondent from Hollywood. He depresses me much more. Perhaps this is because I am more sensitive to crimes of the intellect than to those of the body. They are more dangerous - because they are more lasting.

Jew hatred was the odd hobby of this Prince of Reason - Voltaire - just as a great detective might practice murder on the side. He was the first witty friend of rational behavior produced by the Christians. No more engaging cries for tolerance, for justice, and for an end to irration ever have been uttered by a friend of man. Yet this ornament to reason, this glowing brain, had, as a sideline, one of the most bumptious hatreds of the Jew to be found in literature.

It is not Jew hatred that ever depresses me. There are many writers whom I would not have without it. There are many minds by whom it is an honor to be disliked, and a victory to be hated. This is not true of Voltaire. To find such a hatred in him is to feel doubly its sting - the sting of being hated by a nearly fine fellow and the sting of having to answer back, of having to treat as an enemy someone who has nearly all the charms of a friend.

Monsieur Voltaire was one who enriched the world. It is for this reason that when I look at him I feel a sadness peculiar to Jews. It is unprofitable for the Jew to look at history's heroes or philosophers - without skipping a little. He is apt, if he looks intently, to see only monsters. The corner of civilization he occupies is usually running with his blood and loud with his libel, and never looks to him like civilization at all. Men who are saints to other eyes are often horned devils to his. Behind their white plumes, their wit and benevolence, they have but a single face to offer the Jew - the grimace of hate.

It is no pleasure to say of so fine a fellow as Voltaire that he is a fouler enemy of the Jews than the murderous German of today. It is like reporting of a great beauty who dazzles your eyes that she has not so pleasant an effect on your nose. Ah, this extra nose that the Jew carries! It is an organ out of which he gets little delight and much inconvenience. What he would embrace passionately as a man of the world, is sniffed at by this secondary proboscis and found to reek of aversion for the Jew. He may continue his embrace, despite this depressing odor, but it is the embrace of a lover whose heart must overlook more than it holds.

My letter to the little Jew-killer with his red crayon was briefer than the answer Monsieur Voltaire inspires in me; for this fearsome and anonymous little fellow from Hollywood was a harmless one - even though he might end up breaking Jewish heads in some studio. He would break only a few Jewish heads and land in jail, his crimes forever at an end.

Monsieur Voltaire has never stopped breaking Jewish heads and, as long as paper endures, he never will. Nor will he ever be dragged off, his own head bowed in disgrace, to any hoosegow. He will remain grinning securely on his pedestal.

To boot, Voltaire is not only yesterday, but today, and the finest part of today. He is the great grandfather of Bernard Shaw, Anatole France, Schopenhauer, Mencken, Nietzsche, H.G. Wells, and all the big and little champions of rationality. No man in our time speaks and writes of a sane world but he quotes Voltaire. He is the smiling ghost who presides over our gatherings where companionable understanding of life is sole credential. From these gatherings emanates civilization. And among these gatherings of our most polished and thoughtful citizens we find, as in the brain pan of Voltaire - the same gibbet for the Jew; a gibbet all the more shocking because it stands in so fair a territory.

I shall address myself later in more contemporaneous detail to these "civilization makers" who persist in keeping the Jew dangling over their feast of reason. But here in my answer to Voltaire are a few generalities that fit them as rightly as they do Voltaire, dead two hundred years. The Jew has changed since the time of Barbarossa. But not his enemies. Folly survives by not changing.

THE CASE AGAINST VOLTAIRE

During Voltaire's life many pamphlets were written bringing to light the sorry little fact that he lost twenty-five thousand francs through the bankruptcy of a London Jew named Medina. Another Voltairean tragedy uncovered by the pamphleteers was that the great philosopher had been worsted in a legal battle with a German Jewish lapidary named Hirsch. A number of eminent witnesses, among them Frederick the Great, had brought proof that the brilliant French philosopher had swindled the little Jewish gem setter. The burden of these pamphlet rebuttals was that Messers Medina and Hirsch were responsible for warping the philosopher's mind into anti-Semitism.

A number of these pamphlets attacking Voltaire for his anti-Semitism were written by German Catholic priests who signed them with Jewish names. Nothing in Voltaire's writing is as ironical as the spectacle of these German priests rushing to the defense of the beleaguered Semite - the same priests who had driven the Jews out of Germany and tormented them with libel and murder. The irony is not so much that these monks came to the rescue of Jews, but that these same long-standing Jew-haters saw in the philosopher's anti-Semitism a stain on reason, a stigma worthy of moral rage. Good God, how can minds so crooked put pens to paper!

Voltaire stewed a great deal over this situation. But he was a shrewd philosophical pot, and he elected not to answer the priestly kettle - on these points. The great humanist, accused of inhumanity by the busiest practitioners of inhumanity in Europe, packed up his ironies and moved to other fronts. One pauses to ask: He who attacked all bigots, did he wonder if his Jew-hatred was bigotry? He who belabored the clumsy mind of Europe for bringing injustice and suffering to people, did he pause to figure whether his own clumsy calumnies of the Jews might bring them another pogrom or two (as they did)? How could a man who posed, not as angel, friend of God, confidant of Heaven - but simply as a friend of man - how could such a one practice reason by despising stupidly and illogically the Jews? Where, in God's name, was his reason?

The answer to all these queries is, he did not wonder, figure, pause, or fret. He continued to be what he was - what all men are - a proof of the fact that the unreasonable part of the mind is eternally divorced from all reason. Just as there are oases in the driest of heads, there are trackless deserts in the most verdant of skulls.

FOOLS GRASP AT STRAWS, PHILOSOPHERS AT FLAWS

The theory that Voltaire's anti-Jewish crusades were the product of small personal wounds rather than Olympian cogitation continued to fill the journals of Europe for the rest of his life. It was a logical enough scandal and it satisfied the Jews. Anti-Semitism is often based on this sort of revenge motif. In denouncing some thirteen million Jews as crooked and despicable, the accuser is able to conceal the fact from himself (and others, he hopes) that he was, perhaps, worsted by a single superior individual or embarrassed by a lone Semite. His defeat becomes then a defeat at the hands of an army and not a duelist.

But I doubt this answer to Voltaire. Our Arouet may have owned as small and grasping a nature as any sharper's - but he did not write with this nature. He only lived by it (perhaps). The Voltaire who wrote was a man of acute vision. He may have brought into his writing some slight corroborative distaste for Jews fetched out of his non-literary hours -but even this I doubt.

The blind spot in Voltaire's philosophy came, not out of a bad heart seeking vengeance, but out of bad thinking. He was a bad scholar and a good wit - a combination that usually makes for major errors. Voltaire attacked Jews as an ancient idea and not a living people. Very like the Germans of today, he saw the great sin of the Jews to be that they were responsible for Christianity. But he was even more illiterate than the Germans. He had not the faintest inkling of what the Jews, as an idea, really were. The significance of prophets of Israel never occurred to him. All that occurred to Voltaire was that the Jew was a caricature easy to wave at the Christian for the embarrassment of the latter. The Catholics understood this. They saw in Voltaire's attack on the Jews something much more dangerous than had inspired their own attacks on the Jews. The philosopher was exposing their own roots to ridicule. It was this knowledge that brought the priests to the defense of the Jews - via their anonymous pamphlets. History is filled with such pro-Jewish attitudes as theirs. Burn the Jew, but cherish the soul he has given us - is the cry of the pre-Nazi pogroms.

Voltaire's assaults on the Jews were not out of proportion for a thinker who considered religion a disease. They were ten to one - ten blows for the Bishop to one smack at his prayer-drenched grandfather, the Jew. The lack of proportion lay in the results. Our philosopher succeeded in improving the Christian with his therapeutic pummeling. He also succeeded in debasing the Jew. In this lies one of the minor evidences of his bad thinking. His aim had been to improve the whole world.

To write of Jews, as Voltaire did, as if they were living characters out of the old Testament, is much the same as to write of Englishmen as if they were still Druid fanciers overrunning the world in coats of blue paint. He knew better, but it served his ends to know less. He denounced living Jews, and his mind remained fastened - none too brightly - on dead ones. The injustice of this trick could not have escaped him. But it did not halt him. No less than Torquemada, whom he detested, he was willing to sacrifice humanity in order to arrive at a conviction.

The Jew, along with his neighbors, has outgrown the abortive doings of his Biblical ancestors. He is no more related to the homicides of David or the harems of Solomon than is the modern Frenchman to the mysticism of the Knights Templars. Jewishness, as a faith, is the survival of an ancient collection of fairy tales. But even in this, the Jew is no separate and archaic figure. What is good in these fairy tales has been appropriated by the world. The heroes of these fairy tales are the heroes of Christendom, and the absurdities in those tales are as much gospel to the anti-Semite as to the Semite. There is no abnormality to be found in the Jew's religion that is not shared (and increased) by all his enemies.

But Voltaire had no interest in the existence of the Jews. They were a step in his logic, a ready-made joke for his wit - nothing more. This species of aloof anti-Semite is a more potent trouble-maker than his club-swinging co-worker in the market-place. He preserves the Jew like a patriarch in amber, and peoples the world with Hebraic fossils. He keeps alive the eye for an eye and tooth for a tooth cries of the Old Testament as if they were the breakfast talk of Jews in Paris, London and New York. The Jew has not been in a position to collect eye for eye and tooth for tooth for almost two thousand years. Such bargaining has been practiced usuriously by every people in the world except the Jews. Yet it is the Jews who are indicted by Voltaire as vengeful folk. He is not interested in any changes the Jews may have undergone in the eighteen centuries since the Cross was reared on which they were to be crucified for ages. He was concerned, noble mind, with what he called a philosophical dictionary. That less noble minds than his seized on his ideas and saw in them proof of the abominableness of the living Jew rather than of the occasional chicaneries of long dead tribal chiefs, probably struck Voltaire as one of the hazards of being a philosopher.

He would have been more Voltaire had he seen it as one of the hazards of being a Jew. The stones this most philosophical of men threw at David, Saul and Solomon are still bouncing on the heads of Jews more or less alive in Europe.

SOME ALL TOO FEW SENTENCES ON PREJUDICE

There is a lie in Voltaire deeper than any of his Jewish confusions. It is not a single lie but a whole process of thought.

Voltaire examined ideas and never their human origins. Like many philosophers, who are usually journalists in quest of abstract scandals, the Frenchman investigated crimes against reason as if they were misarrangements of words or lapses of logic. He did not know, as Shakespeare knew, that the ideas of men are the debris of an inner battle fought out of sight of the mind. He had no eye for the forces of passion, greed, terror, and insufficiency that throw our thinking at us. He visualized reason as the vestments of mathematics. It is not that. It is a vestige rescued from mania.

He would have written of Dostoievsky, had he been able to read him, that the Russian was an industrious reporter full of useless tidings from chaos. Shakespeare he did read and of him he wrote - "He would have been a perfect poet had he lived in the time of

Addison. Addison is, perhaps, of all English writers, the one who best knew how to guide genius with taste...I find it somewhat extraordinary that [Shakespeare's] buffoonery and drunkenness count among the beauties of the tragic stage." (I have rearranged the sequence of this quotation so as to make both my and Voltaire's point more obvious.)

He seems to have found it extraordinary that buffoonery and disorder also existed on the human stage. Consequently, he wrote - and this is the great lie behind his thinking - "Prejudice is opinion without judgment." It is a statement worth examining, for in it lies not only Voltaire's, but half the world's misunderstanding of itself.

This statement says that our souls can be purged of evil by the attentions of the schoolmaster. It says that we are unreasonable because we have not been exposed to enlightenment. It says that our passions can be arranged into tasty, Addisonian order by the application of external logic - knowledge. It says that error exists because truth has not been offered in exchange. It says that the prejudices which fling us into stupid, silly, or barbarous behaviors are no more than an absence of judgment.

This is a misconception so deep and so tall that, in making it, Voltaire divorces himself, not only from Shakespeare and all the poets, but from all psychology as well. And without psychology there is no truth any more than there is history without bloodshed.

It is this misconception of what prejudice is - of what unreason is - that made Voltaire an anti-Semite. He thought that truth lay in the exposure of some Jewish and Christian "miracles." He had no eye for the maladjustments of his own Europeans - that made their persecution of the Jew a thousandfold more unsavory than the latter's worst intellectual lapses and a thousandfold more important in the study of human unreason. It is this preference for playing solitaire with ideas - as if that little deck held all the faces of mankind - that makes philosophers often anti-human, or at least anti-social.

Voltaire's sentence that "Prejudice is opinion without judgment" is not a sentence, but a credo. It is a religion that misunderstands, not God, but man. In this sentence there is, even on the surface, a glaring contradiction that should have been obvious to the logician - Voltaire. He should have seen that his credo presupposed fantastically that the mass of humanity was fit for the exercise of judgment. He himself knew better than this. He knew that the history of Europe revealed that no more than a handful of men in a generation were capable of thinking and acting as rational men. And he knew - no one better - that even this handful of enlightened ones remained as full of prejudices as a cow's tail is of fleas.

The study of anti-Semitism is no more than a sidelong look at the human genius for prejudice. I do not mean our superficial prejudices - the ones that are formed by the many wanton winds that blow our personalities together. Our external minds are of minor importance in our own or in the world's destiny. They are dressed mainly out of journalistic dust storms. Those loose fittings that we call our political beliefs or social tenets are not prejudices at all. They seldom array us against reason or send us gallivanting through a vacuum. They do no more than add a touch of eccentricity to our cliches.

True prejudice is not opinion at all and cannot be influenced by the things that make up opinion, knowledge, or sanity. True prejudice is an inner unreason as necessary to us as our outer reasonableness; that is, as necessary to our continuation as buffoons and drunkards of life. Evolution - the same evolution that changes with godlike slowness our bones and tissues - is its only schoolmaster.

Until we are straightened from our Simian mental stoop, prejudice will remain our shield against illness, our buckler against matters otherwise insufferable to our ego.

Prejudice is the bandage that protects a sore segment of the brain. Judgment can neither unwrap it nor enlightenment pluck it away.

Prejudice is our method of transferring our own sickness to others. It is our ruse for disliking others rather than ourselves. We find absolution in our prejudices. We find also in them an enemy made to order rather than inimical forces out of our control.

By our prejudices we pardon ourselves; we excuse our defeats, we increase our stature, we utilize our ignorance which is our major equipment.

Prejudice is a raft onto which the shipwrecked mind clambers and paddles to safety.

The human ocean bottoms where prejudices are formed are too deep for the educators or the precept bringers. There no light can shine. It is into this dark place that the word Jew has fallen. It has become a word, not of historical or religious meaning, but a symbol of obsession - one of the mystic forces by which men are able to outwit their insufficiencies.

The word Jew has in two thousand years been promoted from the name of a people to the name of a symptom. Along with the many hoarier complexes and phobias that disturb and, at the same time, protect the human soul from disintegration stands this new magician in the subconscious - the Jew complex.

It existed in one of its more evil guises in the texture of a man who is called one of the greatest minds of the race. Voltaire, in his antipathy for the "wretched little Jews," proved himself, if proof be needed, that prejudice is independent of judgment. For he was a man of excellent judgment. He revealed, to the contrary, that the prejudice of anti-Semitism is a symptom that can thrive as virulently in the most acute and enlightened of minds as it can in the darkened thought of fools.

ENTER SEÑOR PINTO

I met him in a history book. He is a tall, handsome man with an imperious eye but an unhappy mouth. He is a Portuguese Jew of distinction, and lives in elegance in the city of Bordeaux, France; time, 1763.

The Señor owns a few sailing vessels, trades with the people of the Indies, has a carriage with four horses, pomades his hair, takes snuff, carries an ivory-handled cane, and reads the latest works of the new French Freemason, Arouet de Voltaire.

These are admirable works but they, nonetheless, disturb Señor Pinto, for there is much in them that is unpalatable to a Jew. The merchant of Bordeaux calls in some of his friends. They arrive in velvet carriages drawn by happy horses. They discuss the matter of this Jewish calumny of Monsieur Voltaire over tall bottles of wine. The Jews must strike back at this Freemason. And who is there better fitted than Pinto, so rich, so well read, so talented?

Thus, by acclamation, Señor Pinto is declared champion of the Jews. He seizes his quill, produces in five weeks a fine volume of rebuttal, and takes this volume to Paris to hurl at Voltaire. The rebuttal says that Voltaire is a fool in assailing Jews as if they were all alike. Señor Pinto points out indignantly that the Portuguese Jews, who "are all practically aristocrats," despise German and Russian Jews as deeply as do any of their other despisers. All Voltaire has to say against the Israelites, cries the Señor from Bordeaux, might well be true of these same uncouth German and Russian varieties. But it is in no way applicable to the fine, high-class Semites only recently driven out of Portugal.

I shake hands with Pinto. He soothes me. He reveals that neither Voltaire nor any anti-Semites have a corner on intolerance. It is not good for a people to be too much in the right, too noble, too flawless. It would unbalance them. They would become then like a badly written character in a play - the one who has nothing to do but recite all the long, dull speeches on goodness and honor. The Jew is no such bore.

I applaud Señor Pinto and bring him to the footlights for a bow - at the end of Act Two. He looks around with imperious eye, takes a pinch of snuff and smiles with the arrogance of a Cardinal.

But Señor Pinto's distaste for all Jews but his own brocaded variety has an unhappy Act Three. Attracted by this dandy's boasts, Christendom looks on the towns of Bordeaux and Avignon and is shocked to see Jews living in such high estate, Jews with ivory-handled canes and velvet capes and large sailing vessels full of spices and gold plate. Unlike the Epicurean Pinto, the Gentiles are unable to savor the distinction between Portuguese and German Semites. They launch themselves at once into the bedevilment of Pinto's own people. The Portuguese Jews of Bordeaux are stripped again of their dignity and treasures and sent packing into ghettos.

Another reason I admire Pinto is that he permits me to say, here is one Jew who was victim only of his own stupidity. I imagine there are many such, but Pinto stands in a spotlight. There is a certain relaxation in beholding the Jew as a villain, even if it is only himself he outrages. There is also a historic lesson in Pinto, for he reveals that when the Jew plays villain, there are always better villains around to steal the part from him.

Señor Pinto also helps me to understand many Jews of today who have come to high estate in various lands. These elegant ones are ever ready to repudiate all Jews without ivory-handled canes, collections of fine paintings, or the ear of an archbishop. No more than poor Pinto will these Jewish Fortunatuses know that, in the eyes of anti-Semites, Jews are as inseparable and identical as Siamese twins. No more than Pinto will they learn that even espousing so un-Jewish a cause as anti-Semitism never makes a Jew less a Jew.

But Señor Pinto is not entirely a villain nor yet a fool. He is more the victim of a certain logic that the world refuses to share with him. This often troubles Jews more than the calumnies of their enemies. The logic in their own heads informs them they are not Jews at all, judged by any Jewish standards they know. They are cynics, philosophers, sophisticates, and even atheists. They care no more for Jews than for Patagonians. But there comes a morning when they always wake up - Jews. History stands outside their windows and, in a voice that seems truly that of an idiot, bids them attend a massacre being held for Jews only.

At such a time the Pintos and the near Pintos beat their bosoms and catch a look at the true meaning of the Jew. He is part of a game the world plays. Although it devote itself eagerly to his extermination, it cannot afford the loss of his Jewishness. This Jewishness is not essential to the Jew, who may outgrow and outwit it. But it is to his enemy, who refuses to outgrow a panacea so soothing, so enriching, so ego-inflating as anti-Semitism.

MICE WHO RUN AMOK

The anti-Semites have a flag. It is sadism. I examine the little red land of actual murder that lies under this flag.

The Voltaires alone cannot equip the anti-Semite. In addition to the meditations of sages and the dicta of priests, he has needed always a gun, a sword, a cudgel, a torch, a friendly judge, and a machine that breaks bones. (The Germans, proud of their chemistry, have added lime and gas to his requirements).

The tent of calumny under which the Jew has lived is an unsavory enough residence. It is not as uncomfortable as the abattoir which is his other home. The aberration called sadism is behind his libel and his killing. Not much attention is given to this fact. All the sides involved prefer to imagine it something else. This gives everybody a chance to talk of politics, anthropology, history, theology, and other high topics.

The long practiced murder of Jews en masse is a safe and therefore popular expression of sadism. It is little else. Yet it has not served to alarm our humanists. To them the murderers of Jews are never murderers. They are misguided patriots, misinformed economists, misdirected pietists. It has not yet occurred to anyone to identify even the German anti-Semites as murderers first and politicians last.

The murder of Jews is like the stealing of nickels. It does not fix a criminal record on its perpetrators. There is too much historic, religious and legal precedent to make the murder of Jews a matter outside the humanities. Jew murder has become a crime that neither belittles its performer nor shocks its spectator. A dead Jew remains an historic figure. He never quite becomes a human corpse.

The sadism behind all the libel and killing of Jews is a complicated thing. Medically the disease is identified as an instinct for cruelty. Little boys who wring the necks of rabbits have it. The Germans who wring the necks of Jews have it in almost as pure a form. In the Germans, as in the little boys, it is sort of backward lust. But even among the Germans the pleasures involved do not entirely come from the agony of the Jews. They come from the thrill of being murderers, from the thrill of lawlessness which contains in it always the illusion of power and freedom.

Criminal anti-Semites are usually people haunted by a deep and ulcerous grind of defeat. Dissatisfaction, bleak and reaching into their bowels, is their secret companion, and the companion bears a thousand names. The criminal Jew-hater may be dissatisfied with his religion, his wife, his king, his love life, his virtues - most often his virtues - or his general feebleness. He is the mouse who dreams of being the lion, and whose troubles are those of the mouse. All these troubles are unsolvable as long as he remains within the law and obeys the common restrictions of decency. Life is attacking him and he cannot fight back. He must raise the cry of "burglars" before he can draw a weapon. History has ready for him the Jew as this phantom burglar.

His need, however, is not to kill Jews. That is a sideline, more often a smoke screen. His need is to be lawless, to break the laws of logic, sanity, and good behavior, behind which he is hemmed in, bogged down and mousey. Lawlessness is what he wants. It alone can rid him of the tyranny of his virtues. The moment he is lawless he feels powerful. He is freed of society and as happy as a felon who has broken jail.

CRIME WITHOUT PUNISHMENT

There are numerous ways of attaining this freedom from honorable restriction. One may become a thief, a gangster, a swindler, a bigamist. But these are dangerous callings, and society is ready with scourge and dungeon for their followers. Such callings are not for the anti-Semite. That gentleman has not the true courage of his craving for lawlessness. He desires to be a criminal - but a criminal in fine standing. He longs to defy truth; he longs to avenge himself; he would like to get back at something - to bedevil his fellow man, to rob, lie, run riot. But the little mouse would like to do all these leonine things without forfeiting his rights as a member of society.

Anti-Semitism provides him with the ideal ground for such

transformations and operations. He can climb out of his sense of inferiority by bashing Jews - and, at the same time, line up with the great of history. Anti-Semitism is the one crime for which there is neither a court of law nor a bar of human judgment. It is, therefore, the most popular of crimes. Considering not only its immunity, but its many rewards, I have wondered often that the world was not entirely overrun by anti-Semites. Perhaps this is because there are not enough Jews to go around. Or it may be that civilization is making certain progress. But I doubt this. Our aluminum wings do not move us an inch out of superstition or abnormality. If civilization is to be measured by the progress of human rationality, we can still use the yardstick of the cynic - which is no longer than a sigh.

THE LOVE OF STINKING

The smugness of the anti-Semite, when confronted with facts that disprove his aberrated outcries, is baffling to those who do not understand him, to those who believe he has a "cause." For the anti-Semite has no "cause" other than the need of lawlessness. He is delighted when facts prove he is wrong - because the doing of wrong is his sole objective.

I remember Teddy Webb, who was no anti-Semite. He was an honorable Chicago bandit. He killed three policemen, "for the hell of it," before he was cornered in a rooming house. He surrendered affably. I was with the police when they searched him. They found his pockets stuffed with newspaper clippings that contained stories denouncing Teddy Webb as a cruel killer, a fiend who had violated every claim to human sympathy. They urged that he be crushed like a bug when captured.

Teddy pleaded that his clippings be not taken from him. He knew some of them by heart and he gloated in them. They were the press notices of his success. The anti-Semite thrives similarly on all proofs of his stupidity and brutality. He loves to hear how idiotic he is, how lacking in common sense, how devoid of common decency. Such accusations inflame him with a sense of power. As a man of sense and decency, he was nobody. As a creature who outrages the world, he is a mighty figure. When you convince an anti-Semite that he is a fool, a scoundrel, and a monster, you offer him only proofs of his new greatness. And of the potency of his lawlessness.

Anti-Semitism is unique in psychology as the only form of lunacy with a political future. Claustrophobia, zoophilia, necrophilia, nymphomania, homosexuality, and pyromania are useless to the politician. Anti-Semitism stands alone as a politically usable mania. It can fetch votes as neatly as a High Tariff or a Poll Tax platform.

But though the politicians may use it, it is not they who derive its greatest rewards. The cynical politician can become only a Senator. The "true" anti-Semite can change from a mouse to a roaring lion, which is a mightier transformation.

PUNISHMENT WITHOUT CRIME

As the matador's cape is to the bull, so the Jew has been to the beast horns that lie prettily concealed under the human coiffure. The metaphor is not entirely apt because in the case of the Jew there has been no matador behind the cape, no sword to flash from its folds and pierce the brutal heart assailing him.

In the game of Jew-killing, the beast has always won, and although this is contrary to the code of evolution as well as of sport, little effort has been made to alter the rules - and keep them altered. They are accepted on the basis of their antiquity and convenience.

The practice of these rules has not given their practitioners a particularly bad name. The bad name has gone to the Jew. The continued murder of the Jew through the centuries of Christianity is as much responsible for his ill-repute as any ten factors.

History has rebuked occasionally the murderer. But nobody reads history, particularly the sort that offers uncomfortable reports of mankind. Gossip is a more vital mold of opinion, and the gossip of the world continues to concern itself with the undesirability of the Jew and not of his murderer. His ancient slayers seem somehow to have reformed but the Jew continues obtruding out of the past like an unregenerate corpse. His corpse, in fact, has curiously the look of the aggressor. On this oddity the history of anti-Semitism is founded - that the victim is guilty of the greater crime.

THE PARADOX OF TOMORROW

It is certain that at the end of this war the Jew will have earned a more sinister name than was given him by the fagot-lighters of Spain. A curious evil will have attached itself to him, and he will be regarded with fearsome suspicion by the crowds of the world. This will be due to three odd factors: one, the fact that three million Jews will have been massacred by the Germans during their brief fling as supermen; the second, that gossip will have it that the Jews started the war, not by any political or financial cabals, but merely by the fact that the Germans took to murdering them and that the world rushed to their rescue; the third will be due to the guilt complex already active in the soul of Christendom. I will enlarge on this last only because I think it the most potent.

The criticism of German brutality will subside in a few years - a not very difficult prophecy to make, since at its height, staring into the smoke of massacre, this criticism was never more than a feeble and embarrassed protest.

Gossip will step in to soothe the conscience of the crowds, of the crowds that participated in the great killing and of the crowds and their statesmen that looked on full of abstraction, indecision, and vicarious evil. These latter will be especially open to the seduction of gossip. For they are like the citizen who, making no outcry while he watches a murder done under his window, finds excuse afterward for his silence in the rumor that the victim was a creature deserving his bloody fate.

The crowds and their statesmen who watched the massacre of millions, and broke their silence with hardly more than a "tut, tut," will emerge from the war with a troublesome guilt complex. They already have it, and are already engaged in the medical work of its exorcising. This is done by exchanging the guilt complex for a rage at the thing that produced it.

I see this activity around me today. People are developing aversion for the murdered Jews of Europe. They are beginning to look for foulness in the victim rather than in the criminal. There is another reason for this. To contemplate the foulness of the criminal is to incite oneself to thundering moral protest. This is not easy. Moral thunder calls for the exercise of all the virtues. It is even more difficult than writing poetry. Indifference is the easier way. But though the moral soul is willing to close its eyes to the presence of the devil, it cannot as easily lull its aftermath of conscience pangs. Morality is based less on the poetry we contribute toward it than on the guilt we feel for its violation.

Thus conscience will make white-washers of us all. We will fall to searching, not our souls, but the Jew's, and try to find therein the true cause of his agony. We will add eagerly to his bad name in order to remove the shadow from our own.

Our verdict will be the same as all other verdicts handed down in the case of the Jew versus humanity. We will find him guilty again of having provoked by his alphabet and his ancestors the temper of a very nervous people - the Germans.

There are simple-hearted Jews today who are waiting eagerly the end of the war in order that they may witness the trial of the Germans and Romanians for their treason against the human race, and their fitting punishment for the massacre of millions of its members.

There will be no such trial and no such punishment. For the truth is that nobody warred on the Germans because they were cruel to Jews, nor yet because they were experimenting with inhuman ideas. The Germans were fought because their aggressiveness, like that of the Japanese, threatened the comforts, lives, and prestige of other nations. We battled, not beside the Lord at Armageddon, but at Waterloo and, luckily, on the right side. The defeat of the Germans' ideas will be only an incidental matter for discussion by a few experts in psychology. We will have actually defeated German guns and not German ideas, since it is only their guns we honestly fought.

When the Germans have been beaten, these guns and the

aggressiveness behind them will automatically disappear and there will be nothing visible in the Germans to merit our continued hate. If we have any emotion toward them at all, as Americans, it will be one of gratitude. We will feel grateful toward them for their vincibility. You can see this epilogue in the boxing ring any night. The victor always embraces his vanquished opponent, if he has been a tough one, and beams on him with true love, as if asking him to share the triumph to which he contributed by his toughness, his valor, and his defeat.

Such was the history of our relationship with the Germans after our first war with them, and such will be the history of sequel number two, with the difference that we will have to find apologies for the Germans having brutally slain so many Jews; and for ourselves for not having included the laws of morality in our war aims. The "faults" of the Jews will provide these apologies.

A BIOGRAPHICAL SORTIE

I determined to do little dissecting of Jews, but there is one Jew I have decided to examine closely - myself. On reading what I have written, I find a curious use of two first person pronouns beginning to confuse the syntax. The writer is, apparently, uncertain whether he is I, the Jew, or We, the Americans. And on occasion he offers himself as a citizen of some literary limbo where thought is its own nationality.

Accordingly, I pause to find out just who is writing this book - a Jew, an American, or an intellectual phantom. I am inclined to vote in advance for the intellectual phantom, for that is what an honest writer should be. An honest writer should be able to espouse the cause of any people pursued by misfortune without having cousins or uncles on the run. His fury should be a stranger to any self-interest, and he should wear the colors of no country but of reason.

Literature is full of such fine knights from nowhere who fight always the battles of the oppressed - but I doubt if I am one of them. I doubt if any Jew ever wrote of Jews except as a Jew - inspired by the desire to defend or glorify them (God knows they can use a few ruffles) or by the hope of proving he is no Jew at all.

It would please me to think my own fervor is no more than that of a mind trained in the humanities under the beneficent culture of the United States. For, truly, I have never been anything else but an American, and to find myself at forty-nine writing out of an obstreperous Jewish heritage is as confusing to me as if I had waked up one morning and found an entirely new language in my head. It is also in a way proof of a thing said against Jews - namely, that they are, in a pinch or in the long run, Jews and nothing else.

But this, too, I doubt. I doubt equally whether I am I, the Jew, or We, the Americans. I could make out a case for myself as either or neither, which is another way of saying that I am both. Both I am and both I insist on being, and it will need better anti-Semites than I have yet read to unmarry me.

Were I a Frenchman, Pole, Spaniard, German, Englishman, or Italian, I am certain I would not put in this claim to honest wedlock. History would have too loud a rebuttal to make, even the history of the English.

It was only as little ago as 1923 that Hilaire Belloc - a dull enough fellow to be worthy of representing a fair share of English thought, wrote in his book, *The Jews*: "The continued presence of the Jewish nation intermingled with other nations alien to it presents a permanent problem of the greatest character...the wholly different culture, tradition, race, and religion of Europe make Europe a permanent antagonist of Israel...the problem is, how to relax those strains and to set things permanently at their ease again. There are two ways to such a desirable end. The first is by elimination of what is alien. The second is by its segregation. There is no other way."

Here is a Barkis who is unwillin', an Englishman who would remain, under all temptations, a toothy bachelor and marry no Jews. And, mind you, this was after the original war to make the world a democratic planet had been fought and won. (I am being facetious. I know that wars of human liberation have nothing to do with Jews.)

EXHUMING MR. BELLOC

I have no desire to coax the cadaver Belloc or any of his surviving kith to make the Jew an honest man, since it is as impossible to change the prejudices of the living as it is to alter those of the dead. In this connection I recall the opinion of Epicharmus, a Greek philosopher, whose wisdom has survived only in a single paragraph.

"Why argue with any man's error," said this ancient one, "when it is his error that is he? As well seek to convince a cow that the most dazzling creature on earth is not a cow, or prove to a pig that the finest resident of our world is not a pig."

The philosophy of Mr. Belloc is not as innocent as that of such self-infatuated fauna. It is loud in the land, and Mr. Belloc, dead and returned to his fastidious English maker, must be a happy shade. His notions are now rampant in Europe at least, where the Jew has been pronounced so great an alien that he is unfit even for living anywhere. The odd thing is that Mr. Belloc himself has not prospered as well as his philosophy. He has already dwindled out of literature and become no more than a footnote to yesterday.

Then why do I write about him at all? Catholics who know Mr. Belloc to have been one of the literary darlings of Catholicism will imagine I am slyly belaboring the Papacy. I am doing nothing of the sort. Mr. Belloc's religious affiliation has no interest for me. His choice of a master was more fortunate for him than for the master - this is the extent of my opinion of his religion.

What actually interests me in Mr. Belloc is the fact that he is the articulation of a whole tribe of Anglo-Saxons who are usually mum. These are people whose very mumness is both their social and intellectual distinction. They are the stern, cud-chewing Englishmen (and their American cousins) whose righteousness seldom ventures beyond monosyllables.

Mr. Belloc was one of these word swallowers in reverse. He shared with them the deep fear of ideas that keeps them deaf and dumb. But he was the English monosyllable with the scribbler's itch. His talents, by the way, were not confined to chatting about the Jews. He went after Topics like a man in a frenzy. He wrote books "On Making an Omelet," "On Cats," "On Dressing Up," "On Architecture," "On Mules," "A Guide to Boring," "On Emeralds," "A Record of a Merchant of Tenth Street," "Farrago," a "Heroic Poem in Praise of Wine;" on Hills, on Oceans, on the Thames, on the House of Commons, on Beauvais Tapestry. He has a book called "On Anything" and a companion volume title, "On Everything." It was as if he had plunged into literature with a cry of "Button, Button, who's got the Button?"

THE SILENCE THAT SPEAKS

One would imagine that in the course of flying from pillar to post and setting down a hundred thousand pages of gossip, the pen of Mr. Belloc would point for at least one brief moment inward. It does not. This busy scribe who made a good penny out of rehashing all the biographies he could find in the Club library never turned his eye to the great wealth of material that sat in his own scribbler's chair. It is this silence I propose to examine.

He wrote no word about himself except in a fragment of several pages called "Autobiography." In these he explains his reticence on Belloc. It is because he is gifted with a quality called "Pudor." This is a bit of Greek for which, he says, there is no modern equivalent, and he defines it as "that element of salvation in us which prevents us from singing at the top of our voices in railway carriages." Discussing further his dogged silence on Belloc, he writes, "we preserve a little shrine. We keep a little hedged field....That we should desire to write our lives is inevitable....We are restrained at heart by this feeling, 'Why should I cast these pearls before my snouted fellow citizens?' Why should I open the Holy of Holies?' "

Mr. Belloc, who chattered his head off for fifty years, is proud of having revealed no single secret of himself. I wonder why this incredibly snoopy fellow kept his nose out of the Holy of Holies - his own interior. Was it a Holy of Holies or something quite else?

Mr. Belloc is entitled to his silence. I am certainly glad he did not write any more than he did. But I have still two other questions to ask of his Pudor:

What urged Mr. Belloc to pick up a broom and sweep out Jews? Where was the real dirt that Mr. Belloc mistook for Jews?

ATROPHY AS A SOCIAL ART

I have gone to the trouble of documenting Mr. Belloc a bit because he is one of the flowers that anti-Semitism wears in its buttonhole. He is out of a very fine English bouquet.

I have met a few Bellocs, and I have heard of others. They are as identical as the salmon whom they somewhat resemble. Their noses twitch with disdain (and a touch of hayfever), their voices refuse to finish words (the more left unsaid, the better), they stare a lot as if they were half stunned, and they look as if they had been greased against human contacts. This general terror of life is at the bottom of all snobbery; and all this remarkable paralysis of mind, vocal cords, and motor reflexes is offered to society as evidence of superiority. Superiority to what, forsooth?

There is one credo that operates this by-product group of Anglo-Saxons. It is the Commandment to stand pat on what you know. And if you know nothing, you stand pat on that. The main thing is to use neither your senses nor your mind, and to behave generally as if you were a gifted statue. In this dedication to immobility lies the secret of Anglo-Saxon snobbery. The garden statues that practice it have all the Bellocian fervor for eyelessness. They snort with him: "It is better to decorate yourself than know yourself or (good God!) let anybody else know you."

I am not writing here of the artificial snobs - the ones who borrow the stupidity of their "betters" along with their accents and haberdashery. These are people who know themselves only too well and are miserably dissatisfied with their information. It would be unfair to bunch these synthetic snobs with the true psychotic disdainers of life. They are impostors - even as anti-Semites. The anti-Semitism they put on is a threadbare thing. You can see their hindquarters sticking out.

The Bellocian or true English anti-Semitism is part of something much deeper than any such social pretense. It is an authentic negation, and much more than a highty-tighty refusal to say hello to any odd-looking neighbor. It is a fear of saying hello to itself. It is full of Pudor.

A CLUE OUT OF THE WASTEBASKET

Rummaging through the wastebaskets of history and coming up with lucrative essays on a thousand topics, Mr. Belloc, his labors done, proudly offered the world the statement that, though he had talked his head off, he had said nothing, and that he was that apotheosis of an English gentleman - a pearl in hiding. He closed his literary career with a salaam to his fellow statues - "Nobody knows me."

Had Mr. Belloc stayed away from the Jews, his boasting might have stood unchallenged. But in his book, *The Jews*, Mr. Belloc writes his autobiography. In this volume our author speaks out of prejudices deeper than animated his tirades against Protestants, workingmen or fellow authors. And if you want to hear a man's true name, catch him muttering in a fever or howling out of prejudice.

I shall now sift the evidence Mr. Belloc has left against himself. And if, in doing so, I use the name Belloc too often, it is because it is a symbol to me - just as the name Jew was to him.

THE MYSTERY OF THE MISSING BELLOC

The basis of Mr. Belloc's anti-Semitism was that he regarded the Jew as an alien. Mr. Belloc was at home everywhere - in Europe, in history, in Heaven. But he was not at home before the Jew. The Jew, he writes, is therefore an alien not only to him but to all the world.

It is obvious from this thumping oddity he ascribes to the Jew that Mr. Belloc is bothered by something unusually alien; by an alienism, in fact, that transcends geography, politics or culture. Our author shivers and starts before the Jew as if he had sighted a Loch Ness monster in his favorite tobacconist's shop. It is a Jew, it is a monster and it is alien. But why and how it is these things Mr. Belloc does not say. He has seen it and it is. As is the habit of people who behold monsters, Mr. Belloc does not pause to define, but rushes to attack. He attacks Jews, firmly and courageously, and you would almost think he was an English Knight battling against horrendous odds, and not Horrendous Odds battling against the ancient Jew still on his mule out of Jerusalem.

Mr. Belloc names this monster he has sighted "Jewishness." He sets up his battle cry, that to an Englishman the Jew is adversary. But how can all this be? Knowing nothing of Jewish history (as his book reveals) and having never consorted with Jews (as he says), what in the name of St. George is he attacking? Can you attack something you have never seen or even heard of? Mr. Belloc does just that. He attacks something he doesn't know, something he hasn't experienced, and something he has never suffered from. It is, accordingly obvious that our Englishman is actually attacking nothing. He is defending something. He is defending the purity of his Englishness just as the Germans were later to defend the purity of their Germanism - by liquidating Jews.

But is it purity that needs such defense?

And is it "Englishness" that needs to be protected from all comers like the gold that the miser buries in his back yard?

THE MYSTERY OF THE MISSING VILLAIN

The Jews, says Belloc, threaten him. How? In what club? Does he mean the handful of Jewish actors and liquor salesmen who have been knighted? (And he not.) Or the dead Disraeli? Or a few rival penny-a-liners? Or the Jews of Galicia lighting their faraway candles on the Sabbath Eve? Obviously none of these. And since he knows nothing of Jewish culture, certainly there is no threat there to him.

(To say, as he does, that a Europe whose culture and religion are actually based on the Hebrew Bible must be "the permanent antagonist of Israel" due to "a wholly different culture and religion" is proof that our Mr. Belloc was either a dunce or a liar - or maybe just a penny-a-liner.)

But there is no denying that Mr. Belloc felt a threat - a bad one. People sometimes invent threats just to show how brave they are in overcoming them. There was a touch of this sort of hypochondria in Mr. Belloc, particularly since any threat he could trump up was good for royalties, or space rates in the Catholic magazines. But the Belloc I know (by his book on the Jews) felt actually threatened, even after he had collected his royalties.

As for the whereabouts of this threat, it was evidently inside him, since there were no Jews waving any maces at his head. But there was obviously a "Jew" inside Mr. Belloc. And a very nasty fellow he must have been, to judge from our author's deep dislike of him. Please understand, I am not calling Mr. Belloc a Jew. That would be unfair to both sides. I am merely sifting the matter. The "Jew" inside Mr. Belloc was actually only Mr. Belloc, but a part he disliked intensely. He had another name for it too. He called it his Holy of Holies. Which really means that in addition to disliking the secretive Mr. Belloc, he also adored him. Yea, venerated him. This only goes to show how complicated an anti-Semite can be, if you start sifting him. He comes apart into dust, most of which gets into your eye.

But I shall persevere. What could this ugly secret in Mr. Belloc have been, that he called Jew and attacked outwardly, and also Holy of Holies and defended inwardly? Mr. Belloc himself confused the whole matter by dying. But to his death, Mr. Belloc continued to seethe with certain psychic disorders and unholy animations at which I can only continue to hurl questions. It is the only way you can hold an autopsy over a symbol. Maybe Mr. Belloc's fear of Jews had another twist to it. Does the Anglo-Saxon suffering from wretched dreams and anti-social impulses imagine that Jews are going to see through him?

Possibly, for in the English mind Jews are a polysyllabic people, brilliant, nosy, and as restless as grasshoppers. As if in further proof of their undesirability in and around a fine old British Club, the Jews at that moment invented psychoanalysis. I doubt, however, if Mr. Belloc had heard of psychoanalysis when he began attacking the Jews. If he had he would have been more frightened.

Outside of psychoanalysis and a historical reputation for wit and imagination (which is most irritating to people who disdain such qualities) what was it in the Jew that made him so dangerous an alien to Mr. Belloc? Was it the morality of the Jew? He does not practice it with special fervor, but he is known as its inventor. Or was it the Jew's abhorrence of decadence? Lots of people abhor decadence - bishops, curates, school marms, newspaper editors - but you cannot go around attacking them without seeming a little potty or, worse, revealing dangerously what you are defending. You can, however, attack Jews and not seem to be a man frightened by hidden abnormalities - except to a Jew like me.

What was the deep agitation and disquiet in Mr. Belloc that made it necessary for him to turn castigator of others? This I do not actually know - and will withhold my guess. What I do know is that there is a ruse by which our accusing conscience becomes a mop for the uncleanliness of our neighbor. Instead of losing face by giving ourselves up to the fumigator, we try to find an uncleanly neighbor, or invent one. The Jews are always handy for this role. They cannot sue for libel and their innocence has long been ruled out of court as immaterial.

When you hear the anti-Semite cry, "Out with aliens!" his cry is usually a paraphrase of a deeper lament - "out, out, damned spot!" I know many such Bellocian anti-Semites in life and literature. They make of the Jews a symbol of the thing in themselves that is damned. Then they proceed to call this symbol all the names they can think of - beginning with Jew. A Bellocian title for the Jews in fact would be, "Symbols of Anything and Everything I Don't Like."

A few more questions conclude the autopsy. What is it about ourselves we do not like? Our true worth? Our honest merits? Our decent love for man, woman and country? Not, as the psychiatrists say, by a potful. There are secret and undesirable monsters that disport in the darkness of all of us. In some of us they disport too much and their lair is not so dark. It is the hiders of monsters that have become too bold that are forever driving out Jews. The Jews fly - but the monsters remain. They remain and we stay an Englishman still.

THE SIGH BEFORE THE MIRROR

"*Qu'est ce qu'une nation?*" Renan asked. And then devoted his life to studying the history of the Hebrew people with much tenderness. Usually when this question is applied to the Jews, it is asked by less friendly minds, and holds in itself the answer that the Jews *are* a nation, a people apart and everlastingly alien.

It is a large question - the identity of the Jew - and I do not engage myself to handle it in all its wearisome ethnologic and political aspects. But neither is it to be answered by saying it isn't there at all. Indeed I will confess that, if I have never asked it before, or entered into its endless disputations, I have often experienced its equivalent - a startled look at the Jew.

When I see Jews who bring a note of Babylon into the subway, who intrude an Assyrian haircut into Broadway, whose large, liquid eyes seem to stare out of the palace of Xerxes, I am startled because these faces belong to me. I do not wear them but somehow they are mine. The long cheeks of the Arabs, the curly nose of the Chaldeans, the thick lips of the Memnonites, the cardboard shoulders of the Egyptians, and a thousand other oddities of phiz, body, expression and gesture that seem like an index of all history, offer themselves to me out of Jews. My heart says always I am related to them. My mind frowns at so large and diverse-looking a family.

How disturbed am I? Not too much. For they are not exactly alien. I remember uncles and aunts in my own home, who, when they assembled for a holiday, looked like a congress of nations. Some of them had faces five thousand years old and some of them had ideas untouched by thirty centuries of science.

They are not alien. Their trick is that they make *me* seem alien for a moment. They pull me out of my conceptions of myself as an American full of the history of Bunker Hill, John Paul Jones, and Covered Wagons. They remind me I have a secret - the vague, half-romantic secret of Jewishness - in me.

When, added to the oddity of face, there are also the sound of broken English, the dress of a gypsy, and the obtrusive mannerisms of poverty, my disturbance is a little deeper. I do not then criticize these gaudy and uncouth kinsmen of mine. I feel, rather, a pang of worry - the fear that in the eyes of others I am part of their alienism. It is a little fear and a fugitive one - but I have noted it. It has helped me understand many Jews I know who close their eyes entirely to all Jews as if they were a bad dream. Close their eyes as tightly as they will, the dream will not vanish, nor will they, themselves, step an inch out of it. They have nothing to gain by closing their eyes but a psychosis. But they seem to prefer a little madness to the hello of their kinsmen.

Such are some of the thoughts I have when confronted by Jews with a faraway look and sound to them. I have never run from this little surprise nor closed my eyes, nor grieved, nor sought to hide myself in an artist's smock or in an infatuation for other people's origins. Nor have I ever hurled myself into Jewishness as the only way of hiding from its troubles, as the shrewd way of making the best of a bad bargain. There are many Jews who do this. Unable to stand up alone in their Jewishness, frightened by the look in the eyes of others that calls them alien, they rush for protection to the lodge of the Jews. They borrow eagerly from the history and tradition of the Jews and dress themselves up as Hebrew scholars and Semitic chieftains. In this way they are happy, rather than unhappy in their alienism.

But for the most part, the Jews I know are more or less like myself. They have healthy minds, and they answer the smile of curiosity that sometimes touches the mouth of the Gentile with a smile of their own - who says a little alienism is a sin? Who is the judge of these matters? You, my fastidious friend? Who appointed you judge?

Nobody, good fellow - nothing but the oddities of your own ego. The oddities of my ego do not doff their hat in your courtroom. Judge away all you want, but you are not my judge. I am the only jurist I know. And, as jurist, I know that alienism is a fraud. A man has only to travel three hours in an aeroplane to find himself full of characteristics considered outlandish. I know that it is out of aliens that nations have made their own faces and laws. The English took in the Saxons and the Saxons took in the Danes. And the Danes, Saxons and Angles took in the Norman, the Celt, and the Castilian (who was already part Jewish). And the combination of all these took the Teuton into its royal house. And God knows what else went into the goulash called English - let alone the bouillabaisse called American.

I know that all this taking in of aliens is not always accompanied by welcoming committees. The alien who comes to nest in strange lands is often resisted as if he were an ogre or a plague. As an invader he is greeted with cannon, as a philosopher usually with a prison cell, and as a humble citizen in quest of a roof, very often with special laws that fill his roof with holes.

All this I know, and if, for an hour a year, I feel a certain pang of alienism in me, it has not yet inspired me to renounce my kin - or to affirm hysterically my difference from them.

AN AMERICAN WEDDING

I have written that in nearly all the lands of Europe a Jew must think of himself - if he be a reasonable creature - as a Jew only, for he has been repeatedly singled out for special disfavors as a Jew. He has been seldom and but briefly embraced as a European.

In the history of the Jew it takes one to make an auto-da-fé and two to make a wedding. His delusion that he is German, Polish French, Spanish, or Italian, his readiness to write their tongues, increase their cultures and die for their peculiar national ambitions, have nothing to do with his ultimate status as citizens of these lands. His deeds, however valiant and talented in behalf of foster lands, are fineries quickly stripped from him. Loaded with medals and diplomas, he is sent packing into ghettos, exile or death, and if he is not a Jew in the eyes of God or the rabbis, he is always one in good standing in the eyes of misfortune.

But in my own country, there is no history to give my illusion that I am a full citizen the lie. There was originally some discrimination in Maryland and in a few other colonies - where Jews were denied the rights of citizenship as well as fellowship. This, though, was at the beginning before we had become a nation (I am we again) and not since our emergence as the United States.

Their being present at the birth of a nation is no novelty for Jews. They were present at the accouchement of Poland, Spain, France, Germany and other nations. They have fought for the freedom and founding of many such states and achieved nothing by their efforts but the building of yet another house in which they were not welcome.

This has not been the fate of the Jew in the United States. Here he has been embraced politically and socially, although the heartiness of the embrace has sometimes been questionable. Nevertheless, he has never been shown the door or even ushered out of the parlor. As much as the man from Sweden, Ireland, Greece, Italy, or the islands of the moon, the Jew has been given fully the inner and outer garments of our democracy. He is an American and the rites of honorable assimilation are performed over his cradle or his citizenship papers.

Why then, any doubt on the subject? Why raise an issue of whether Jews are Americans when they so palpably are? I raise no such issue. What I raise is the right of Americans to be Jews. And I raise the issue, perhaps, more for Jews than non-Jews. Though we have tribes of anti-Semites in America, busy with all the fantasies of Jew-hatred, our country is as used to our Jewishness as it is to the shamrock-studded parades on St. Patrick's Day. It is only we assimilated Jews who are not used to it, who desire to run from it when it signals in our nervous systems. Run where? Usually to the psychoanalyst's couch.

I see the facts as follows. If I do not defend myself as a Jew, who, then, will? If I do not attack the enemies of Jews, who will have at them? My fellow Americans busy on other fronts? Why should they, since they are not Jewish, and I am? Since I hold my peace, why should they raise their fists? Do I prove my Americanism more by hiding behind its flag and muttering falsely that calumnies against Jews are none of my concern, and they do not touch me? Here is a lie, for all Jews are touched by the libel against their kind, the destruction of their distant kin in Europe. They are touched, darkened, and sickened, whether they stand praying in the synagogue or sit on the many red, white, and blue thrones of our country.

If my sense of outrage against the Germans is a Jewish one, do I lessen my Americanism by voicing it? Americanism is founded on a hatred of tyranny and on the belief in man's humanity to man. If tyrants flout the laws of human rights, and murder the weak, and I shout against them, am I more Jew than American? Even if my anger is Jewish, loudly Jewish, and makes no bones about the fact that it has gathered its violence from the spectacle of a people swindled out of happiness and tormented into near extinction?

My Jewishness does not belong to any other land. Despite the activities of the back-to-Palestine patriots, the Jew of America has no secondary homeland - except his face, and the history of his face. Unlike the man from Ireland, Germany, Sweden, Italy, France, the Jew of America is never to be seen floundering in divided loyalties. As a Jew, he is loyal to the same ideas to which he gives his American loyalty. He cries for the rights of man, and for the decent, unperilous operation of government. If he cries more loudly for these than the American next to him, is he not, perhaps, more American?

"WHO AM I?"

I would be wrong if this question gave the impression that I am confused. I am not confused and have never been confused about who and what I am. It is my enemies who are confused on that subject. I write about their confusion, not mine.

I will describe myself, briefly, and sketch my background. It is the habit of writers to offer their ideas as if these were orphans belonging only to truth. This may be a fine way to write if you are writing about the shape of the heavens. But when you are writing about the shape of your own soul, I prefer Montaigne's way. He threw in accounts of his arms and legs and even bladder. My discourse on anti-Semites does not rise genie-fashion out of a bottle of truth. My ideas are the product of my personality and not of magic. They will acquire more import if I acquire more outline.

I lived forty years in my country without encountering anti-Semitism or concerning myself even remotely with its existence. This is, perhaps, a record for a Jew, or more likely, for a country. There were no false contributions to this record such as an un-Jewish face, an un-Jewish name, or a mixed heritage. My family, including all the uncles, aunts, cousins, of which I ever got wind, were all Jews, all immigrants from Russia, and all people of lowly origin.

I have some uncles nearing ninety who have begun to mutter of learned forebears - sages and rabbis allegedly responsible for our line. I put little stock in these twilight reminiscences for I can remember no learning or even much literacy in the great troop of relations that surrounded my boyhood. I recall mainly that they were a noisy and impoverished lot and saltier than any people I have since encountered.

I was born in their midst in the ghetto of New York, and embraced forthwith with a somewhat mysterious devotion by all of them. It is, in fact, the memory of these Jews of my childhood who draped me in gaudy vestments and filled my days with fervor and entertainments that has held me constantly in my mind as a Jew. Although I traveled far and in many curious directions, I was loathe ever to leave those who had loved me so happily when I was weak and full of demands.

At the age of eight, speaking Yiddish almost as fluently as English, and also a little master of the fiddle - as what Jewish child of that era wasn't - I was plucked out of the ghetto and toted off to the Wisconsin town of Racine. The change of environment was startling, but I cannot remember noticing it. I was placed in a public school which contained only two Jews. I made no friends with them. My discrimination was a matter of circumstances and not of social nervousness.

I remember the two Jewish boys as somehow unfit for the diversions of Lake Avenue, which was the street in which I lived. These diversions consisted of loud, and often dangerous, games of pirate and Indian play - of making and sailing sixteen-foot catboats, of practicing to become circus acrobats - (I became one at fourteen) - of playing stump on the ice cakes in Lake Michigan, of breeding rabbits, hunting crows and frogs, building huts, and doing tricks on a bicycle.

During this time, my parents, who had established a store on Main Street called "The Paris Fashion," discovered a moody scholar from Kiev on the outskirts of Racine and ordered me to his side twice a week. His duties were to teach me the Hebrew language and the prayers necessary for the salvation of the Jewish soul. He did this abominably, for he was a complete fool - a fact which I understood at the time. He instructed me in the reading of Hebrew but indignantly refused to confide to me the meaning of the words I read. I thus leaned to read Hebrew but never to know a whisper of what I was reading - a piece of rabbinical sabotage that has kept me from enjoying the marvels of Sholem Aleichim, Hamm, Hirshbein, Bialik, and other untranslatable Jewish geniuses.

My parents, who were honorably, but vaguely, fulfilling a Jewish tradition, had small interest in the fact that illiteracy and not culture was being pounded into my skull. They were concerned only with the fact that on my thirteenth birthday I would be confirmed in the presence of all my aunts and uncles come from Chicago and points east, and be able on this occasion to repeat in Hebrew words the prayers necessary for my knighting as a Jew. Immediately after my Bar Mitzvah, the whiskered and foolish rabbi was dismissed from my life.

My visits to the rabbi of Racine were known to my fellow Indians and pirates, as was my Jewishness. They had often seen my towering and billowy aunts, and heard the dialect comedians who were my uncles, come to visit us and make merry over tea glasses in family reunions. Yet I remember no hint or whisper from any of my companions or their families that I was an alien in their eyes or a member of a race, people, or cult to be looked at askance. The only derogatory name I was ever called was "book worm," an epithet which I bore with secret pride.

My years in the town's high school were similarly missing in any Jewish consciousness on the part of my companions or myself. My own sense of being a Jew stopped with the love I had for my parents and my noisy troop of relations. I attended no synagogue, read no Jewish history or literature, never heard of the Spanish Inquisition, and listened to no discussion of Jewish problems. Had anyone asked me at that time for a statement on the "Jewish situation" I would have been floored completely.

There was no Jewish situation in my world of redskins, buccaneers, and acrobats. Jewish history consisted only of my folks who had, after many hardships, arrived in the USA, and who considered themselves happily to be Americans with a slight accent. My mother had picked up a sort of Samuel Weller diction in London's Whitechapel and, to the end, was baffled by V's and W's. Otherwise, she spoke fine English with the exception of an occasional double negative. My father's talk was a little more that of a Russian-Jewish immigrant. It was also that of a man whose imagination was too large for his vocabulary, a fact which made him a bit unintelligible, regardless of accent.

THERE WAS A LAND OF MILK AND HONEY

In all the time of my boyhood I can recall no utterance by my parents that they were aware of anti-Jewish discrimination. If it existed around them they were, like myself, too happy to notice it. They looked on the United States as a land of bright promise and vast cordiality. I had some uncles and aunts who, to the time of their death, twenty and thirty years later, conducted themselves as if they were tourists on a picnic in a strange land. The longer these lived in America the less they seemed to master the pronunciation of English and the less they, apparently, found out of what was going on around them. Their Jewishness was a sort of preferred entertainment, and the older they grew the more Jewish they became.

But even these Hebraic picnickers had only one phrase for America. They loved it. They loved it, perhaps, even more that those of my uncles and aunts who became "Americanized." For America allowed them to remain themselves and offered no calumny or peril to their oddity as Jews. They lived and died full of the simplehearted belief that they were human beings in good standing.

My father's Americanization, though it did not include a mastery of English, was fulsome. He enrolled himself as a member of as many lodges as he could afford. I recall that he had a drawerful of equipment that identified him as an Elk, a Knight of Pythias, a Mason, a Modern Woodsman, and a Loyal Moose, and to his death he liked nothing so much as marching in fraternal parades, accoutered in symbolic regalias. (He had an intellectual side, which reached a climax when he delivered a speech on Anatole France to a ladies' clothing Designers' Association, of which he always assured me he was President). My mother looked down on such diversion as nonsensical and possibly leading to sin. She found relaxation in swimming and dancing. She had learned to swim in the Dnieper but dancing was a talent she acquired at the many festivities of the New York ghetto.

At seventeen I went to work as a newspaper reporter on the Chicago *Journal* and continued in this profession for fifteen years. Here, again, circulating daily through underworlds and upperworlds in quest of scurrilous data, I met no hint or whisper of anti-Semitism. The newspapers of Chicago in this time did not attract many Jews. I can remember only one, an elegant gentleman from London who wore a black ribbon on his glasses and who considered all his colleagues uncouth. He, however, was highly esteemed for his exotic manners.

My intimates during my newspaper days were predominantly of Irish ancestry, although one of my closest friends was a cynical son of Germans.

Among all of them I was never an alien. In fact, it was my belief that I was regarded by all the newspapermen I knew exactly as I had been by my parents, my uncles and aunts. I felt nothing but love and fellowship around me and would have been startled to learn that, in this whole newspaper realm of drunks and scholars, poets, bar-room fighters, and dusty egoists, there was one who was not fond of me and pleased to have me for his friend.

I remember this world of 1910 to 1925 from almost every point of view but a Jewish one. Whether the host of people I knew avoided talking of Jewish matters to me, I cannot tell. My impression remains that there were no such matters around.

MY GOSSAMER HEBREW SCHOLARSHIP

Three Jewish things I recall from these young years. One was a swindle I practiced on my editors that my parents were religious folk and objected to my working on Jewish holidays. This always netted me from three to five extra days off during the year, which I usually spent in saloons waiting for my indignant Gentile colleagues to join me. Another was a morning I spent in Maxwell Street, the Jewish quarter, looking for a murderer. Unable to come upon the slayer - an every-day failing with newspaper sleuths - I decided to telephone my office. I was unable to get to a phone, for all the stores in that block, and for blocks around, were closed.

I found one finally in an adjoining neighborhood and, after phoning my editor, called an uncle of mine and asked him what sort of a Jewish holiday was being celebrated. He said it was no holiday, not even a minor one, and that there was no reason he could think of for Jews closing their shops on this day. He himself was busy in his ladies' tailoring establishment, and trade was thriving.

I returned to Maxwell Street to solve the mystery of the closed shops. An old Jew explained to me that this day was the twenty-fifth anniversary of the publication of Bialik's poem, "The Eagle."

Bialik was a name I had never heard. The spectacle of hundreds of Jewish merchants paying their highest obeisance to a poet in

Palestine startled me. I wrote a story about it for my paper and was convinced, together with my editor, that the Jews of Maxwell Street were a little daft.

Nevertheless, this Maxwell Street matter haunted me. My own family could throw no light on it. None of them had ever heard of Bialik, or any other poet, for that matter, and the name Palestine also caused them to shake their heads. The last reports they had on Palestine were that the Romans, a despicable people, had blown up the temple of Solomon and killed all the Jews.

The third incident was my meeting two of the most brilliant men I had ever been sent to interview. They were Louis Brandeis and Shmarya Levin, both attending a Zionist congress held in the Auditorium Theater.

I was assigned to cover the conclave and instead spent four days listening to Messers Brandeis and Levin talking in their hotel suite. I remember only of their talk that it enchanted me. I was used to wit and men of learning, for there were many talented people on the newspapers of that day. (They and their successors are still there.) But I had never heard the likes of these two Jewish delegates.

Listening to them, my own notions of culture, which consisted mainly of contact with Russian, French, and English novels, underwent a blasting. These two were learned in law, history, anthropology, science, knew twenty languages between them and were familiar, apparently, with all the secrets of man. To boot, they were witty and intelligible on all these subjects.

I recall only one brief conversation of our last meeting. Shmarya Levin was speaking. He had a bold black Van Dyke, bold black eyes, and a voice designed for humor.

"My boy," he said to me, "you will some day write about Jews. Well, I ask you to remember this advice. When you write about Jews, write with humor. Make jokes."

When Brandeis and Levin left Chicago, I was a slightly muddled convert to Zionism. The mood lasted two weeks. During its flush I wrote a one-act play called (why, I forget) "The Red Door." It was performed by a Little Theater group. In writing it I failed to take the advice of the witty Shmarya. I put no jokes into it. Its plot was the "crucifying" of a Jew, who was a brilliant Zionist, by other Jews who were stupidly averse to Zionism.

A month after the leaving of Brandeis and Levin, I had forgotten entirely the Zionist movement and all the witty and dramatic arguments that had been poured into me by the two evangels from Palestine. For almost thirty years that followed I never read a word on the subject or had a thought in my head concerning it.

A GLASS OF BEER WITH CAIN

I spent the years 1919 and 1920 as a foreign correspondent in Berlin, taking charge of its German office for the Chicago *Daily News.* During these years I adventured about Germany, covering a dozen revolutions and colliding with hundreds on hundreds of Germans. And here, no more than in my own country, did I encounter anti-Semitism.

It would seem from this that, despite my highly considered talents as an observer, I was the victim of a curious blindness. But I doubt this to be the case. I have been always a sensitive fellow, and not only easily offended, but quickly outraged by hints of criticism. And since I was engaged in studying the character of German people and reacting to its oddities with the excitement of a Chicagoan, I am certain I would have heard, smelled, or seen anti-Semitism had it been offered my senses.

What I did see of the Germans left me with two memories of them, only one of which operates today. I found them, after their defeat, a people full of appeal - polite, wistful, and a little mad with politics. It was impossible to escape German politics, even in bed. The ladies sighed themselves to sleep with murmurs of "Die Unaphängine Socialistische Partei." Through tea parties, saloon brawls, picnics and musicales sounded always the theme of politics. Everybody I met, from former Chancellors to porters and street car conductors, crackled with political philosophies. Even the homosexuals in their private and swanky Offizier Klubs talked like aldermen on an election eve.

I was much depressed by this monomania. It was as paralyzing as if I had come upon a nation of Stamp Collectors, all with albums and chatter to match. I was also a little stumped by the homosexuals.

I met more of them in one day in Berlin than I had encountered in nine years in Chicago. What was more, unlike the Chicago variety, who were sort of a nervous lot, these Berliner Fallatians were full of sneers and social dominance. They did not seem at all interested in aping women but in adding a new sort of arrogance to the male. I could never quite get over the fact that they always looked down on me as lacking something - as if homosexuality were some sort of literary and spiritual triumph instead of an ailment.

There was also the matter of culture. I had never encountered so many people who knew about knowledge. I met few poets and fewer musicians. But everybody recited poems or whistled movements from Bach. I found this dull, as if I had wandered into a land of parrots, and I spent many hours arguing with Germans about the significance of their culture. I felt it went with their stiff collars and was a reflection of their monkey-like vanities rather than of their love of art or interest in thought. These arguments revealed a curious thing to me. I never met a German who, in Germany, was willing to stand up for anything German - for more than fifteen minutes. After fifteen minutes he always struck his colors and fled to England, France, and even Africa in search of a superior culture. After fifteen minutes he was always ready to admit that Germans were fools lacking in the true sense of life - or any other equally pompous *mea culpa.* This attitude fascinated me at the time. I wrote that the Germans were a philosophical people - for they were able to see their own shortcomings and confess their failings - much more readily than Chicagoans.

And most of all - for this part of the ledger - they struck me as a cool people who took their four years of military travail and the defeat of their grandiose dreams with no inner sense of disaster. They seemed almost whimsical about the war.

Along with these qualities I responded to another phase of

Teutonia - its stark cruelty. I also wrote of this at the time. The Germans, with all their affability and political philosophy, seemed to me completely lacking in a moral sense.

BEELZEBUB AT PLAY

I will tell a story to illustrate this. The story was printed at the time in the Chicago *Daily News.* I was run out of Germany for cabling it to the United States but slipped back in a few days under the protection of Hugo Haase and his Independent Socialist party.

The story runs - I came into the bar of the Adlon Hotel at two o'clock one morning and saw standing alone a young German lieutenant. He was staring pie-eyed ahead of him and methodically tossing brandies down his gullet. I knew that this was a curious way for a young German officer to behave, for nobody outside a Chicago newspaperman with a grudge against his editor would stand by himself at a bar and hammer his liver with slug after slug of brandy.

I spoke to the lieutenant in English, asking him to join me and was pleased to flush, at such an hour, a native speaking my tongue. We stood for a time drinking together until I noticed that the lieutenant's hands were shaking and his eyes shedding tears. I asked him what was the matter. He slid to the floor, without replying, and I helped carry him to my room. Here he recovered in a half hour and, sobbing with shattered nerves, told me his story.

He had manned a machine gun in the courtyard of Moabit Prison (in Berlin) for three hours. During that time he had assisted at the execution of nine hundred men, women, and boys. They were German workers, their families captured during a recent putsch in Alexanderplatz where the proletaire had made one of its foolish and abortive essays to overthrow the government of Ebert, Scheidermann, and Noske, the last a forerunner of Hitler. These prisoners had been captured in fair fight and a week later placed before the machine guns in Moabit. My lieutenant was unable to bear the memory of the cries of his manacled compatriots as they fell before his machine gun. They had all - even the boys, shouted, "Long live God and our

Fatherland."

I left the lieutenant in my bed and hurried to Moabit Prison, armed with binoculars. From the branches of a tree some distance off, I watched the last of the two thousand prisoners tied together and driven with bayonets into the courtyard and shot down by the lieutenant's successors at the machine guns.

This story I cabled in the morning to my paper. I called it The White Terror. It was cabled back to the continent from London, and appeared in French and German newspapers under my name. Soldiers from Wilhelmstrasse arrived in the afternoon at my hotel and presented me with an order to quit their land. I was, at that time, in possession of a German bombing plane stolen for me by the German ace, Franz Knerr. It had been his for three years of combat. In this plane I went to Austria and from Austria flew to Wiemar, where the first National Assembly in German history was to open. I placed myself under Haase's wing and Herr Haase addressed the opening session of Germany's first republican forum with an account of the doings in the Moabit prison yard. He submitted the names of the two thousand who had been executed and said, at the end of his speech, "Germany can never take her place among the civilized peoples of the world until it unlearns its savagery."

His countrymen failed to achieve this mood, for they assassinated him a few years later while he was on his way up the steps of the Reichstag to take his seat in its councils.

The barbaric indifference to the laws of humanity of the German officials, that enabled them to execute two thousand political prisoners in a single night - and political prisoners who were their own kind - is one of my chief memories of their land. That and their political garrulity and homosexuality.

I saw innumerable times evidence of what seemed to me, despite my youthful indifference to ethics, a layer of barbarity in the German soul. In that day the Germans were still a generation away from canonizing this side of their natures and making their bid for world empire on the grounds of their talent for cruelty. But the making of their future "greatness" was already visible as it has always been to anyone looking on the Germans with German-cleared eyes. Nietzsche, whose eyes were thoroughly rinsed, wrote, at the beginning of the century, that there was no hope for Germans because they had brutalized themselves beyond cultural repair by their conduct in the war against the French in 1871.

At the time I was in Germany I knew nothing of its anti-Semitic history, knew nothing of the dead and tortured Jews of Cologne, Metz, Freiburg, and the many other place names where anti-Semitism had repetitiously struck. I left Germany in 1920 without having heard the word Jew mentioned during the two years I had prowled its towns as a reporter.

"SING NOT THESE OLD GRUSINIAN SONGS"

I dislike to remember the past for I am haunted then by a fairer world and younger faces than I now know, and by an innocence which, though it differed from that left behind by Adam on the Euphrates, was, in a way, Edenesque. There is nothing more enviable in the world than the fine misknowledge youth has of it. It was not so much Chicago I left in 1925 as a robust misunderstanding of men, women, and events that had kept me happy since childhood.

Some years after I had come to the city of New York I wrote a rhyme, hundreds of pages long, that began,

> "With a pencil and a writing pad,
> A suitcase and an overcoat,
> I came to town like Galahad -
> I wandered in like Don Quixote -
> Pensive and a little mad
> And hungry as a nanny goat."

My disillusion did not include unsuccess. In New York I flourished as a novelist, playwright, and composer of movies - which is often the same as being under bombardment by air, sea, and land forces, for there are critics (God, what a swarm of them!) guarding the approaches of those three arts. I was glad I had allowed my mastery of the fiddle to lapse for I understand that the music critics are submarines.

I had been under critical guns for my literary work in Chicago.

But the criticism you got while living in Chicago did not count; I do not mean from the local critics, who were all either enlightened or cowed, but from the boys at the catapults far away. Their shouts of battle were the mutterings out of Limbo. Not only were there no anti-Semites in the world. There were also no people of importance beyond this city of my youth.

I remember the critic Francis Hackett - a man giddy with learning and worldliness - objecting wittily to my first novel because the thing was a lie from beginning to end. He had lived many years in the city of Chicago, described in my book, and a more dreadful locale he had never known. It was a place, he contended, devoid of all beauty, including starlight. He feared that the beglamoured rains and snows and romantic highways I put in my novel were apt to entice people to the Illinois metropolis, which was the same thing as coaxing them into a herring barrel.

Of all the calumnies my book unloosed from the world that was over the hill and far away, this one stung the most. I did not mind being called a "degenerate," "a young man who should have confined his literary efforts to the walls of toilets," or being labeled "superficial," "sex-mad," "cryptic and humanless." But Mr. Hackett's inference that I was a Hillbilly disturbed me. It came as a clincher on top of Federal persecution, bankruptcy, and some domestic troubles, and I packed my writing pad. I left the city of poets and thinkers, of enchanted lamp posts and glorious sleet storms, and sought residence in New York. I was, perhaps, bored with Elysium.

One of my first impressions of New York - and the only one I will discuss as fitting into my thesis - was that I had come to a foreign country (like the Turkoman empire of the fifteenth century) in which all the courtiers were Jews. During my first year I met only Jews and half-Jews - with the exception of four transplanted Western friends - Messers MacArthur, Fowler, McEvoy, and the Dutchman Rosse.

These Jews in New York were not like my aunts and uncles but like myself, Semites far away from Semitism - writers, publishers, theatrical producers, journalists, wits, actors, and mighty drinkers whose only synagogue was Broadway. I imagine that there were also clever and accomplished Gentiles in the city, but I did not meet them. If I did, I probably mistook them for Jews, as I did Alexander Woollcott for a long time. MacArthur finally convinced me that this persnickity aesthete had not been Alex Wolfson originally.

There is nothing intellectual Jews dislike so much as to read that they are in the ascendancy anywhere. Such a statement seems a sly reflection on the caliber of the world they dominate. It also challenges their sense of social prestige. To be top dog in a world of Jewish top dogs is like winning a race on a treadmill. Having by their talents escaped their not too satisfactory origins and proved themselves disciples of Art rather than Jehovah, they are a little disturbed to find their new Temple seemingly a Jewish one. This is one reason why American-Jewish writers are inclined to write about Hindus, Chinamen, Negroes, Russians, Slavonian peasants, factory hands, and the nobility - anybody but Jews. A lucky fellow who has been invited to a ball doesn't appear in a suit of old clothes. Our American-Jewish writers like their new clothes better, and I am not arguing - although there is such a thing as being too dressed up - even for a ball.

I understood the slight disturbance in the Jewish soul. We who met at dinner tables in New York were not Jews, except possibly in the eyes of the butlers. We all had aunts and uncles like my own but they were tucked away in neighborhoods incalculably distant from our fingerbowls and our epigrams. ("Forgetfulness is always with us," a muddled Hebrew wrote a thousand years ago.)

Our disputations were as free of Jewish topics as if we had descended from the moon, where there are perhaps no Jews. If there was any nervous self-consciousness in this omission I did not know it. There was none in me. I had not been a Jew in Chicago, and I continued in New York not to be one. It seemed to me only normal that all the Jews around me should be also not Jews.

I MEET THE BOOGIEMAN'S FOOTPRINTS

It is the tradition of a great city that sins are to be found in it that do not flourish elsewhere and that innocence is stricken in its environs. Such is the sorrowful thing that befell me. In New York the world reached my ears that had before listened only to the bird songs of the ego.

I heard now rumors of anti-Semitism - not of German origin, for the Germans were still flirting with sanity - but of an American species. Word came that there were certain hotels where even Jews of great distinction and fine tailoring were not welcomed and that there were certain Social Sets that held out firmly against the induction of Jews.

My first reaction to this gossip was that it was a thumping lie indulged in by masochists in search of pinpricks. I said that it was not Jews who were being discriminated against but obviously individuals too ill-favored for social appeal. The Jews, I said, are able to leap a little more readily than most people from rags to riches, and they often bring into their wealthy estate the manners and accents of poverty. Greeks, Italians, and other strongly defined nationalities also do this, and there is no anti-Jewishness involved any more than there is any anti-Hellenism or anti-papacy in the aversion to such changelings. As for the rumors peddled by these offended millionaires who could not get into certain hotels or Sets, I said it was obvious that the scorned individual solaced his ego by placing the scorn against his "race" rather than against his own failings.

I was answered that the truth was otherwise. It appeared that when a high society figure did not cozen to a Greek or Italian he said merely, "Protopopolis is an ass," or "Giovanni is a fearful bounder." But when this same croquet and polo player was offended by the manners of Max Lapidus he did not say, "That fellow Max Lapidus is really a stinker." Instead he said, "The Jews, you know, are really stinkers." There, I was told, you had the nuance called anti-Semitism. (These were the happy days when anti-Semitism was still a nuance.)

My second emotion, on being thus convinced, was one of anger, and my anger was for the Jews who had begun to murmur these facts of life to me. Why, I asked, did they want to go into Sets where they were unwanted? Why want something that did not want you? Particularly something so vastly unimportant as the good will of a total stranger who was also an ass? Such as attitude not only belittled you but increased the stature of your enemy. You pumped him up with your chagrin. It made him at once your superior, and his anti-Semitism became a social crown which you, yourself, had clamped on his silly noggin.

When a man's an anti-Semite, I said in that cherubic time, he is automatically a jackass, and who gives a damn about his Social ýSet? He has hung a smallpox sign on it and it's he who has the pox, not I. And why feel depressed about the whole thing? If a man dislikes me for being Jewish, where is the humiliation? Who is lessened by this calamity? I have lost the companionship of a creature who has proved himself a fool. He has lost much more. Jews, I said, were inclined too much to fall down like dominoes. When a Jew in Pasadumkeag heard that a Jew in Albuquerque was disliked, he, too, immediately toppled under this displeasure or sat stewing in the Maine woods over a woe as distant as the Texas prairie.

Here was no way to be, I said. The Jew was no bit of flora that must give endemic response to air currents. We were individuals and must put aside our masochistic kinship. The way to fight an anti-Semite was not to fall down when he aimed at a Jew three thousand miles away. This sympathetic collapse did not help the Jew under attack. It merely knocked out the reserves before they had actually sighted battle.

My answer at that time to anti-Semitism was, briefly, it doesn't exist unless I say so, and to hell with it.

LITTLE BOY BLUE, GO BUY A HORN

There were flaws larger than elephants in my logic. For one thing, I was talking not to Jews but to anti-Semites - frustrated ones. That is what my fashionable Jewish friends actually were - Jews with an unhappy distaste for their kind. This distaste made them automatically look on bona fide anti-Semites as their betters. They suffered from anti-Semitism because it was actually a goal denied them.

There was an even more elephantine flaw in my logic than the error of my trying to comfort such fashionable Jews by talking to them as Jews. My confession of it will likely make me sound a playful and posturing fellow. This I am not nor was I ever. My misunderstandings came honestly out of my nature which was full of trust and of juvenile enthusiasms that often sharpened my style but left my ignorance intact.

My confession is that I looked on anti-Semitism only as a high society phenomenon - a sort of social fracas between two millionaires, one with an accent. I had read no Jewish history at the time and listened to no Jewish thinkers other than Brandeis and Levin. These had spoken only of the exciting future of the Jews, which was, perhaps, why I admired them so much. I was willing to be part of any exciting future but had no interest in joining a miserable past.

My failing was not merely one of education, which is always easily remedied, but part of my unworldly character. I had no awareness of what is called the Struggle for Existence. It is true I had come from poor people and been surrounded for many years by a toiling and often desperate troop of relatives. But this had never stirred me to any interest in the working classes. I regarded all poor people as somehow part of my family. I was ready to love them, champion them and be fascinated by them. But my sympathy fell short of interest in their actual troubles.

It is obvious to me now that I was molded in a rather childlike pattern, and that my early years as a man were spent in preserving about me the happy world I had known as a child. You cannot do this and become excited about what Karl Marx defined as Economic Determinism - that bedrock of one's relations to one's earnings on which many philosophers would rear the Soul of Man.

This missing sense showed up often in my writing. There you

found my heroes usually living in luxury - not gaudy luxury, but something even better - a happy unconcern with the problems of making a living. As a writer, I always gave them plenty of cash and dropped the whole business of Economic Determinism right there. They were then able to concern themselves with more vital matters, such as psychology, biology, and the manufacture of similes.

These economically untroubled heroes of mine were no escapist's creations. They were actually like me. I, too, had never rubbed noses with any grindstone. I was always able to make large sums of money without giving money any thought. The money I made never turned into riches, for it disappeared as mysteriously as it came. And the manner in which I made it had no relation in my mind to any struggle for existence. I felt, a little vaguely, that I was being rewarded for being what I was. Money seemed more like applause than part of an Economic System.

This attitude was responsible for my ignorance of the grimmer and wider aspects of anti-Semitism than were to be found in the wounds of a social climber. I had not looked into the bitter toil and competition going on among my family - the poor. Thus it was hidden from me that among those Jews who grieved about non-membership in clubs were not only social climbers but lawyers of talent who knew that law suits were most easily arbitrated in such fraternal settings. There were gifted doctors to whom anti-Semitism meant insurmountable handicaps - not in social life, but in the fulfillment of their work. They were barred from university chairs and kept out of all hospitals except a small percentage that permitted practice by Jews. And there were also countless bright youths barred even from medical or other professional schooling, for Jewish student quotas prevailed in most of our colleges and trade schools. There were big and little businessmen locked out of deals, as well as golf lawns, and there were even trained and eager warriors who would never be allowed to fight for their country in their most skilled capacity. And beyond all these people of talent was a larger and more helpless group. This was the army of the young - clerks, artisans, and unskilled workers who haunted the want ad columns and were denied needed jobs because of their Semitic origin.

Of the ugly side of anti-Semitism I knew nothing during my first years in New York. And, such is the tenacity of illusion, I was still surprised to learn in 1943 that Meyer Levin, one of the American war heroes, had been a victim of such corrupt discrimination. In his obituary I read, with astonishment, that, after being graduated from a government aeronautical school, the second highest in his class, Levin had been denied any work in the aircraft industry for three years because he bore a Jewish name. He had enlisted finally in our army, then at peace, and struggled to a lowly position in a ground crew in the Philippines. Here, his spirits undimmed, he rose to the status of pilot and bombardier. Four years after being graduated from school as a brilliant, but undesirable flyer, young Levin celebrated his victory over anti-Semitic industrialism by dying heroically for his country.

Such was the confusion, misunderstanding, and indifference which made up my first responses to anti-Semitism. They were based a bit on the failing of which Nietzsche once wrote, "the malady that I carry in me is the love of human beings." My misplaced affections have not broken my heart, but they have made me older.

THE RICH ARE ALWAYS WITH US

I find, after all, that I cannot dismiss the rich from the arena. They will have to enter it once more. In fact they have, of late, re-entered it themselves. When I first arrived in New York, anti-Semitism among the rich was a truly minor business, affecting only a handful of the more neurotic hostesses. The phobic dowager who shied at Jews was usually a lady so granite-faced and ill-favored that even Jews refused to have anything to do with her. The prettier people were in the main unaware of the "menace" of the Jew, and found neither tics nor belittlement in his presence.

But those pleasant days are over. The unearned increment fraternity has taken to rolling a Gestapo eye at the Jew; not all of it, or most of it - but a sufficient lot to menace the dinner parties of the rich Semites. And though the woes of such afflicted millionaires leave me as unmournful as when I first heard of them (and denounced them), I am moved to take a new look at the swells whom I left in my younger years happy with their ping-pong tables, their riding habits, and necking parties. I may help them to understand their new diversion of anti-Semitism.

Much has happened to the rich since the days when I first peered into their penthouses and summer palaces. Not as much as their yells of despair would indicate. These would almost convince you that the rich were being shot down on sight in their boudoirs, and clubbed to death nightly in all the better cafés. They have, in truth, raised more of a din over the curtailment of a few privileges than have the Jews over the bloody business of their extermination. But this is only natural when you consider, historically, the infantile sensitivity of the rich. They always have howled louder and carried on more frenziedly over the loss of a few luxuries than have the poor under the most fatal of blows of misfortune. In fact, the bad manners of the rich - their endless screaming and saliverous catfits - have confused the economic systems of the world since the beginning of government. They have convinced most of the philosophers that our highest human function lay in keeping the rich content and quiet.

The death rattle which our own rich have been uttering piteously for the past two decades has been considerably premature. They are not dead yet. All the rich people I knew twenty years ago, after twenty years of moaning and groaning, are still rich. Some of them are even richer.

NARCISSUS WITHOUT A FACE

Nevertheless certain things have been happening to the rich. They have been robbed of distinction and a point of view. The loss is not fatal but debilitating.

When I first encountered the rich (in the guise of a somewhat nerve-racking young iconoclast) I observed almost instantly that there was actually nothing distinguished about them at all. They were not even villains. They were, for the most part, amiable people with good diction and a flair for bad art. (I used to write like this when I was younger.)

I next observed that the business of being distinguished lay not in the heads of the rich but in the heads of others. On their own verandas the rich were a group of people hard put to keep from boring each other to death. But on the back porches of the poor, these same rich were a fabled folk. And I observed further that many of the rich (most of them) were content to sit about in their drawing rooms and be thus admired from afar. That a vast and lesser world considered them distinguished and enviable was enough excitement for them. Only the most wanton of them went looking for further diversion.

With this lazy business of being distinguished went a point of view equally pleasurable. The rich in that day were permitted by logic and tradition to look down on the poor, and to dream nobly at the same time of doing something nice for them.

All this has changed. It is indeed a most archaic and misinformed rich man who would sit around today dreaming about how to help the poor. The poor have risen. They have their eye on his silk hat and not his handouts.

These are important factors in the growth of anti-Semitism (as I shall reveal in a moment), particularly among the wives of the rich. It is chiefly the wives who run the dinner parties at which anti-Semitism is a centerpiece.

Robbed of their window dummy distinction and their Lady Bountiful point of view, the wives of our wealthy are the eeriest group of humans to be found in the world, as far as I know. They are all practically lunatics, and suffer from the shell shock of idleness - although I hesitate to call it suffering. Their recent activities as war workers - doughnut peddling, bandage rolling, benefit giving, and bed pan swabbing - aggravate their inner doldrums. For the work that the war has to offer the rich is no healthy thing. Work out of vanity and not necessity is an empty practice that leads to quicker and noisier breakdowns. There is a contingent who work out of an inner patriotic necessity but I ignore these in the happy belief that anti-Semitism is not to be found among honest patriots.

The truth is that the more excitement there is in the world, the less do the rich feel part of it. It is the poor who always come into their own in time of disaster. A war such as ours turns all the values of the rich to nothing, undermines their snobbery by filling their lawns with soldiers and sailors, strips them of glamour and meaning and leaves them without a Society leg to stand on. And there you have the secret of their anti-Semitism. What other distinctions remain open to them?

CONQUISTADORES FROM JERUSALEM

And now it is time to open a few reference books and look at history. Historians, as a rule, do not delight the mind. They have usually the manners of the stranger in the frock coat who knows his way too well about the funeral. Death seems to inspire them only with efficiency. But there are some historians who have in them more the joy of life than the pompousness of data. They come to picnic in the graveyard. Plutarch, Suetonius, Gibbon, Carlyle, Prescott are of this tribe. These recite an almost ribald tale of human misadventure.

In their tale, evil triumphs as often as virtue, the good are vanquished, the honorable are swindled, and the weak gleefully destroyed. But we read them, nonetheless, with pleasure. We find in the many preposterous wars they recount more than defeat or victory.

For on reading them we look rightly on the conflicts of the past and we become like a spectator who watches two teams engaged whose objectives have no meaning for him. We have no interest for the foolish goals that spell triumph or for the lesser score that registers defeat. We are fascinated by the players and we marvel at their cunning, their valor, and their great health. The game itself seems often more than half crazy but these players who dart and leap and are never tired of storming across the field seem almost half divine.

When we look rightly into the past we see and hear our predecessors - the people of history - hurrying toward senseless places. We do not applaud their goals but we smile at their liveliness.

This is the only test of nations or peoples - were they lively enough; did they pay their respects to their Creator by using their arms, legs, lungs, eyes, and possibly their brains, to the fullest degree?

To the little tribe of historians who answer "yes" for the past, I add the name of Graetz. He wrote a "History of the Jews," and a gorier tale has never been put to paper. He recited all the mishaps that had befallen Jews from the days they first engaged the displeasure of the Egyptians to the days that witnessed their many troubles at the end of the nineteenth century.

During this stretch of time, the largest occupied by an unconquered or unchanged people in history, the Jews tasted of the barbarity of a hundred nations. They were harried from one end of the world (the civilized part) to the other. They were whacked at by Babylonian, Chaldean, Greek, Roman, French, Spanish, German, English, Russian, Portuguese, Polish, Turkish, and Arabian potentates, armies, rabbles, statesmen, lunatics, saints, and scientists. Never was there such a battle and never so one-sided a battle.

When I had finished the last of Graetz' five heavy volumes, I felt a little stirring of sympathy for Europe, Christendom, and the lands of Islam. To have fought tirelessly and with so many ingenious and powerful weapons, and to have fought so small a foe as the Jew, and to have lost always - impressed me, fleetingly, as a debacle calling for some sympathy.

VIVA FROGS!

It must be confusing to anti-Semitism to have planted victoriously a thousand standards over the heads of Jews - usually through their skulls - and to see these heads rise constantly higher in the world. Never was there a land so stamped out as that of Israel. Nebuchadnezzar took it apart stone by stone and threw it to the winds like dust. Rome cleared the air even of this dust. And the game of centuries became to lay the ghost of Israel, to exorcise the world of it. Incredible ghost! Shade that blossoms on curses!

When I was a boy I hunted frogs in the marshes outside my town. I used to stun them with a long stick as they sat pondering in their green and cabalistic silence. I carried one of my mother's stockings for a game pouch. Into this I would drop the dozen comatose frogs and start for market. The little Saurians fetched a nickel apiece from the butcher. But I never earned a nickel by this enterprise. No matter how tightly I clutched the top of the stocking, the frogs escaped. They squeezed through my fist one by one as I sprinted toward the market. Never have I felt anything as maddeningly active as these frogs in the stocking. Even the dead ones escaped. I used to come home at twilight and lie on the grass, exhausted and bewildered - as any anti-Semite.

AROUND HIS NECK HE WORE

The history of the Jews is not like the history of any other people. It is more than a tombstone or a fairy tale. It is an identity tag that hangs like a tidy bit of haberdashery from the neck of every living Jew.

Most Jews are not aware of this tag any more than I was. When first the realization of this difference came to me I used to wonder at the vividness that attached to the word Jew - a greater vividness than seemed to illumine any other name in Europe. You said "British" and thought of adenoids and Trafalgar. You said "German" and thought of music and bad elimination; Russian meant a dancer with a knife in his teeth; French, an inkwell with a flag stuck in it. And so on through the world - the names of the nations have different sounds but they make a chorus. Jew is a name apart. It fits no motley pattern and you cannot introduce it into any chorus. You say "Jew" and it is a word that stands apart - either triumphant or lonely, as your mood will have it. But always apart.

I used to think that this apartness was entirely due to the lunacy of the anti-Semite. Looking into myself, the only oddity I felt was a separation from fools. I saw no other significance in myself. I was compounded of a prevalent culture and normal human relationships.

Look as I might, I could see nothing that entitled me to shine with the word "Jew." Logic answered, therefore, that the word "Jew" was a mote in my neighbor's eye.

I discovered late the tag on my neck and the thing written on it. It is written in a deep language and is exceedingly hard to read. I have managed to decipher some of it. It has taken a number of years and I am not unaware that others have been busy with this tag and made excellent translations. What I offer may well be only what is already to be found in any scholar's library. But I have never been in one of these. I have only my wit, my Jewishness, and Herr Graetz for consultants - these and the anti-Semites.

A TRUNKFUL OF GHOSTS

When I first read the history of the Jews I was as excited as if I had discovered radium. It seemed that many things had been revealed to me. The toughness and indestructibility of the Jew was not a "racial" phenomenon, but a mental one. The Jew was not part of world history but of the human mind. That is why armies could never vanquish him. That is why his enemies resorted so often to casting spells. The Jew was truly a ghost - and his haunting grounds were the corridors of the brain. These were among the revelations.

The history of the Jews reads like a trick done by the late Harry Houdini, master of illusions. They are captured, bound in chains, bashed with hammers, pierced with knives in all their vital places, jammed into a trunk, and the trunk, before your eyes, is lowered to the bottom of the sea. After an impressive interval, the trunk is hoisted to the surface, the lid unbound and opened - whereupon the Jews step out - refreshed. There is no mark on them, and they are not even wet.

The effect of this trick is stupendous. Yet it is a very simple trick. The Jews, you see, were never put into the trunk at all. They were never bound, hammered, pierced, or drowned. That was all illusion. It is always an empty trunk that is lowered to the sea bottom. As for their seeming to step out of this trunk, all beaming and refreshed, that is also a simple bit of deceit. They only seem to step out of the trunk because the foolish anti-Semites believe so avidly that they were in it.

To explain this whole matter of the untouched and constantly refreshed Jew is going to command all my wits. I don't think God has anything to do with it nor do I think that the Jews have even much to do with God. The tag on my neck says nothing about God. The whole business of miracle and hallucination with which the highly dramatic instincts of the Jews have offered their meaning to the world can be put aside and with no harm done to truth. The violent God of the Jews was the violent ego of the Jew. The oneness of Jehovah and His unmeasurable powers were the intactness and dream of power in the Jewish ego - a dream of human individualism and the ego's supremacy over tribes, states, and kingdoms that came sounding out of the first Jewish poets. There were other egoists in the world of the Prophet Samuel. But they were the accidents of circumstance or biology. Or they may have been artists who are happily everywhere and always. They were not a religion of egoism. The Jews were that. They said God was all-powerful but they meant something quite otherwise. They meant that the mind that could conceive of Him was all-powerful. They meant that the human spirit that could dream of its own perfection was a mighty spirit.

ON TIPTOE THROUGH THE BIBLE

I am no historian and less theologian. I am an admirer. I admired all the Jews of whom Graetz tells. They seem often as mad as Hatters, as monstrous as bad dreams. But their mission is clear. It is an admirable mission. It is the mission to think - to think as an individual in the teeth of all Kings and Causes. It is the drive to separate the human from nature, to rear his ego above the perfection of the ants.

Any nation intent on the perfection of the ants must automatically hate the Jews. Any nation whose power is its statehood, whose glory is its subservience, must immediately hate the Jews. The Jews say no to the ants. They say it in confused and fantastic terms - but their "no" is the health of humanity.

On this Nietzsche writes - "It was Jewish free thinkers, scholars, and physicians who upheld the banner of enlightenment and of intellectual independence under the severest personal sufferings, and defended Europe against Asia...The Jews are the opposite of all decadents....They are the health of Europe."

My admiration for these no-sayers to the Glory ants, the Power Ants, and the Ants who love strait jackets, begins with Abraham. Abraham is obviously a somewhat legendary fellow. But he can be seen plainly by the eyes of the spirit, which are the only eyes we can bring to the study of the remote past. He stands in a wilderness beside a road he has hewn and invites strangers to come eat with him in a new house he has built. He is the father of democracy.

I found Abraham admirable because of his smallness. He is the first small hero, the first to stand up in history and beckon for attention as a non-king, non-warrior, non-greatness maker. He is also the first recorded human famed for good deeds rather than evil ones. He tends sheep, he goes on a long trip, he finds a congenial place to live, and he has an idea. The greatness of nations had not touched Abraham. He saw no kings when he studied the stars, and dreamed of leading no armies when he fell asleep in his new house. He was as unworldly as Adam, but with a new type of unworldliness called introspection. He wondered who he was and, after some confusion, figured out he was God. Whereupon, he saw no reason to care or to wonder about anyone else. I admire Abraham for his twin invention of psychology and the Jew.

It is pleasing to be descended from such a man or such a legend. It puts one in the royal line of egoists. This is the miracle of the Jews today, not that they have somewhat preserved their God, their rituals, and their slightly Phoenician faces, but that they have kept the egoism of Abraham as a trademark on their souls. The anti-Semites have helped preserve this ego. Egoism is the one human attribute that thrives on disaster. When I hear of anti-Semites today muttering to one another of the unfitness of the Jew for their civilization, I know that this yeasty ego is in for further improvements and enlargements.

My admiration for Abraham's descendants is not inspired by their feats of magic or their many fables by which they seek to assure the world that they are God by posing as His favorite magician. My admiration is not for angels and miracles nor for other matters I cannot understand. This will likely make me seem full of irreligion, now that I am about to wander off into the Bible. The Bible is an old house and we are all its housekeepers. We do not like to see its curtains disturbed or its curious appointments questioned. I will disturb and question as little as possible. I have never admired those iconoclasts who smugly match wits with the dead.

I have no irreligion except that which lies in an absence of religious faith. I am willing to be God without fearfully putting a Substitute in the heavens. As God, I find myself surrounded by enough mysteries to keep me awed and wondering. My thoughts are candles that I light. They illumine a very little space to be sure. But they make a steady light.

The Prophets in the Bible assure me that God is all-Mysterious, all-Inconceivable. I nod. That is just the way I am. I have not the faintest idea even of why my liver functions as it does and who suggested that it function at all. All is mystery, all but the ants. Them I understand a bit. They are here to make systems and governments designed to chase Jews and egoists off the planet.

I read the Bible with Abraham's eyes who, I am certain, would have been as full of psychology as I am had that hurly-burly book been set before him.

THE FIRST BLOODSTAIN

In the tale of the Jews to be read in the Bible (and Professor Graetz) I admire most their liveliness. I do not mean their liveliness in flight or in their art of dodging disaster. I mean an inner liveliness, a most fantastic aliveness that bubbles away like a Jewish sap in civilization. It is against this aliveness that twenty-eight hundred years of enemies have launched themselves - and lost. It is as rife, as capering, as stubborn, and as drunken today as it was when the world first decided to be rid of it - because it offended the Glory-ants.

This was a world ruled by an amiable ancient named Ahab, King of the Phoenicians. He presided in the city of Tyre and he had for a spouse an overactive glandular female named Jezebel.

I go looking into this time because the trail of anti-Semitism begins there - the official trail. The Jews go much further back - another five centuries - but the anti-Semites have a less venerable history. They begin only with Ahab. Those modern mutterers against Jews who would like them all removed from the earth but who are, at the same time, fearful of offending them - are Ahabites. And the Pogrom, that has no such divided feelings, is bloodthirsty Jezebel - spouse of all half-hearts.

In Ahab's time, 940 BC, the greatness of the Jews as a nation was already gone. It had lasted two hundred and fifty years and flaunted twenty kings, among them two fine poets - David and Solomon.

When Ahab ruled Phoenicia, the Jewish Kingdom was already an epilogue. Its story had become a chronicle of minor mischiefs. The Jewish genius for disorganization had begun fully to assert itself. But though its greatness was gone, there was a quality lingering in its ruin that excited the King of the Phoenicians. It did not excite his cupidity for there was hardly a single candlestick to be grabbed by battle; nor his lust for warrior deeds, for he was neither warrior nor even a royal sadist. He was an amiable man and interested chiefly, like any schoolboy, in learning to read and write, which was the new diversion his fathers had brought into the world. Ahab's sires - the Phoenicians - had invented the alphabet, not as a means for writing poetry, but for keeping their business ledgers straight. Nevertheless, this invention opened a continent as big as the world itself - the continent of writing. Ahab rightly considered his collection of stone tablets the most important thing under the heavens, next to his fleets.

What excited Ahab and his lusty spouse, Jezebel, was the Jewishness of his neighbors. This is the first time in history that the Jews, or any people, are singled out for disfavor because of their spiritual characteristics. It is an interesting hour to look at for this reason. It is the beginning of the remarkable battle between Kings and Jews, governments and Jews, psychiatric quirks and Jews. It is anti-Semitism in its originally pure state.

It is not yet a complex signaling a hundred human lunacies, but the naive glaring at an idea that insists on donning the name Jew. The idea is a revolutionary one. It will take on many names in history and confuse and bedevil mightier men than Ahab. After many centuries it will shed entirely its ornaments of angels and Ventriloquial Voices, and become an unmystic matter called Moral Ethics; called also the Rights of Man. That which began as Ego, affirming the power of the individual, will, in a later day, affirm the power of all individuals.

All ideas have an artist who begins them. The idea that there was something more powerful in life than the whim of Kings, that there was a justice that the mind could impose on the might of nations, began with the Jews. The Jews were the artists and egoists of this idea. It was so powerful an idea that they, with artistic modesty, had to attribute it to God rather than to themselves. And to one God rather than a dozen who might scatter it into a fairy tale.

In Ahab's time the Idea was still in its first stages. Justice was so strange a concept that it made an egoist out of anyone who spoke it. King Ahab, who was part Jew, felt the idea in his bones but, with the rest of the Semitic tribe of Phoenicians, he was a little vague about it. He could feel that it contradicted his Gods, his fleets, the importance of his palace, and the meaning of life viewed from his vantage place of a throne. But as an idea he could identify it chiefly by negatives. It was not military ambition, nor trade competition, nor was it even what is called the Jewish religion.

THE LURE OF LITTLE GODS

This is one of the most interesting points in anti-Semitism - that it was not started by the religion of the Jews. At the time it began, the Jews had mostly discarded their religion. They still believed in one God but had put the head of a Bull on Him. They were not as impressed by this Jehovah with horns and a steaming snout as their fathers had been by the little flame that had burned day and night on their altars. This little flame had been their first picture of God. It was a reproduction of the Great Fire that had spoken to Moses and the children of Israel from the top of Mount Sinai. Having beheld God as a flame on a mountain top, the Jews had vowed never to picture him as less. Their eternal light on the altar was to be their only portrait of His inconceivability.

But they had come down, nevertheless, to a Bull with Horns. When I was reading about these matters the first time, I was not surprised to find El Toro usurping the holy place. The Jews had lost almost all their Jewishness in their adventures with power and dynasty. The little flame of God was the concept of ego. It had no face or expression. It was anonymous. It was the fire-picture of the individual soul. It said that this soul was supreme, and that its concepts of behavior were the future of man.

But two hundred and fifty years of Jewish glory had sapped the ego of Abraham and Moses. The Jews had found greatness in a Kingdom instead of in a shepherd's soul. They emerged from the business of half ants and half Jews. If Ahab had left them alone, they might have vanished altogether as Jews. There's a history I would like to read - the history of a Jewless world! It would sound like Shakespeare with most of his adjectives missing.

The matter of what God looks like is a vital part of religious history. I have not studied it deeply, but certain things became obvious to me as I pursued the Jews through Graetz. The moment God looks like anything at all, He ceases to exist. He becomes not God, but an objet d'art, a thing. This is one of the secrets of Ahab's excitement about the Jews. He wanted wistfully to own some Gods and not be owned by them.

The Phoenicians, like the Egyptians and all civilizations preceding or contemporary, had believed firmly in a worship downward. They worshipped Gods whom they were careful to make less important than men. This was the first wisdom of the world - the wisdom of kings. Their lesser Gods could not interfere with their bad habits. Nor could they send telegrams demanding revolution and disaster. Neither were they waiting in Heaven ready to punish them for villainies that seemed the charm and salt of life.

AMIABILITY VERSUS ECSTASY

Ahab shared, with all un-Jewish antiquity, the aversion to the ecstasizing of man. A man might become a great and heady creature through the plots of courtiers, the valor of armies, the manipulation of enterprises. But it was dangerous to imagine that he could leap willy-nilly into greatness by pronouncing a benediction over himself. Man, in Ahab's world, was a slave until proved otherwise. In ours, thanks greatly to the Jews, he is a master until demoted by events.

Ahab's amiability also inspired him against Jehovah. Said Ahab, if there were gods, they should not be anything as mysterious as man, but a pleasant collection of Kittens, Pigs, Foxes, Snakes and a few Sexual Symbols to give the galaxy a wider appeal. The Jews were about ready to trade in their almighty God for this set of wall ornaments. Yet Ahab and Jezebel, looking on the Jews, decided they needed further humanizing.

The Phoenicians of Ahab, though the first anti-Semites, were almost the cleverest. They did not resort to great violence - a thing that usually becomes a forge for the spirit and produces a blade of steel out of a handful of dogma. Instead they followed the tactics of Balak, King of Moab, in the time shortly after Moses had brought Jehovah and the Israelites into history.

GIRLS ARE ALWAYS BAD FOR DREAMERS

Balak, seeing the Israelitish host outside his city as being too great for his armies, had dispatched Balaam, his most gifted magician, to halt them single-handed with spells. Balaam consorted with the Israelites, studied their astonishing character, and brought back a report which has never been surpassed in history for truth and prophecy. The Israelites, he said, were a people who never could be overcome by arms, magic, or argument.

Balaam maintained that their peculiar nature was impervious to all assaults - but one. This was assault through the senses. Obviously, Balaam knew that the mind, however strong, never stands guard at the approaches of pleasure.

King Balak launched this assault. He sent his Midianite maidens to mingle with the Israelites and to worship their God, Baal-Peor, in the presence of the Hebrews. The worship consisted of sacrificing their virginity to Baal with the aid of any passing stranger. This rite was performed on a couch, according to scholars.

The Israelites, beholding these religious observances, grew restive and, with unusual tolerance, began assisting at the rituals of these pagans. In a short time the tents of all the Hebrew chiefs and rabbis were full of Midianite religious activity, and the great work of Moses seemed certain to be undone.

There is a brief account of how Balaam's classic plot was worsted. It is reported that Phineas, grandson of Aaron, saw one of Israel's holy men skipping toward his tent with a Midianite maiden on his arm, eager to make a sacrifice to Baal-Peor. Whereon Phineas, waxing wroth at this spectacle of vice, stabbed the two worshippers before they reached the sacred sofa, and by this deed brought about a moral awakening among all the Israelites.

I do not doubt this story. Moral awakenings are almost a habit with the Jews. But there are usually contributing factors. In this case I suspect that the supply of Midianite virgins was running low and the wily Balaam had begun to throw in substitutes.

THE HERO WITHOUT A SWORD

Ahab, King of the Phoenicians, pursued the course of Balaam in his first anti-Semitic plot. He sent an army of priests into the land of Judah, accompanied by the hand-maidens of Astarte. Their theology consisted mainly of fornication. These rites attracted great crowds of Hebrews and it seemed, for a time, that the triangle of Astarte would replace the Ark of the Covenant in the affections of Abraham's children.

But, as always when Jewishness is in danger, whether from inner or outer deviltries, there appears a Prophet. The Prophet of the Jews is the single swallow who makes a Jewish summer. There came into the midst of Ahab's great plot a man from nowhere named Elijah. He was not a man for fornications. He wore a heavy leather belt and a black hairy cloak. He drank no wine and he was busy organizing a sect called "The Nazarites." These were Jews who pledged themselves to renounce the pleasures of life and never to cut their hair. They spurned also all work as vain and belittling. They went about declaiming fiercely, "Jehovah alone is God, and Baal and Astarte are dumb, lifeless idols."

What did the Phoenicians stand to lose by the whoopings of Elijah? Not their own pleasant religious practices, for Elijah was hallooing only at the Jews. And history could already have assured Ahab that Jehovah was a God with an appeal so limited that He had never yet crossed a frontier.

It becomes obvious, therefore, that Ahab, derided in the Bible as a silly man, is actually a man of some vision, and his anti-Semitism is based on this vision. He can see obviously that the worship of Jehovah is no religion at all but a great social bomb. Ahab has built a new city, Jezreel, and in it raised a palace made of ivory. Here he comes to enjoy the winter months with Jezebel, with his stone tablets and sundry painted fellows. He has also a father-in-law who is in charge of a thousand priestesses of Astarte. These are beautiful young women whom the Bible describes briefly as abominations.

Under all these pleasant matters the words of Elijah are a bomb threatening explosion. The Nazarites, or Jews, or Israelites, or Samarians, or Hebrews, or whatever they are in this day, are a threat, not to false gods, but to society. Ahab sees this nervously. Therefore, he listens to Jezebel, who is no philosopher like himself, but a woman scorned. The preachings of Elijah cry avaunt to her abominable thighs.

Both Jezebel and Ahab are naive people. Jezebel can think of no way of out-arguing the Jews except by murdering them. Ahab also is too naive to resort to any hypocrisies. He lives before a day in which the worship of morality and its continual violation will become the religious norm. Man of vision though he is, his eye does not extend to rich men worshipping a God who loves only the poor, to warriors prostrating themselves to a credo that admires only peace, to sensualists with as many bedfellows as himself chanting in the houses of God that the flesh is vile and only the spirit is noble.

Haltingly, and with a feeling that he is not quite doing right, King Ahab launches the unended battle of anti-Semitism. He gives orders to his soldiers to hurl spears at the Nazarites on sight.

There have been a myriad of dead Jews in the world, but these long-haired ones who fall before Ahab's soldiers are the first humans to die for speaking poetry. They are the first men to be killed for voicing a human ideal.

Elijah escaped the soldiers and hied to the ivory palace of Ahab where all his enemies dwelt. Here Elijah challenged single-handed the newly born soul of anti-Semitism. He offered to engage in a contest with all the Astartean priests in Jezreel and see which of them - the idolators or he - could induce God to make a sign.

Ahab was fascinated by this proposal and considered the contest fair enough since the priests of Astarte outnumbered the Jewish entry four hundred fifty to one.

HOW THE WORLD OUTWITTED JEHOVAH

King Ahab hopefully gave his consent to the praying contest. He was, perhaps, curious to see if these unlikable people had any standing in Heaven. This was a folly few of the anti-Semites who came after Ahab permitted themselves; for they quickly learned the paradox that it was not in the eyes of God the Jew is unholy, but in the eyes of man. On this curious fact the twenty-eight hundred years of anti-Semitism are completely agreed. The Jew is the father of their morality and piety, but these children slam the door in his face. They even call the police at the sight of him.

Voltaire touches on the matter. He does not understand, in one of his ironical flourishes, why all Christians did not become Jews, since their God and their Savior are both entirely Jewish. Voltaire merely asks this so as to annoy the Christians.

Voltaire offers no answer, but the answer is simple enough. The Christians did not become Jews because the Christians did not become Christians. Christianity took over from Judaism not only its God and its Prophets, but its basic human ideas. The Jews had been unable to peddle them anywhere. They had succeeded after the fourteen hundred years between Moses and Christ only in keeping these ideas alive and warm. The Jews had become like a hen sitting patiently and fanatically on an egg that refuses to hatch.

That this egg did not hatch out a world of Jews is no miracle. The miracle would have been in its doing so. Then we would have had the miracle of goodness and justice triumphing everywhere instantly.

Quite another thing happened. The Christians removed the dangers of Judaism by divinizing it some more. When the egg hatched, its contents were taken immediately to Heaven. The Jews had been worldly egoists. They had demanded, to the consternation of Kings and Powers, that right and wrong, good and evil, be based on the needs and talents of the humble. The practicality of their requests had made them anarchists.

In taking over Judaism, the Christians confused the issue with so many new angels, miracles, and hallucinations that the worldly significance of democracy all but vanished. The rights of man were removed from the egg of Jerusalem to a place beyond the stars. "We'll eat pie in the sky, by and by," sang the Christians.

Thus Christianity removed the entire problem of revolution from the earth. It built an annex in which the dreams of goodness could disport themselves without discomfiting too greatly the evil of the world. The rulers and the ruling classes were quick to see this. Where Jewishness had bellowed at them to abdicate, Christianity whispered to them only to sing a song of tomorrow. Christianity contained in it a great solace for the humble and the seekers after justice. It assured them that their cause was in the hands of the angels. More than this, it satisfied the deep cynicism that lies in the souls of the lowly. The lowly know that, however powerful are the forces working for them, little will be accomplished in their lifetime. They were overjoyed to hear the more reasonable story that justice, righteousness and goodness would set in immediately on their deaths. The Kingdom Come became the riches and the triumph of the poor. It interfered in no way with the kingdoms of the rich. Thus Christianity reconciled the enemies of the world by a magical distribution of riches.

The Rights of Man proclaimed by the Jewish egoists were now for a long time to remain hidden in the new incense of Christianity. They were not lost and they were still Jewish. But they were inside another egg, as it were - an Easter egg more fetchingly and exuberantly decorated than the Judaic ovum. And the Jews were not allowed to sit on it any more. Nor did the Christians sit on it. It was an orphan egg and it incubated slowly in the areas of time.

When all the new miracles were finally in place, the words and music written, and the Christian incense sweetening the world, the great fact to be observed was that kings and their admirers had found a way unknown to Ahab of rendering the Jew powerless. They had added to him. They could show him page for page where the Christian Bible was finer, nobler, and even more Jewish than the Bible of the Hebrews. And, having won this battle of books and contest of poets' sayings, the Christians could cry avaunt to their father as a reprobate. They could proceed to live neither as Christians nor Jews by the ruse of paying homage to a dream of goodness happily placed beyond human reach.

I APOLOGIZE TO THE CHRISTIANS - WITH MY FINGERS CROSSED

I have done no more than call the Christians hypocrites. It is very obvious that they are, and that they have managed to remain Christians chiefly by practicing hypocrisy. It is also obvious, not only in the Bible, but in the streets around me, that the Jews are also hypocrites when they are lucky enough to be in any situation that calls for hypocrisy. David and Solomon were in such a situation and perjured themselves as valiantly as any Pope or King. They agreed that God was all-powerful and disproved it daily by working for the all-powerfulness of a kingdom and a court.

Thus it is obvious that hypocrisy is not the stamp of any faith. It is the stamp of faithlessness, and we are all, Jews, Christians, and Mohammedans, inclined to be faithless to our dreams when we can improve our properties.

GOD CAN MAKE MISTAKES, BUT HIS INTERPRETERS, NEVER

King Ahab gave the command for the praying contest. The Astartean priests erected a magnificent altar hung with expensive fabrics, shining with a thousand jewels, and no doubt enlivened with the finest pornographia to be seen in the world.

Nearby, Elijah built his altar. It was made of twelve crude stones representing the twelve scattered tribes of Israel, and had nothing about it to stir the senses - nothing but the wild eyes of the black-cloaked figure that stood beside it.

The painted priests whirled and danced before their wondrous shrine, cut themselves with knives, let their blood cover them as they rolled about in fornications, crying out, "Oh Baal, hear us!"

Baal failed to answer. After a time, the Astartean entries came to an end of their supplications and lay exhausted on the ground. They turned to watch the hairy cloak.

Elijah placed a bullock on his alter of stones. He spoke the words of the Hebrews that offer homage to the many virtues of Jehovah. And even as the bullock lay on the stones, an astonishing thing happened. Out of the bright sky came a bolt of lightning that smote Elijah's altar and crumbled it as Nebuchadnezzar was to crumble Jerusalem, scattering it to the winds and drying up even the water in the trench around it.

Ahab and his court, watching the contest, were overwhelmed by Elijah's miracle. I am also, twenty-eight hundred years later, a little startled - but not by the bolt of lightning that smote Elijah's pile of stones. This may well have been a poltergeist incident and no more miraculous than a meteor falling into the silo of a Kansas farm. What does amaze me, after these many years, is to learn that Elijah won the contest. I would have reported the matter differently. I would have written that Jehovah was angered by Elijah, that He lost His temper, in fact, to such a degree that He hurled a bolt of His fire at the prophet's altar and destroyed it utterly, and dried up all the water in his trench for good measure. This seems to me pure logic.

That Ahab saw the incident as he did is truly a miracle of that illogic by which divinity seems usually to win its victories. That the priests of Astarte were so defeated by the destruction of Elijah's altar that they hung their painted heads and moaned, reveals to me how far my own is from the religious mind. I would have shouted with glee in their place.

Elijah, flushed with his debatable triumph, demanded the immediate murder of the vanquished priests as a reward. Here is something that finally approaches rationality in the episode. Elijah was disposing of some enemies - a sane thing to do at any time. And there is never a better time for quick and pious murder than the hour in which God shows you His favor.

THE EGOMANIA OF ELIJAH - AND ITS DISDAIN OF PROOFS

But Elijah's rationality goes only a little way. Why did Elijah, with Ahab gaping in his palm, content himself with the riddance of only a hundred enemies? Having proved to Ahab and all the court of Phoenicia the inferiority of Baal as a God, why did not the hairy-cloaked one boldly demand the overthrow of the entire Astartean priesthood? On that afternoon, with the miracle cowing every mind about him, it could have been done. Elijah could have ordered not hundreds, but all the thousands of androgynous priests of Phoenicia to be thrown into the river and stoned to death.

I know the answer to his modesty. It has to do with the quality of Jewish liveliness before which I sit admiringly. This liveliness flooded the spirit of Elijah as it had of Samuel and Isaiah, and all the other egoists who made Jews out of nobodies. It is a liveliness that does not cry for conquest, that does not seek for glory, that does not desire monuments of dead bodies or of carved granite. It fancies only one monument - itself. It can imagine nothing in the world that can add a tittle to its importance. It is content to call itself God - and let others flounder about as Kings, Plutocrats, and Heroes.

Elijah called for no rewards from Ahab because his Jewishness was a distaste for all the things by which the Phoenicians measured greatness. Elijah, in his leather belt and hairy cloak, and his mane flowing down his shoulders, was the apostle of man's sufficiency unto himself. He was the prophet of man's destiny as an individual. He, Elijah, the ugly lone one was his own king. He would continue to move through deserts and cities proclaiming this fact to the annoyance of the amiable peoples who were delighted to be somebody else's subjects.

It was the prophets, says Renan, who put the stamp on the brow of Israel. Before that the Jew was anonymous. Since then he has been the troubled anarch, the Individual around whom events, dynasties and systems whirl in vain, like a rapids around a stone.

THIRTEEN MILLION UNHAPPY ELIJAHS

I write this of Elijah because I see him as one of the perfect Jews. There are few like him in the world today. His ego and its lordly scorn of its seeming betters are not easily come upon, even in the most pious of synagogues. There are certain artists in garrets who look down on the rich and mighty, and look up only to the vision in their own heads. But these are not necessarily Jews. Art is older than Jewishness. It has built many temples, but it has none of its own. It can be Jewish, but it does not have to be.

Yet Elijah does exist today, undiluted and unbarbered. He exists in the heads of the anti-Semites. They hear his thunder, no less than Ahab, and are frightened. They hear a man affirming himself as greater than thrones and pacts and plausible powers, and are angered. They call this man Jew because he was once Elijah, Samuel, and Jeremiah. But he is no more Jew than Kentuckian. He is part of an evolutionary foment in the human mind.

As a Jew I am flattered to be identified as the Egoist Anti-World. I have no such towering quality but it is a crown that looks good, even if it does not fit my small head.

Many Jews, however, are disturbed or wearied by this identity - as much so as if they read of themselves in the papers as being mad poets with long hair. They are not mad, nor poets. Their hair is cut and they have no more ego than is necessary for a pedestrian.

But they have the Prophets. And the Prophets are still wrestling with Phoenicia in every corner of the world. I have heard few hosannahs rising from the Jews watching this spectacle. But I, for one, have a little exultation in me.

TIN KINGS AND GOLDEN EGOS

The swaggering Elijah wanders off, his modest hundred enemies disposed of, and it never occurs to him to doubt who actually won the miracle contest.

The liveliness of the Jew has ever been of this half-mad sort. The lightning bolt that strikes him is always a sign in his favor. He is punished for no reason, burned, mobbed, humiliated, and all these wretched bolts of lightning are manifestations in his favor. I see in this the simple logic that the Jew does not believe in God at all. If he did, he would long ago have been impressed by His inimical Doings - and bolted to Christianity. This the Jew never did because he was too deep an egoist to be impressed by a friendly or unfriendly God. He dreamed of a heavenly earth, and affirmed a single mystery - himself. The heavens might fall on his head without disturbing his belief in the divinity of his soul.

When I use the word Jew, I hardly mean any Jews I know excepting myself and a few friends. I mean Jewishness. I meant the psychology that bedevils the anti-Semite.

I will finish now with Elijah. He had a mission and he moved fiercely and erratically over the land to fulfill it. He desired to find some lowly, plodding fellow tending sheep or cleaning camels - and anoint the startled laborer as King of the Jews. Samuel and others had done just this before him. They had dug kings out of dung and thereby sought to insure, at least, the lowliness of royal origin - its inferiority to themselves. They could never be certain of commanding its powerful finales - although this never much depressed them. They knew the most glittering of kings and the most powerful of systems obeyed the exit sign on the mighty temple of Karnak - "this, too, shall pass." They knew that all was vain but the bubbling, eternal ego of man.

I leave Elijah in quest of a king to disprove kinghood, in fierce search of his eternal enemy - the greatness of nations.

THE JEW AS A TORCH

The line from Phoenician anti-Semitism to its present Nordic child in Germany is unbroken. It makes a spiral through time but it never breaks. It threads the councils of dead and living nations, wraps itself about the steeples and minarets of new religions, crawls in and out of the windows of philosophers, and grows like a moss on the paving stones of villages and cities. Its outer tracks are easy to locate. The historian with a strong stomach can follow it neatly. (Name the cities of Europe and you have the tombs of the Jews.)

My hero Graetz makes such a pilgrimage. He pauses at every bloody stone and points a lyric finger. For Graetz has ever an ear for Jewish agony. He hears its most distant sobs. He watches all the funeral pyres. He moves, sadly, like Dante, through a shambles.

Here Jews burn themselves alive in their synagogues in Coblenz, Munich, Magdeburg. Here they flee down Spanish roads to the sea and the peasants seize them and cut open their bellies looking for hidden gold. Here they hang in the villages of France, guilty of having slyly attacked Christendom with the Black Plague. In Basle, Freiburg, and Cologne they make an almost continual bonfire. Cossacks to the east bash them to death against stone walls. Englishmen to the west halloo at their heels and go home at night with tales of their day's bag, a hundred Jews, a thousand Jews.

I have never liked facts, even pleasant ones, so I will pause with Graetz only at a few of his paragraphs. They are typical. Multiply them and you can become a Jewish scholar. On the 14th of February,

1349, the two thousand Jews of Strasbourg are all taken to the burial ground, tied to stakes, and burned alive. Around this time the Emperor Charles IV gives the cities of Worms and Frankfort a royal gift. He proclaims to their citizens that they can do anything they want with any Jews they can find. The Jews, hearing of this largesse, lock themselves in their houses and set fire to them and perish all. In other towns, Mayence is one, Jews rush into the streets armed with cudgels and die in a less despairing manner. There are hundreds of such Thermopylaes in Jewish history, a handful battling against armies and dying to the last one (and who says they lost?).

THE MIRACLE OF JEWISH GAYETY

But this tale of Jew-killing that runs through the centuries and is, apparently, still running through them, is a little misleading. On my pilgrimage with Graetz, I was fascinated by other matters than the lists of dead and foully-done-by Israelites. I was fascinated by the curious animation of the living Jews.

Here is something that, when I met it, had the odor of miracle. During the eighteen centuries in which hate, humiliation, and massacre boil constantly around them, my kinsmen, the Jews, reveal a single, unwavering characteristic. They are not impressed. Let alone they are not exterminated or driven into lunacy or filled with an incapacitating sense of horror; they are actually no more impressed than if it were raining. For centuries the Germans clap horned hats on them to distinguish them as a scurvy people; the French and Spanish - but I will not go into more of their troubles. Suffice that they are endless, bloody, and fantastic. Yet, surrounded by a demented Europe, by the hate and contempt of a perpetual lynching mob, the Jews perform neither as victims nor pariahs. They fill the lands with universities. They invent new sciences. They widen the fields of medicine and law. They open trade routes. They write great books. They are busy as beavers attacking each other as if there were no enemies at all baying at their heels. They are as industrious, sprightly, and inquisitive as if a sun were shining and not even a rain falling.

They remain part of a world toiling to disgorge them. They remain its friend.

Not only is their victory one of survival, in itself a notable one, but one of intellectual increase. Their troubles seem only to improve them.

Christendom is a jungle full of Papal tigers and Lutheran anacondas, yet Israel flourishes. Murder and calumny are its constant neighbors, and yet Israel grins, exults and makes its mark on all the eras. It is not the mark of martyrdom but of scholarship and of a bewildering genius. Robbed, it is always rich; blasted, it is always exuberant; hounded, it is always full of a baffling poise.

AN ANCIENT GALLOWS COMIC

While poring over my reference books, there was one time, in fact, that I laughed out loud. I had turned some of their darkest pages and my thought was staggering a bit with the details of so much murder and calumny. Whereupon, I met a Jew named Abraham Aboulafia - a learned friend of angels and demons.

The year is 1280 and Aboulafia, the Kabbalist, is on his way from Barcelona to Rome, a trip that takes him ten years, for he is often beset by ruffians and pursued by whole counties of Jew-haters. But Aboulafia allows nothing to deflect him from his mission. He is going to call on Pope Nicholas III and convert him to Judaism. Modestly, and with a humor undimmed by the centuries, Aboulafia, himself, writes of this matter -

"My plans were to look up the Pope the day before Rosh Hashana. The Pontiff, however, who was then in Suriano, a day's distance from Rome, upon being informed of my coming, arranged for a stake to be erected near the inner gate of the town so as to be spared the inconvenience of an audience with me. When I heard of these solicitous preparations in my behalf, I retired to a lonely chamber where I beheld the most wondrous visions and composed diligently one of my finest works - 'The Book of Testimony.' The book finished, I pursued the Pope to Suriano, only to learn from the heralds that he had died suddenly on the eve before I entered the town. Such are the miracles which continue to befall me."

I doff my hat to Aboulafia and to all his kin of Europe. Incredible Jews, it is obvious that they are as unchanging as the smell of their leather books. Nothing horrid that mankind can devise is able to lessen their enthusiasm for breathing, thinking, plotting, wrangling, and disporting themselves in the ever-blooming pastures of their love of life.

I understand all this even better when I regard these phenomena personally, through my own senses. It is through these and not through the data of history that I write. For I am a Jew in a world that hates and kills Jews even more actively than the world of Luther and the Popes, and I am unimpressed. In my world the knights of unreason still circle through the dark astride their sharp-winged bats and I am alive and sharp with words. I do not have to go to history to study the meaning of the Jew, or of the hate that seeks to engulf him, or of his incredible gayety; which (in a way) is lucky, for I am a poor scholar and would tire quickly fumbling among parchments.

THE SICKNESS CALLED WRITERS

Much has been written to explain the recurrence among the Germans of their old and bloody hobby of exterminating the Jews. But it has been an oblique writing. Looking on the blood-drenched massacre hands of the Germans, our writers have continued to discuss the political holes in the Nazi ideology. During the time of the massacre of 1940 onwards, I have read every day vibrant disputations on almost every subject except Germans. Our soldiers are allowed to fight Germans as fiercely as they can. But our writers are not allowed to discuss them. Not allowed! Who dares stop our writers? Wheel him out for Congress to pillory!

But he is a hydra-faced villain, who stops our writers. He is anti-Semitism and he is Semitism. He is also what the psychiatrists call "ambivalence" - a secret love of the thing one hates. Half of our most rabid anti-Nazi journalists are secretly infatuated with the Germans.

That is the way of many writers: there is too much sickness in them to make them of any use in a Cause.

The villain who halts our pens is also called by the name Good Taste. Virtue is to an ugly woman what good taste is to a stupid man - a false riches. Writers who are too timorous, too vacuous, too thin-hearted, to set to paper anything but the dullest of matters are usually full of the greatest of pride. They are proud of not writing. This pride in not being able to say anything is flaunted by all the votaries of good taste. They are obviously not people to tackle the Germans.

Nor are the anti-Semites.

As for the Jews who hold back, I will not say too much about them. They are full of many foolish ways of deadening the sting of German hatred. Too timorous to fight the enemy, they try to minimize him, by lessening him as a horror. Cowardice must always turn a back, either its own or its enemy's.

There are a few writers who concern themselves with a deeper look at the Germans than is to be found in a shifty and ambivalent eye of our political commentators. They see that the Germans are not evil politicians, but evil men. They see that the Nazis are not a street full of bad boys who have led the noble German astray - but the startling unmasking of all Germany. They see that a cancer flourishes in the body of the world and in its mind and soul, and that this cancerous thing is Germany, Germanism, and Germans.

They see the disease but they are its superiors, not its eradicators. The disease inspires them only to stick out their own chests. Looking on evil, such writers devote most of their energies to examining their own virtues. They are Narcissus who carries only a mirror into battle. And thus we have had an outburst of self-love in our country that has sickened our soldiers when they see it in the movies or hear it over the air. The Germans have this minor flaw - they are able to inspire nobility in people who are not entirely entitled to it.

More irritating than the saints who preen themselves in the presence of evil, however, are those writers (and readers) who cling to reasonableness at all costs, usually at the cost of reason itself. It is the fancy of such cud-chewers that not losing your temper makes you a philosopher at once. Most of the intellectual Jews I know are of this high-fallutin' ilk. They desire to be "fair" to the Germans.

I can understand this intellectual "fairness" of the Jew. It is often found in Jews in search of a way out from uncomfortable Jewish emotions - pain and vengeance; and in search also of a more comfortable identity. This identity they find equally in the clouds of "philosophy" or in Russian Communism. As "philosophers" they can escape the gnawings of anger. They do not have to respond then to the Germans as vicarious victims or men of righteous violence - both moods being difficult for attenuated souls. It is easier to tut-tut like Aristotle's son than to hurl rocks like the descendant of Judah Maccabeus - even mental rocks.

Even much easier than the flight into "philosophy" is the simple journey into Communism. Here there are concrete and human pleasures to embrace. The Jew, as a Communist, graduates from worrying about the enemies of Jews. He can enjoy the nobler anger against the enemies of man. He can escape his personal pain by disdaining the murder of three million Jews as being unimportant - compared to the wider injustices practiced against hundreds of millions of workers by the capitalist system. And he can wangle out of Communism something even more soothing to his battered Jewish spirit. He is able to look on the Germans not as today's murderers, but as tomorrow's Communists. They are, therefore, not enemies at all, but friends in the making. Thus he has lessened the horror of the Germans for himself and at the same time provided himself with a perfect future. To boot, in achieving all these things he has had the satisfaction of not thinking like a Jew, but a Russian; of not belonging remotely to any Jewish situation but to a much more positive and more socially (as well as mentally) desirable one - the Communist situation.

I have no great criticism of this pogrom-acrobat who has landed safely on the radical stage. He is often a valuable battler in that important cause. He gives to it the heroism and talent that he is incapable of giving to his own kind. His cowardice is not quite like the cowardice of our important and wealthy Jews, who turn their backs entirely on the Germans or who hide in the folds of the American flag. (God knows what they hide there.) I am not for vilifying these or any other Jewish non-combatants. It is a little foolish to berate sick people for not running and leaping.

The "fair-mindedness" of writers (and readers) who are not Jews is more disturbing because they make our majority of "thinkers." They are the ones who are elegantly proud of keeping a cool head amid disaster. It may be that they are reluctant to attack something evil as evil because they are secretly related to it. This may account for the eagerness with which they hunt down the villain's hidden virtue.

When such writers (and readers) contemplate so horrid a disaster as Germans, they like to turn it over and look at all its sides; observe Beethoven, Goethe, Maternal Instincts, Bruderschaft, Thomas Mann, and the discovery of 606 (by a Jew). This is a most unscientific way of studying a disaster, this contemplating of its undisastrous sides. It is like poring over the love letters of a murderer.

BORGIA WITH A COO

I remember doing this myself once as a young reporter. A voluptuous young woman of Chicago had slain a dentist in his office. I arrived with the police to find the shapely slayer still kneeling over the dentist's body. She held an emptied revolver in her hand and was moaning, winningly, "Oh, I love him. Oh, I love him so."

This declaration fascinated me. I spent much time with the unhappy girl in her cell discussing the ins and outs of love and hearing from her the long tale of wrongs done her by the wicked dentist. He had refused to marry her on finding out (in a hotel room) that she was not a virgin. This narrow-mindedness had shocked the young woman. She asked me, tearfully, how could a man scorn someone who adored him because of some foolish and forgotten accident in her past? She allowed me to read the ardent correspondence that had passed between them, and I shed a tear beside Juliet. To the day she was sentenced to imprisonment for life, I considered this young woman a romantic figure, a poor sweet creature driven to murder by the greatness of her love.

I was astounded three years later to read one morning that my heroine had tried to stab to death one of the guards in her prison. My editor, who considered me an authority on this case, due to the reams of misinformation I had already offered our readers, ordered me to rush to the scene. The young woman remembered me gratefully. She wept again for amorous wrongs done her, this time by the prison guard. The lecherous turnkey had seduced her by words of love, unmeant. She had discovered that his affections had strayed to a newcomer, in durance for having beaten her child to death. What could she do but what she had done, she cried.

When I left the prison it occurred to me that this young woman was a murderer - and that I had been taken in by her other talents.

I am not taken in by the other talents of the Germans. That they exist, is obvious. But they are the talents of humanity. They are the talents that make human beings and not those than make Germans.

Our reasonable thinkers are always assuring us that it is a sin against reason to condemn a whole people as evil when only a part of their soul is at fault; since it is obvious that, in addition to being murderers, they are also music lovers and very efficient with test tubes.

I am not interested in the Germans as musicians or scientists because you do not have to be a German to be either. To be a murderer, bold and gleeful, you have to be a German. It is in this specialty my interest lies. The tiger is of the cat family but we do not woo him with a saucer of milk and consider his kittenish charm - not all of us, anyway. The Germans are members of the human family, fully equipped with legs, lungs, arms, eyes, philosophers, and a modicum of reason. But I bring them no saucers of milk, and I am not allured by their charms. However they coo and weep (as they will soon), I see them standing over a dead body. I read in the fatness of their necks the mark of the murderer. I read in their watery eyes, their faded skins, their legs without feet, and their thick jaws, the fulfillment of a crime and the promise of another.

THE SICKNESS CALLED GERMANS

In reading the journalists (and philosophers) of my day, I notice that what impresses such writers chiefly is that the Germans have elaborated a style of government that all good Americans consider to be lacking in the virtues and charms of democracy. Under the German government, I am informed daily by our own finest thinkers, men are not free to think and act honestly, and all their social maneuvers are dependent on the whims of a dictatorship. I do not understand what is wrong with this sort of government - for Germans.

I am told that the efficiency and power generated by the Nazi economic system is a menace to the world. It piles up armament and brings on wars and almost wins them. This I do not believe at all. The Germans, under an economic system handed them by the angels, would pile up armaments, bring on wars and almost win them. The Germans, like the poor, have in them a need to assert themselves, and this need is as independent of economic systems as a wolf's howl is of music critics.

In fact, the only thing I like about the Germans is their Nazi government. I have my own reasons for liking it. It makes the German obvious, easy to understand, and infinitely less a menace than when he is posing as a zither player in a Tyrolean hat.

Our battle against the Nazi form of government is like throwing stones at a man's hat and taking care not to hit him. When we have knocked his hat off, he will only put another one on. I prefer him in his true native topper. It is not a pretty hat, the Nazi bonnet, but it is a German one, and when he wears it, the German is a true German, and we are safe from his wiles.

I consider the Nazi government not only as suitable for Germans, but ideal from the point of view of the rest of the world as a German government. It should be left them, after they are defeated, as a gift from Tantalus. They should be allowed to remain Germans in the open, with a good spiked fence around them such as is used in rendering a zoo harmless. Within this Nazi zoo maintained by the world for the diversion of philosophers, the Germans could then listen to Beethoven and dream of murder, and inconvenience no one. When their claws had grown too long and too sharp we could send in manicurists.

I offer this plan as the only one that can satisfy all sides - Germans, policemen, and humanitarians:

The Germans, now that they have tasted the wonders of pure dictatorship, will never be content with less. They will pretend - but they will plot and suffer - until they can be Nazis again. The name does not matter, nor the name of their leader. The important thing is the surrender of human rights and the existence of diversion. The Nazi government provided them with both. It is a very stimulating system. The Germans are a torpid people and need much to stimulate them into any kind of activity. As individuals, there is no hope for them. They would all sit around and become cases of obesity and melancholia, and their professors - whom Nietzsche called "Germany's national disease" - would end by strangling the thought of the world. The Germans need Nazism just as the man who, having no natural potency, needs high-powered drugs. Their Fuehrer was their Spanish Fly. I see no reason to deny them the only diversions possible for them - rape, murder and lunacy - providing they are forced by the police to practice them on each other.

Locked firmly in the middle of Europe as Nazis (with storm troopers, concentration camps, hangmen and Gestapo intact) the Germans would handle their own problem of extermination in their own way. Their massacre would not have to be on our conscience. At the same time, they could be watched and studied as criminals, and contribute much to our understanding of abnormal psychology.

But such sensible things never come to pass in the world. Our statesmen will insist, after our soldiers have defeated the Germans, that the enemy resume its masquerade as members of the human family. Thus we will reap from victory the reward of allowing the Germans to delude us again. It is the same reward we reaped from our last victory over them. Having taken their militarism away from them and restored them to an outward pattern of unmenacing government, we were able to forget happily that they were Germans.

This was an unwise thing to do. It will be even more unwise tomorrow. I know I am speaking into a wind and my words will carry no further than my nose, but I say them anyway; if not for the guidance of nations, perhaps for the diversion of students yet unborn.

Tamerlane, the conqueror of the great Persian monarch Bajazet, was wiser than our statesmen. He put the mighty Bajazet in a cage and studied him for many years. He never went anywhere without taking Bajazet in the cage along with him. The indignant Persian finally managed to batter his head to a pulp against the bars of the cage.

Such would, undoubtedly, be the end of Nazism, locked away in Europe and deprived of all outlet. It would be only medical justice if the only people who died from Germanism were Germans.

GUESS WHO WEARS THE DUNCE CAP IN MYTHOLOGY?

Ever since the Nazis took over the unmasking of the Germans, only the blind (who are always present in large numbers) have been unable to see them. To all others they have loomed, as we used to say in Chicago, like a sheisshouse in the fog. Although my thesis is anti-Semitism, I am lured from it to sniff a bit at all that is German - over and above its anti-Semitism.

Nietzsche, who never heard of Nazis, described them well in 1900. He called Germany "Europe's Flatland." He identified the spirit of Germany as "soft, swampy, slippery soil." The Germans, he wrote, "love all that is crepuscular, damp, and shrouded....They have not the faintest idea of how vulgar they are....The Germans are the most backward among the civilized peoples of Europe."

This backwardness goes back a long time. It is a constant thread in history and is the great national secret of the Germans. They have been full of backwardness longer than any unit of people, and they have been always proud of the fact. Their pride reminds me of the line from Bret Harte, who tells of the manner in which the editor of a western boom town paper reported a flood than engulfed the community. "The editor," Harte wrote, "proclaimed, with pensive pride, that an area greater than the State of Rhode Island is now under water." The Germans have been equally impressed by the area of their submergence and its longevity.

Their backwardness begins in the records of mythology. Sir J. G. Frazer relates that, at a time when the Franks, Slavs, Visigoths, Scythians, and early Greeks had progressed in their religion to a worship of birds, foxes and reptiles as their totem-ancestors, the German inhabitants of the Black Forest still held firmly to the theory that they were fashioned out of trees.

Their religious rites consisted of tying themselves up into the semblance of logs, and their priests would roll them, thus thinly disguised, into the forest to commune with their arboreal parents. It is not entirely an accident that the term "wooden head" has survived as the most trenchant description of the Germans.

This backwardness has persisted. Through all German history one fact remains apparent. Their souls do not quite fit them - nor do they quite fit the world. They are always nervous toward themselves, full of the insecurity of the badly dressed. They do not like themselves and are inclined to hold themselves cheap. That is why they are so eager for greatness. It is a thing not in them. It is a food for which they have a great appetite but no larder. And though they have developed a talent for confiscating greatness, they have none for possessing it. The English have become heroes by their conquests. The Germans remain clowns on the outskirts of all their victories. They cannot digest their loot. In their attacks on their neighbors, they wind up always like hoodlums with delicacies not meant for them. It is this that makes the triumphant German look always grotesque.

DISCOVERIES ARE DANGEROUS FOR FOOLS

The German rage against democracy is based on many German factors but also on a few democratic ones. The German hates democracy because he does not like himself. He has only one political ideal. It is based on his fat neck, his watery eyes, and his faded skin. It is the ideal described by Nietzsche: "They [the

Germans] first of all wish to see their genuine craving for obedience idolized." And described by Bismarck: "The Germans make the best soldiers - and the best waiters." A German living in a Democracy is like a fish out of water. He can only lie on the pier and expire. His natural element is power, not his own, but his tribe's. He dreads initiative as if it were a pox and he blubbers like a lost child if called on to depend on himself. "Submission, conformity, whether public or private, are German virtues," wrote Nietzsche.

This backwardness, this underdevelopment of ego, make the Germans enemies, not only of the Jew, but of the form of life which Jewish egoism has helped create - democracy. Democracy is to the German a truly evil thing since it robs him of his profession as a servant.

But the rage of the Germans against Democracy was not based entirely on their own incapacities for it. If it were, it would have been an unsuccessful rage, and would have attracted the attention only of psychiatrists and not historians. It is a rage based also on the deficiencies of Democracy. They were able to pounce on these deficiencies and thus seem to direct their talent for murder toward the destruction of false gods.

What the Germans perceived was that Democracy had lost its bloom in an industrialized world. The inventors of Democracy had worked without knowledge that the soul of man was going to end up pouring out of a smoke stack.

The inconvenience of Democracy in a world engaged in manufacturing rather than living has been apparent to many of its friends as well as foes. I, for one, who am its friend and its beneficiary, believe that Democracy is not entirely for tomorrow. It will continue always to make the best literature but it is doubtful whether it will continue unaltered to make even fair government. (The prospect is that Democracy will survive as a religion, as a sort of earthly version of Christianity and Judaism. That is the future Renan predicted for it. He wrote, at the end of the last century, that England and America would continue the work of Christ and Moses.)

Machines need arithmetic as well as covenants for their operation.

The Germans, who are always a little more up on arithmetic than covenants, were able to see this some time ago. They discovered that the world (for which they were unfit) was not a perfect one. There was great solace in this for the more sensitive Germans, who prefer an idea or two mixed with murder. However, the novelty of finding themselves in the van of anything unnerved the Germans. They are not a people used to the first gleams of Eldorado. Nietzsche wrote: "Everyone who has to live among Germans suffers from the dreadful grayness and apathy of their lives, their formlessness, torpor, and clumsiness; still more, their envy, secretiveness, and impurity, their innate love of the false and ignoble, their wretched mimicry and translation of a good foreign thing into a bad German one." Obviously a people unused to the cry of "Eureka!"

Their discovery that it was time to change the economic world a bit - a discovery they were kicked into by their first World War defeat - went to the sodden German head. They made the miscalculations common to drunkards. First, they visualized themselves as larger, prettier, and more irresistible than they were. Second, having discovered that arithmetic and not covenants made wheels go round, they considered it an ideal time to knock all the humanity nonsense out of the world.

The Germans, who once fancied themselves as logs descended from bigger logs, were able, after many centuries, to promote themselves to ants. The spectacle of so many machines in the world convinced them that the world belonged to ants. And that a little propaganda and a few blitzes would transform the world into a sensible ant hill.

The news from the Berlin of 1935 that the Germans had discovered they were a master race (of ants) served to bewilder chiefly the Germans. And perhaps a few Americans for whom all advertising matter is a tonic.

The Germans were bewildered because, despite all the torch-light processionals, they knew well enough who and what they were. Nietzsche had summed them up - "in things that really matter, the Germans are no longer worth considering." And added later, "If you consider the bestial quaffings of the ancient Germans [and not of the ancient ones alone!] then the origin of the German spirit can be understood - intestinal depression." A patient thus diagnosed must feel some confusion when he is handed a certificate as world champion.

For it was not Nietzsche alone who saw the sickness of the Germans. The Germans themselves have always known their liver was off. Like true invalids they have always admired the doctor who gave them the worst diagnosis. That is why they venerate Nietzsche.

In all their history, the Germans have never felt much self-affection. Such mood requires too much egoism for a German - and a little more blindness than he can command. The German can love himself only if there are enough of him around to drown out his misgivings in large and noisy cries. As a hero, he is the chorus boy, never the soloist.

German affection has always scattered itself to other lands. When I was in Berlin in 1919, I found two such German love cults in progress: one doted on the English, on English clothes, accent, poetry, politics, and mannerisms. The other was devoted to the French and sought to imitate the graces, wit and insouciance of the Gauls. The result was chiefly homosexuality. I met almost nobody among the hundreds of German officers, statesmen, revolutionists, poets, and industrialists with whom I talked, who had any love of anything German - except possibly for its indigestible food and unintelligible philosophers.

German self-love proclaimed suddenly by the Nazi microphones was an entirely trumped-up affection. It was based on the facts that both the English and the French had removed themselves as objects of devotion. They had fought him, beaten him, and called him so great a variety of names, that no German, unless he were an idiot, could go around saying he loved the Franzosen and the Englander any more.

There was nobody left for the German to love but himself. With what travail and confusion he planted his unwanted kiss on his own brow is now a matter of history. The entire hysteria of the Germans can be laid to this simple social fact - that they could not love themselves without going mad first.

KEGS OF DYNAMITE IN A WINDOW

I was once in the town of Carlinville, Illinois, on a Sunday afternoon in June. The coal miners of Carlinville were on strike. My editor, on hearing this news, had been certain that the State Militia or the regular Army would be called in to end the strike by shooting down a few score of the malcontents. This solution had been tried in the towns of Herrin, Illinois, and Ludlow, Montana, and turned out very well. In both these mining towns it had been demonstrated that unarmed miners, however angry, hungry, and full of complaints, were no match for infantry. That was a happy time in which rich people allowed policemen and rifle squads to straighten out all their economic problems.

I forget now the number of workers who were killed in Ludlow and Herrin. It was large enough, however, to fill my editor with the goriest of expectations. My instructions were to keep on my toes.

On this Sunday afternoon, I walked the Main Street of Carlinville with a weather eye out for violence. A no more idiotic pastime could be imagined, for there was no hint, smell, quiver, or promise of violence within a thousand miles. There was not even a prospect of rain. The striking miners were all in their Union Hall listening to the oratory of their leaders. I had sat there dutifully for an hour and gone away feeling sorry for the miners. The hall was jammed and hot, the oratory was without charm, and the cause of the strikers looked a little shaky.

A prairie sun lay on Main Street like a washerwoman's iron. The town sizzled under it. Prairie towns in Illinois looked always the same in those days - blank as the sky above them and full of a dust that made you dream of the South Seas and other places of escape. There were no movie theaters, no radio; the hotel lobby was an ill-kept oven; there were no ice cream parlors, and the saloons were all closed.

There was nothing to do but walk down the empty street and sneer at my editor who, like all editors, was full of stark idiocy. Violence, forsooth! There was not even a dog barking, a drunk snoring in the gutter, or a cloud in the sky. I was a sentry in a wasteland.

I stopped to look into a window. The window contained chiefly wallpaper samples, cans of paint, a few farm tools and alarm clocks, and a large pile of bottles guaranteed to cure constipation. I was moving on to other diversions when I spied in the window corner a row of six books, standing like a little troop that had lost its captain. I grew happy with the thought of buying them all and devoting the rest of my stay in Carlinville to the improvement of my mind.

A second look revealed that the six books were all of one title. They were six copies of "Thus Spake Zarathustra" by Friedrich Nietzsche. Nothing could have astonished me more. The only book on sale in this dust-bitten prairie town was a great, wild, half-intelligible work of philosophy!

As an avid admirer of Nietzsche, I was thrilled by this evidence of his unexpected popularity. But as a reporter, I was full of cynicism and curiosity. I entered the store, open because of its commerce in constipation cures. I expected to find some eccentric old scholar who was slyly peddling intellectual anarchy to his townsmen. A mid-western chromo rose from behind the counter - the bleary, toothless storekeeper who is as inevitable a part of a prairie town as its Civil War monument and its Sunday doldrums.

"I'd like a copy of that book in the window."

The weary merchant-druggist looked at me a little furtively.

"'Thus Spake Zarathustra.'"

He nodded, cocked a suspicious eye and shuffled off. He returned with all six books.

"How many of 'em you want?" he muttered.

"They're all alike, aren't they?"

He nodded, reluctantly.

"One will do."

He sighed and handed me a volume.

"Are they selling pretty well?"

He shook his head.

"Have you got any other books?"

Again a shake of the head.

"Only this one," he said.

"How did you happen to lay in a stock of 'Thus Spake Zarathustra'?"

"I saw it advertised," he said, "and I fell for it."

"I take it you were misled."

He nodded.

"Yep, I was misled. I thought the thing was a sequel to that Tarzan book. The names are practically the same. That Tarzan book went like hot cakes. Sold twenty of 'em last year. Only book I handled. When I saw this advertisement, I thought it was Tarzan who was talkin' and not somebody nobody ever heard of. So I ordered eighteen of 'em."

"Where are the other twelve?"

"Sold 'em. When I found out I'd been stung I kept my mouth shut. I just put the damn things in the window and let people figure it anyway they wanted. Twelve of 'em fell for it, same as me."

"Have you read the book?"

"You can't read it. It don't make sense."

"Did any of the customers return their copies?"

The merchant's eye lit up.

"Not a one. I figure they were too ashamed to come back with 'em."

"Ashamed of what?"

"Ashamed of being took in. Or maybe of admittin' they were too dumb to understand a book that was written plain in black and white."

"Do you remember the names of any of the people who bought the book?"

He weighed this for a while and then came to a conclusion.

"I ain't tellin'," he said.

I spent the next hours at the writing desk in the hotel lobby composing a feature story for my paper - Nietzsche in Carlinville!

My editor handed it back to me unused when I returned to the office two days later.

"The next time you put anything like this on the wire marked rush," he said, "you will be called in and handed over to a lunacy commission?"

THE GOLEM AND THE ROSE

I tell this anecdote because I have always liked it and because this time it will not be thrust back at me with insults, and because I have always seen a symbol in it - not only of Nietzsche's relation to Germany, but of all high literary men's relation to the world. They are there by mistake and they inspire chiefly embarrassment or confusion.

Germany was Nietzsche's Carlinville during most of his life. The man went mad sitting like an impostor in its store window. And I think it likely he would go out of his mind all over again were he to peer from his grave and see all the Nazis playing ride-a-cock-horse with him. For he was never a cool head nor one given to laughing at jokes. The only joke he knew was Germans, and he did not laugh at them. He stood in their midst and cursed brilliantly, lyrically, and until the day he dropped dead.

He found a certain cheer in this for he fancied that some day the Germans would read him, blush with shame, and mend their ways. It is the weakness of all philosophers that they dream of making the world more honest. They succeed usually in providing the Devil with more Scripture to quote.

I write of Nietzsche because he is more than a philosopher. He is a German phenomenon. A nation is revealed in him. He is German in the same way that Shelley and Swinburne are English. Like these and other English poets who gave expression to something that did not exist in the English - to wit, poetry - Nietzsche was the voice of a non-existent thing among the Germans - egoism and awareness.

These anarchic and repudiating voices are to be found in all lands. They are the few eagles hatched by the many hens. In the days before politics obscured all other values, they bore the proud name of artists.

There is a historical value to these artists. It is by studying them that we can locate the missing side of a people. The artists point always in the same direction - to the absent virtues.

It is for this reason that they are loved (almost as soon as they are dead). The people find a completion in them. The dullest and most inarticulate of Englishmen add Keats and Shelley to their bookshelves and become presto! part of a race of soaring lovers. That they remain quite the opposite is of no importance. Keats and Shelley are not alive to contradict them. They are no longer anarchs, but assets. Their genius becomes something everybody can own. The Russians, who are the most addleheaded of people, think they are Dostoievsky. The French, who measure life by sous and francs, think they are the Latin Quarter. And just as the most unromantic Englishman (of whom there are quite a few) dreams of himself as a creature in Keatsian mold, so it is with the Germans and Nietzsche. The German with the mustachioed Friedrich on his bookshelf can be an egoist and a "superman." He is as little that as he would be a king if he put a paper crown on his head. Nietzsche, being dead and silent, his scorpion whips buried with him, is unable to intrude in the matter. He becomes a crown for fools, a flower the Golem raises to his nose for a whiff of life not in him.

It was inevitable that he should die full of torture and mania, for his birth was too difficult a one. He died in a madhouse screaming that he was being crucified. His biographers see in this evidence that he felt guilty of his long attack on Christianity and was atoning mysteriously by dying on a phantom cross.

This is grandiose nonsense. Nietzsche never attacked Christianity or Christ. He attacked only Germans and their various intellectual belches that they called by different names.

All that I write of Germans was known much better to this lone Teutonic eagle. He wrote: "He who is well-disposed towards the Germans must consider how he may more and more grow out of what is German. The tendency to be un-German has always been a mark of efficient members of our nation."

Throughout his life, Nietzsche strove to remove the stigma of Germanism. He hurled rodomontades at German slavishness, thundered lyrically at German impurity and vulgarity. No artist ever called more names. He was like a man of wit and delicacy mysteriously hatched in a cabin full of grunting uncles and shoeless aunts. He was too honest to flee from them - too fascinated, also. He tried instead to wipe their noses and, in other ways, unvulgarize them. He wrote twenty-three books of etiquette.

But he saw always deeper than he wrote - a fact that sometimes makes his paragraphs unintelligible. At the end he saw the pool of blood in which the German sat. ("The Germans are barbarians - and worse.") He saw that his aunts and uncles were not only kin of vast vulgarity, but that they were gifted with a secret talent for murder unknown to other people. He saw the backward sadism, the killer stare in the watery German eyes. And all his thinking went to pot when he confronted the German criminals sitting around his own kitchen table. They were his kith and he must sit among them, shuddering and crying out at the end, "Oh, these Germans, what have they not cost us already!"

A TALENT FOR MURDER

One million Jews were massacred by the Germans in Poland. Another million were disposed of in Germany, France, Holland, Hungary, Austria, and Romania. A third million Jews were murdered in Russia, Serbia, and the Slav countries. These three million were not slain obliquely by starvation or overwork or on any battlefront. They were done in according to a plan.

The Germans sat at desks and held conferences, discussing the most economical way to murder Jews. The Germans at these desks were not fantastic Germans. They were usual Germans. They were German professors, officers, city planners, businessmen, German writers, German heroes, German musicians, German scientists. At these desks were all the German students and leaders and polite citizens whom we will see again when, as tourists, we visit the streets of conquered Berlin. They will be walking in these streets, bowing to one another behind the plate glass windows of restaurants, hurrying to the universities with ponderous text books under their arms.

At these desks in all the briefly conquered places of Europe, these human-looking Germans, these bakery store and beer-stube Germans, sat and discussed ways and means of murdering Jews expeditiously and economically. The German governor of Warsaw was decorated and promoted to a General for thinking up the idea of the lime kiln freight cars. Each freight car was equipped with enough lime to eat up two hundred Jews. By the time the hundred freight cars arrived at the burial ditches, twenty thousand Jews were dead in them. In addition to being inexpensive and killing Jews, lime possessed another property that endeared it to the Germans discussing these matters at their desks. Lime hurt Jews more than bullets or even fire. It ate their faces off and removed their bellies slowly.

In captured Odessa another of these desk-planners won high distinction. He thought up the idea of using Jewish men, women, and children as targets for the youthful bombardiers to practice on. This was more expensive than lime, but it helped the Fatherland. After bombing and machine-gunning twenty thousand Jews in the roads outside Odessa, the young German heroes had learned two vital German virtues - marksmanship and a contempt for the rights of humanity.

There were other desk geniuses who figured out ways and means of killing Jews that might save the Fatherland money or contribute a little to the education of its sons. Civic gas chambers were set up, dynamite dumps for Jews were constructed.

I have read many reports, not only from the undergrounds, but from the German police books. The murder of unarmed Jewish men, women, and children in lots of a hundred, a thousand, five thousand, twenty thousand, proceeded since 1940 with ever-increasing efficiency.

In conning the reports of this extermination of Europe's Jews my mind has remained never long on the screaming lime pits nor on the crackling synagogues filled with burning Jews. Nor on any of the piles on piles of dead Jews in the rivers and ditches. My mind moves always to the Germans at the desks inventing new ways of murder, giving orders for murder to be done, and receiving the reports from the lime kilns, the gas chambers, the machine gun and arson squads.

Good Beethoven lovers who will laugh and caper again when these troublesome days are over! Watery-eyed herrenvolk with tight, womanish mouths, and the grease of German politeness still bending their fat middles - my mind goes to them - to the burgerliche German at his desk, for he is a man of fascination. He has no gun in his hand, no danger and no enemy before him, no profit to make, yet he is a murderer. He is not even a sadist, in the more dramatic sense, for he does not care particularly to watch the lime kilns and the arson squads. He is a pure murderer. The thought of killing defenseless people brings a glow into his fat German neck. He needs no more than the thought to gladden him, no more than the police book reports of more and more dead Jews to give him a sense of achievement.

When I look at this German at his desk, I understand more about anti-Semitism than when I read a hundred histories. I understand that anti-Semitism is not part of history at all. It is part of man - a version of an old appetite that has found new delicacies. When I look at this seeming human at his desk, I know that there were no Dark Ages. There was only Dark Man. And he is still with us.

The German at his desk, ordering more lime for the lime kilns, gives the lie to all the historical arguments about anti-Semitism. This German citizen, this proud and modest little human unit of the German people, is not "avenging" Christ. He is done with Christ, for the time. Christ was a fool, an Oriental and a Jew. He does not care whether the Jews killed him or not.

The little German has outgrown all that nonsense about walking on waves and turning the other cheek - for the time. He is bristling with mythologies better designed to add a little gaudiness to his goose-stepping. He has dusted off the ancient tribal bric-a-brac Siegfried, Wotan, Gnomes, Fire Maidens - and placed them on the mantelpiece. This is no relapse into paganism. It is a slide into stupidity. He has not gone to his spirit for sustaining dreams but to an official fortune teller. He has had his palm read and been told it is lined with Siegfrieds and Valkyries and that the markings around his thumb show that he is a hero. His new religion is a thing you can buy for fifty cents at Coney Island.

Nor is this little German concerned with dinner table anti-Semitism. He is not a social bounder such as we have in America, who, unable to find any aristocracy in his suburban lineage, takes to excluding Jews - as the only proof of superiority open to him. No, he is not a social bounder and he does not hate Jews because he wants to get into a Blue Book or into a Golf Club where the servants are more elegant than himself. American anti-Semitism usually thinks of German anti-Semitism in this light - that it is a logical development of its own little parvenu games of Who's Who.

Nor is the little German bürgher concerned with arguments such as Mr. Belloc and his evasive kind have to offer - that the Jews are eternal aliens who can never be assimilated. He knows better. He knows that the most German-loving people who ever lived are (or were) the German Jews. They looked, talked, thought exactly like Germans. Even their names sounded exactly like German names. And they even shared with the Germans an aversion for Jews - that is, the Jews of other countries. There were never such obedient and appreciative Germans as the German Jews. They swooned with German culture. And even when the Germans loved English or French culture, the German Jews loved only German culture.

Yes, this watery-eyed one at the desk, calling for more lime, is not concerned with the "alienism" of the Jew. Nor is he concerned with Jewish gold. The robbery was done long ago - in the first happy days of Nazi conquest. All the money, works of art, factories, houses, palaces, automobiles, coal mines, steamships, owned by Jews were soon taken from them. These millions who were being murdered were all paupers. It was not, as the detective-story writers say, murder for profit.

As for the cry of "racial purity" that has been ringing for a decade in the ears of this little German murderer at his desk, this has taken in no Germans to speak of. He knows, as well as anybody, that the best and finest Germans have always been hybrids - Goethe, Wagner, Mozart. (Wagner, whose father was a cobbler in the ghetto. Mozart, of whom Marie Antoinette said, when she heard him play brilliantly on the piano as a child of four - "A Jew cannot be a genius." And ordered his baptism from the little Jew Azar to Mozart, the mighty German.)

He knows that the best Germans have black hair and that the Nordic semi-Albino is not a fellow to throw roses at. He is German, but the dumb German.

This little murderer at the desk is himself proud when he is mistaken for something other than German (just as many Jews crow inwardly when it is said of them that they do not look at all Jewish). He is not a man brought up in a rain barrel. He has read many books - mostly non-German - and he knows the psychology behind the cries of "racial purity" fully as well as I. Possibly better. He knows it is a foolish scientific tugging at your own boot straps. It will never lift you up, but make you look only a little sillier. He knows that there are no pure races - only purified ones. And he knows, too, how homosexuals, like the author of "Mein Kampf" and the inventor of the Luftwaffe, become obsessed with the idea of some purity outside themselves - in which to hide the impurity of their crippled souls.

I am not giving too much credit to this little desk murderer. I think one of the reasons the Germans always laugh at our propaganda is that it always presumes they do not know what Truth and Decency are. We bring them this news a little wildly as if we were missionaries with plums for backward children.

The Germans know about Right and Wrong. They have made an extensive study of it and often even set it to music. They know all our tracts, all our mottoes, all our visions - the fine ones as well as the comic ones. It is not from any lack of enlightenment that they sit at their desks and order lime for the lime kilns, order the murder of millions of unarmed, unmenacing, and unimportant human beings. It is because, over and above everything else he is, the German is a murderer. There lingers, in his fat neck and faded skin, the pleasure of the kill gone out of other anatomies.

German brutality is not passion. It is not usually attended by cries and facial distortions and sexual manifestations such as marked the anti-Semitism of Streicher. The Streicher cult of Jew-haters were really Jew-lovers. They mated with Jewish girls, using whips and branding irons instead of debilitated phalli. German brutality is a backwardness, an insensitivity that lingers like a cold spot on the fat German neck. Out of this cold spot rises his need of subservience. Subservience warms this German goose neck. Murder warms it also.

The little German bürgher at his desk telephoning for more lime does not quiver with low pleasure at the vision of twenty thousand more dead Jews. Instead he sighs with spiritual satisfaction. He feels a sense of relief, as if he had said his prayers over the telephone.

What I write must sound, to a degree, unbelievable, even to Jews. Jews have seldom been able to believe that they are killed by murderers. They have imagined usually that philosophies were killing them, bigotries, arguments, greeds, and political plots. To those who look on at the extermination of Jews from non-Jewish sidelines, the theory that Jews are being killed by murderers is even more untenable. There is a matter of history involved. For if the Germans who do the massacring today are murderers, then it follows that the Jew-killers of other eras were also murderers - and this is difficult to believe - for there were Popes and Kings and Cardinals and noble Knights among them. And always the simple honest village folk called, piously, the People.

Yet it is true. Nothing else about the Jews is truer. Many factors serve to make them a target. Many moods and motives seemingly combine in the minds of the anti-Semites to make the Jew a candidate for the gibbet and the lime kiln. But these are superficial moods and motives. They are social excuses for unsocial behavior. They are apologies to civilization for betraying it. These moods and motives change with the years. They change from religious to financial, from financial to national, from national to biological, from biological to financial. These are not reasons. They are alibis. Hence their shiftiness and transparency. Every pogrom scribbles a little footnote for the historians to study. It is a foolish study. For the moods and motives behind the killing of Jews are always something else. They are no more than the bugle-calls with which murder blows itself to action.

It is murder, foul murder, that stirs the anti-Semite. It is the foul need of warming the dead places in the human skin with the sight or thought of blood spilling that stirs him against the Jew. It stirs him sometimes only to oratory, sometimes only to the bird-brained chatter of the "exclusive" dinner tables, sometimes only to the cousinly deeds of calumny, robbery, and political action. Sometimes the anti-Semite is too civilized to kill, and murder degenerates into a tic - a spasm of distaste, a twitch of arrogance. Or he is too pious, too purring, too masked, with love and learning, to shed blood. Then murder becomes books of theology, anthropology, and unpretty fiction. But it is always murder. It is always murder that bubbles under the mask of anti-Semitism.

The little German bürgher at his desk, receiving reports of another seven thousand Jews run over by heavy motor lorries (this money-saving device was thought up by a German General in Romania); receiving the reports and entering them in a book as fastidiously as any accountant - this little blood fancier is the most perfect of the anti-Semites who has yet appeared. He is without delusions and as cool as the butcher behind his counter. He is the pure German relieving himself - as in an outhouse - of his German vulgarity, stupidity, and insensitiveness. The deed of murder unconstipates him. The deed of murder elevates and enlivens him.

It is by murder done that the German proves something important - perhaps that he is better than a corpse. It is by murder that the German reduces the world fleetingly to his own measure, appeases his lack of ego, makes his bid as an artist (a strong man) asserts his crudity over the finesse of human manners to which he is an unhappy stranger. Murder is his only escape from his damnable subservience. It is the only deed open to slaves. It is the only strength possible to the docile and frightened mind.

It is by being part of the murder of three million human beings that the German feels the stimulating warmth of successful Germanism about him - successful insensitivity, successful backwardness.

MURDERERS WITH DIMPLES

I think of Berlin restored, of Auslander once more sipping cocktails in the lobbies of the Adlon and the Bristol. I hear the elegant English of the maître d'hôtel promising a better suite beginning Monday. I see the bulbous-faced German matrons on the street cars, and the high-class albino clerks behind the counters. These are good people, say our journalists, then. These are fine people, say our war-tired politicians, then. Let us show them that we are not ourselves savages who harbor hate against the innocent.

I remember the journalists and the politicians after the First World War - the liberal ones, the milk-of-human-kindness thinkers. I remember how they filled the world with the tale of honest German worth come out of the four-year-war eclipse. This tale will come again. The little murderer, returned from his desk in Warsaw or Prague or Amsterdam, will see again the hand of human fellowship reaching toward him. He will shake it, listen to Beethoven, lick his chops, and bide his time. Murder is not a profession you can practice constantly. It is a tune you play for yourself when things are just right. A good German can wait ten, even twenty, years before treating himself to murder - a fine, big murder.

I see and hear the way things will be and I have no hope that they will be otherwise. I have no hope because I know that pity is a greater force in the world than intelligence. It is a deeper, more complex, force. By pity we share the evils we forgive. We embrace them undangerously with forgiveness.

MURDERERS ARE NOT ALWAYS HAPPY

I remember many murderers in the death cells of the Cook County Jail in Chicago - twenty-two of them. I knew them all well, listened to their life stories, and sat on a wooden bench and watched them hanged. I remember several generalities about these murderers.

One was that they all received flowers from anonymous friends - not admirers, but forgivers. The sheriff used to get angry and steal the bouquets for his own parlor. Blackie Weed (not a colored man), who had killed a few policemen and two neighbors in the line of fire, received some thirty-five bouquets of American Beauties from the time he was captured to the morning he was hanged. With the bouquets came many sentiments, most of them of a religious nature.

The forgivers sent in their blooms as a signal that God was all-merciful and that the hand of fellowship reached everywhere. The Sheriff knew better. He used to call these forgivers "those God damn morbid minds." And the guards, in the death cells, knew better. They used to say when another armful of blossoms arrived, "Those God damn fools who send flowers to murderers are murderers themselves."

There will be flowers in Berlin. Great masses of diplomatic blooms and statecraft roses will pile up on the desk of the little bürgher who used to telephone for more lime for the lime kilns.

I remember another generality about the murderers themselves. No matter how depraved or low they were, they all exhibited one common human trait. They were all ashamed of the crime committed. Blackie Weed and Teddy Webb were sorry they had killed several policemen. Frank Piano regretted honestly that he had chopped a woman's head off. Dr. Hoch was much depressed by the memory of the three ladies he had poisoned. Mrs. Vermylia wept when she thought of the thirteen baby corpses in the cellar of her baby farm. Morno, the truck farmer, shook his head and whispered to me that he couldn't sleep because of the peddler he had strangled. Carl Wanderer assured me he should never have shot his wife, whose pregnancy he had found unbearable.

Much of this post-murder ruefulness was inspired by the prospect of punishment, much of it by the fact that these were not murderers at all but common folk betrayed into murder by the dysfunction of their glands or nervous systems (or the Economic System.)

But much of it was also due to the fact that these Cook County murderers were conscious of having performed abnormally. Their bloody deeds were not the routine of their fellow citizens. They suffered from the sense of being human "isolates," a sense only very brilliant people can enjoy, and only artists turn to profit.

My murderers were neither brilliant nor artistic. They were related basically to the crowds about them. They felt that by their deeds they had divorced themselves from the homeland of crowds. They suffered from a social regret, much as lesser misdoers writhe in a lesser way at the memory of a dinner table *faux pas.*

They could not continue loving their crimes. However dear the deed had been to them, the world had repudiated it and made its memory undesirable. They bowed to the opinion of the critics (the roses were always kept from them). They were left with the remorse that is more aching than true repentance - the wretchedness of having sinned in the eyes of others. This was the agony of their villainy.

It is this agony of villainy that is spared the Germans. Unlike all other murderers, they are proud of their crimes. There are no eyes of others to stare them out of countenance. Around them are only German eyes, the eyes of German thinkers, philosophers, businessmen, leaders, scientists. The understanding of murder, the belief in murder, the need for murder are in all these eyes. Wherever the little German bürgher looks as he wipes his hands of murder he sees only murderers like himself - a city, a county, a tribe, a nation, a history of murderers. He does not have to repudiate his crime. He does not have to shudder at its abnormality. He is normal. Three million Jews have been murdered around him, and the cries of their dying and the reek of their bodies do not disturb his normality. Jews are not his judge. His judge is the spirit of Germany - and it smiles at him and says, "Well done."

Well done, little bürgher! Return to your bakery shop and your wine stube. Put a fresh linen collar around your fat neck, and a new pair of glasses on your watery eyes. Beam on the world again. Sleep beside Brünnehilde - the Venus without ankles. Germany is defeated once more - but the little German is never conquered. He has a thing that sets him apart from the world - a secret riches that makes all the victories of his enemies without meaning. He has red hands.

Put gloves on them, little bürgher, and carve toys with them again. Turn the pages of books with them again. Beat time with them to Bach and Beethoven. There is no need for worry even though the enemy polices Berlin. You can smile to yourself, little bürgher, because no policemen are going to arrest you. You can smile safely into German eyes and be safe in the smile they return. The policemen are going to take many things away. But they are going to leave you the best thing untouched - your red hands.

As long as your red hands remain, the Fatherland - the great tribe with little cold spots in its neck - is safe. Quiet flows the Rhine, and tomorrow you take the gloves off.

MY DARK PRAYER

The Jews who have been murdered by the Germans - a whole continent of them - are vague people to me, not as vague as the Chinese or the Greeks, but sufficiently diluted by distance and separate cultures to seem almost strangers. They never quite lived in my mind, and they never quite died. What lived and died was the beating of hearts, the warmth of faces and the rights of man.

I never mourned them as racial familiars. My heart did not weep over Europe's Jews as at a family grave. To tell the truth, it has not wept at all. It has felt only outrage. I doubt if any man has ever felt more.

My outrage is not for the innocent ones who died defenseless. It is for those who slew them. Do I live to be a hundred, I shall remember these Germans. I shall keep their name in a lime kiln of my own until I am dead. And I shall bear witness after I am dead - if there are any ears to listen then.

The Germans outraged me because they are murderers, foul and wanton, and because they are fools such as gibber at a roadside, with spittle running from their mouths. They outraged me because they raised little pig eyes to their betters and sought to grunt and claw their way to the mastery of men. They outraged me because they fouled the name even of war, fouled the hopes of man, fouled a generation that belonged to me. And they outraged me because I am a Jew.

That this most clumsy and backward of all human tribes - this leaden-hearted German - should dare to pronounce judgment on his superiors, dare to outlaw from the world the name of Jew - a name that dwarfs him as the tree does the weed at its foot - is an outrageous thing. It is an evil thing for the world that factories can supply fools with what God has denied them - greatness. It is an evil thing for the world that there remains in it a tribe that has only one dream - to cut the wings of others.

That these little pig-eyed Germans should have condemned and executed, not only three million Jews, not only the name of Jew, but the very name of humanity - condemned and executed every dream and hope of honorable men from Moses to Socrates to Christ, to Washington, to Garibaldi, Kosciusko, Bolivar, Pitt, Burke, and Lincoln - is an outrageous thing.

They brought nothing to their century but the cry of an evil hunger. They left nothing of their century but wreckage.

In this book I write no epitaph for the Jews in their graves. I write over each of the three million graves of those who were murdered the news - "The German is an abomination."

Wherever I go I shall carry this epitaph with me. I shall plant it on German brows and German desks. Wherever a German sits or stands, weeps or laughs - there is abomination. The years will never clean him. Nor will the whimpering and oaflike silence into which he will soon fall change his name and his epitaph. The German remains in defeat as in victory, in his cringe as in his gloat - an abomination.

I leave the Germans for a fairer topic. I return to the Jews, and to myself.

TO CONTINUE MY AUTOBIOGRAPHICAL NOTES

The scholar is at home everywhere, the reporter only in his memories. It is for this reason I push off my desk all the books about Hebrew culture and anti-Semitism and turn to Hollywood.

If I read all the books and make notes on them I will end up as full of sawdust as a German professor (or any other kind). In the presence of books my mind walks slowly as if it were a-stroll through a museum. Books impose manners on you more than ideas. They stiffen your legs, flatten your syntax, and put a belly on your imagination. They fill you full of good taste, which is a substitute for impotence. I have always been a disciple of illiteracy- carefully selected. It is like loneliness - good for you. And if I have any intelligence I lay it as much to books I have not read as to any other single factor.

You have only to listen to a professor to know there are too many books in the world- and too many professors. There are too few mariners and too many geographers.

So I go to Hollywood, rather than to the library of Hebrew culture I have accumulated (in my lazy hours), because much of my thought and theory about Jews has come from my experience in that Santa Claus town. Let the professors read *me.*

A GHOST IN THE GHETTO

I lived in New York several years without sticking my nose beyond its borders. I wrote several more novels and a play, enjoyed myself more each day, and found this plate-glass galleon of a city full of swashbuckle, profit, and delight. Six months after I had wept on leaving Chicago I could never imagine returning to it. I had wept, years before, on leaving Racine - and never put foot in it again although it was only two hours away from my newspaper office. This sort of infidelity is easy when you are young and carry the world around in a basket.

But I am not writing of New York or my adventures - only of my Jewishness. There was only one expression of it in these days, and a rather odd one it was. I will relate it before boarding the train for Hollywood.

My ignorance of Jewish matters had increased, if possible, during these first New York years. My concern for any Jewish problems remained unborn. I was full of no-man's-land iconoclasms, and was regarded by all who knew me as one of the most un-Jewish Jews who had ever sortied into Gotham. In fact, so un-Jewish did I seem that people refused to accept me as a New Yorker. I was referred to always as a Chicagoan.

And at this time - at the peak of all my shaygetz activities - I elected to move to the ghetto. God knows what sent me and my furniture to Henry Street. It was not my wife - a new one - who was a Russian girl recovering from childhood contacts with the Intelligentsia. She was still a-mutter with the Brotherhood of Man and the Iron Law of Wages, and as divorced in manner and mood from Jewishness as if she had been born on Tolstoy's desk.

I recall that we were riding with MacArthur in a taxi looking for an apartment we might share. The taxi was heading southward. At Twenty-fifth Street MacArthur announced that a foot further in this direction meant exile. He alighted at Twenty-third Street, wished us luck, and headed back nervously for civilization.

Madam and I continued to cruise up and down side streets and a spell came over me. As the neighborhoods grew more shabby and depressing I remembered my tantes and uncles and fell to chuckling. I became full of anecdotes and recited a rhyme I knew,

"Oh but life went gayly, gayly
In the house of Ida Dailey;
There were always throats to sing
Down the river bank with spring."

Spring and the river bank were the ghetto. I looked out of the cab window and saw sidewalks crawling with infants, push carts hung with ties, alarm clocks and bananas, old gentlemen in linen frock coats smoothing their whiskers, mothers screaming out of windows, little boys and girls playing hide-and-go-seek in refuse barrels. In the midst of all this stood a house To Let.

We moved in. I had returned to my childhood and felt blissful. There were no tantes and uncles, no parents and troops of cousins. But there was the scenery of Jews. And a magic lay over the frowsy streets.

We lived here seven months, until driven out by summer smells. Among these were chiefly the complex odors of rats whose corpses studded the plastering. During our residence it occurred neither to my companion nor myself to look inside any synagogues, commune with any neighbors, or pry into the secrets of the hullabaloo around us. I was a reporter only when employed by a newspaper. Unemployed, I never looked at monuments or conducted inquiries. I always slid back into a tunnel of self. Thus in the ghetto I met no Jews. I spoke to none. I found out nothing of their activities. I merely looked at them - drinking tea behind their shop windows, strolling in dusty parks, jamming the carnival shopping streets. I looked at them and was pleased, and might have lived forever like a Peri without the gate of my childhood - if not for the complaints of my nose.

We returned "uptown," and my Jewish activities were over. My sojourn in the ghetto was regarded by my Jewish non-Jewish friends as a burst of eccentricity. This it was not. I loved something faraway and had spent a while looking at its ghost.

INDIAN LOVE CALL

One of my New York newspaper friends, Herman Mankiewicz, had migrated west with his family. He had gone as an author to Hollywood. This was in the happy day when the Hollywood author had little more to do than to think up something for Lon Chaney to look like.

Here, finding himself wondrously solvent, ensconced in a house as magnificent as a Rajah's, surrounded by Movie Chieftains who considered him an oracle, my friend Mankiewicz bethought himself of me. We had, in New York, engaged together in several unsuccessful schemes to outwit a few millionaires we knew. My friend signaled from Hollywood that a minimum of effort was needed for greatness and riches in that domain - and that if I came there I would find all the highways blocked with millionaires in Santa Claus suits.

I was startled by this news. I had seen almost no movies and given them no thought. Lured by my friend's revelations and a contract he had wangled for me out of the studio in which he himself chewed the lotus leaf, I took train for Eldorado.

I have made the trip often since, and it has been my habit to arrive always with a scenario half in my mind. Now that I go there for the first time as a philosopher, I dislike to break this habit. On the train of thought that leads me to Hollywood I make up another scenario.

FOR SALE - A MOVIE

This is a movie I would like to do. I offer it to my mogul movie-making friends as a work for the screen. It has nothing to do with Jews, so they need not wince in advance. It has to do, however, with a mood which a Jew can understand a little more quickly than other people.

This is a mood contrary to the one the Jewish genius of Hollywood has peddled rhapsodically to the world. For the Jews of Hollywood are all Platonists and not Talmudists. They have followed religiously the theories of that timorous Greek (without having bothered to meet him): "Reveal to people only what can make them happy. Set before them only examples of the profits of good behavior and the victories of virtue." All else, said Plato, quoting his dead master, Socrates, and, as like as not, misquoting him hellishly - all else is a danger and a trouble to the development of man and must be banished.

Plato's precepts lay in the libraries for twenty-two hundred years. Artists shuddered at them. Philosophers praised them apologetically. Hollywood embraced them. Plato's Ideal Republic, a dusty fiction in the minds of scholars, became a reality in the studios of Hollywood. Nothing must trouble the illusion that people are sweet and loving, nothing must trouble the illusion that only sweet and loving and honest folk find happiness, nothing must trouble the illusion that the world rewards only the good and the virtuous - this Platonic credo became the soul of Hollywood. God help any anarchist who brings an opposite cry to movieland.

LISTEN TO ME AND GO BANKRUPT

Yet I bring one. I have long served Plato as a scenario writer, but I come this time with a script from Diogenes - the one with the lantern. Before I write it down I have a selling talk to make. I say to my friends of Hollywood, what good has your forty years of Platonism done? What goodness has come out of your tireless peddling of Greek goodness? What virtues have triumphed out of your relentless sale of Virtue Triumphant?

It was a good thing to try, for it might have done good. That the world was left a darker, uglier place after your forty years of fanatic cooing is no fault of yours. The cooing itself was often a pleasant thing to hear. But even the doves grow silent in winter. There is winter now on the world. It is time to change the sound machines. It is time to trade in Plato for Schopenhauer - or Elijah.

The world is an ugly place and grows uglier with each generation. Goodness does not come into it - though you coo till you explode. Evil and vileness thrive like wild vines around its throat. The more ideals that appear (and they appear like locusts and June bugs), the more viciousness increases. For each ideal generates angry partisans. Every new philosophy promotes murder and not thought. Every new invention renews greed and selfishness. The world is a wretched and contumelious planet. And this its inhabitants do not know. They sit in an ever darkening jungle and listen to the flute solos and the bird calls that rise from Hollywood.

Dear friends in the cinema capital, your forty years of playing the lark have proved that your lark song is of no avail. Not that you are Messiahs who dream of saving the world. But you are businessmen of a sort. And artists of a sort, and leaders of a sort. And there is always great excitement for those who have a little moondust in their heads in the discovery of new themes. Here is a new theme. Why not pam down to the jungle? Why not put a new villain on the screen - the mind of man; a new gangster - the stupidity of man; a new Public Enemy Number One - the brutality of human thought? If people could see how black they are - rather than be lied to about the whiteness of their souls - there might be great profit in it - at the box office and on Judgment Day.

A few readers of stray books know the secrets of human perfidy. Why not let the masses know them - the masses who are blindly part of them? And sometimes not so blindly.

Such is my selling talk. And here is my scenario, taken from the book called "The Life and Work of Semmelweis," written by the Russian, Louis-Ferdinand Celine.

A MOVIE SCENARIO

(RESEARCH NOTE): Ignatz Philip Semmelweis was born in Budapest on the Danube in July, 1818. He was the fourth son of a grocer. There were eight children in the house. They were noisy and full of song.

(HISTORICAL NOTE): Napoleon was through with pulling Europe through his ego and there was an end to all foolish warring in the world.

(EDUCATIONAL NOTE): Philip Semmelweis was sent to the Pest Academy where he learned Latin, won no prizes and left behind no memories of Minerva passing. It was his father's dream that he should be a lawyer.

In 1837 Philip went to Vienna to obtain his degree as a barrister

NO CAMERAS YET

Philip, the young law student, has an aversion for the legerdemain of legalistic philosophy. There is in his mind a pre-echo of a line Sandburg will write: "Why does a hearse horse snicker carrying a lawyer's bones?"

No hearse horse will snicker at Philip. He will hear, instead, the guffaw of a lynching mob. He will hear the world shriek with derision as he rides to rest behind the black plumes. But this he does not know. And, with broken heart (to be explained in a moment), and full of the love of humanity, he goes to become a doctor. He attends courses under Skoda, the greatest surgeon in Vienna.

NOTE TO PRODUCER

I would begin the picture with Semmelweis getting married. His bride is shy and pretty. I would show them during the year that follows. They are happy. Philip is full of love and hope because his wife is to present him with a child.

I would show the scene in which Semmelweis waits for his first-born. He is a poor law student, and his wife has gone for delivery to the big hospital in Vienna.

He waits at the end of a dark corridor. He hears a bell tolling. Two figures appear - a priest in vestments and before him an attendant tolling a little bell. They are going with the viaticum to the bedside of a dying woman. This is prescribed by the rules of the hospital.

Semmelweis sees the little procession stop at the door behind which his wife lies.

A doctor emerges and tells young Philip that nothing can be done. His wife? Dying. The child? Dead. The bell tolls.

Semmelweis looks wildly around. Two, five, nine, fifteen priests move down the corridors. Each has an attendant in front of him who rings the soft bell. Each procession moves toward the bed of a woman dying in childbirth.

Semmelweis weeps - and the bell tolling is his heart beating against iron tragedy.

APOLOGY TO CELINE

This is not in your book - the marriage, the tragic death in childbirth. But it is a case history from Hippocrates, medical ancestor of Semmelweis, written down by Hippocrates twenty-three hundred years ago - the case of Philinas, who stood by with the Greek physician and watched helplessly the dying of his beautiful wife, Thasus, in childbirth. She died of childbed fever. I add it to your book because it fits. Trust me.

OPENING SEQUENCES

Philip enrolls in the medical school under the great Skoda. He is moody, haunted by the shy face of his bride, by the tolling of the little bell in the corridor.

He has come to a school where the professors will teach him the answers to death, rather than legal answers to greed and vengeance.

Skoda is a renowned man. He is strong, audacious, experimental. He laughs at controversy - and medicine is a controversy almost as vicious as politics. A corpse runs for election and always wins. The doctors conduct the campaign.

Philip venerates Skoda. He will learn everything from him but his laughter.

Our Philip works like a steam engine. It is not grief that makes him work. It is the avidity that is always the first disordered sign of genius. He pries everywhere. He travels through miles of viscera. And a bell is always tolling faintly over his books and his cadavers.

A new character appears - Professor Rokitansky. He occupies the first chair of Pathological Anatomy in the school. He is not as famous as Skoda, but he has a deft hand with a scalpel. He is a beer drinker and a man who roars poetry at the night.

Skoda and Rokitansky are the ordained Godfathers of Semmelweis. Says Celine: "They will follow with anxious eyes the labors and efforts of their unforgettable disciple. With anguish they will watch him staggering along the road of his Calvary - and they will be able neither to help nor yet always understand."

CHARACTERIZATION

Philip Semmelweis is not an easy character, even now. There is a hole in his heart. He has looked into a grave and never quite looked out of it. This is the beginning of his new love story - his hunt among the cadavers.

Philip's eyes are not on the world. He is insolent to his superiors. He explodes easily - like all concentrated matter. He is oversensitive to the ancient jokes of medical students. He toils, broods, snarls, and behaves like a man full of slivers. Yet there is only love in his heart.

The trouble with Philip is that he has the genius for smelling out stupidity in others - which is unpardonable in a man who has as yet no other gift to offer the world. (It will be even more unpardonable when he brings the unwanted gift.)

Harassed by his own nature, by his own ignorance, by the strutting ignorance around him, Philip abandons the clinics and cadavers for happier surroundings. He becomes a beachcomber in the Royal Botanical Gardens. Here he meets Herr Bazatov - a shy man and a great expert on plant life. He talks with Bazatov week after week about the wonders and secrets of blossoms.

Philip is delighted by the flowers. He is never to know any other sweetness for the rest of his life than these garden months. No faces will ever smile on him as do the petunias, the roses, the calla lilies.

It is of flowers he writes (in Latin) when he submits his doctorate thesis to the medical school. Skoda and Rokitansky smile. It is bad Latin and worse botany and has no bearing on the medical arts. But they are in a beer stube. The music is playing. The brew is good. And Semmelweis is a stormy one who touches their hearts. They give their wayward Godson an official diploma. In May, 1844, Semmelweis is pronounced a doctor.

SCENES IN SHADOW FOR THE CAMERA

Philip's personality continues to stand in his way like a hippopotamus. But with the aid of his Godfathers, he manages to vault over it. He becomes an assistant to Rokitansky.

He becomes one of the death dealing surgeons of that era. It is the time before Pasteur and asepsis. Nine major operations out of ten terminate with immediate death, or infection - which is death walking.

Young Semmelweis watches the other death-dealers at work over the tables with their little guillotine knives. They are neither disturbed nor ashamed. They are full of strut and wisdom. Young Semmelweis sees that this is the way of the world - to be smug in error, content with stupidity and hateful of all that challenges it.

He listens to learned discourses in which the death-dealers explain the mystery of the tolling bell. They speak of "thickened pus," of "benign pus" and "laudable pus." Celine calls these phrases "the sonorities of impotence."

Semmelweis has also something to say. Vague words, but not smug ones. Remember that he is a man of his times, that he sits among the satraps of ignorance, that he has not seen tomorrow. Yet he writes (out of tomorrow): "Everything they are doing here seems to me quite futile, deaths follow one another with regularity. They go on operating, however, without seeking to find out why one patient succumbs in exactly the same circumstances in which another survives."

Rokitansky sighs over his beer mug as he reads this heresy. Skoda frowns and is thoughtful. Their godson is a question-asker. Dangerous calling. They have flirted with questions themselves. But they know how to laugh and drink beer.

ENTER THE VILLAIN

Master Surgeon Philip Semmelweis, with a hundred dead patients already in the bag, moves to a new department. It is new only to his science. His tears were there before. It is the department where women die in childbirth. The professor at its head is the gallant Dr. Klein.

Dr. Klein is now known in medical history as one of its super villains. This is unfair. Medical history, like world history, likes to condemn the great error-makers of the past. This gives the present always the illusion that it has progressed beyond admiring and defending error. Vain boast! With error constantly disproved and exposed, what remains triumphant in the world? Only this - the genius for admiring and defending further error. The trouble lies in our education. It doesn't begin till we are almost ready to die. Except for a few precocious people like Semmelweis.

Dr. Klein was no villain at all, for he was the friend of his time, the associate of current error. This made him an authority. Patients adored him - on the few occasions when they survived his ministrations. The medical press fawned on him. He was not the kind of presumptuous booby who knew more than the Editors. Nobody defends ignorance as savagely as an Editor. His job depends on holding off tomorrow - like the little boy with his finger in the dike. Editors always stand behind authorities. Authorities are the dikes.

To boot, Professor Klein wore a frock coat and his beard pointed the way to righteousness. He was all-knowing. Nobody could win an argument from him. His was a firm mind. But there was nothing in it. Nothing but yesterday in a coat of armor.

NOTE TO THE CASTING DIRECTOR

To cast this man right in our movie, we must have him played by the most dignified actor in all of Hollywood and the most heroic. Gary Cooper would do if he could sigh like Charles Boyer and beam with indulgent humor like Clark Gable. He must win the hearts of the audience at once. For in our movie, he, and not Semmelweis, is their man. He is the robust, clever, chuckling, fascinating Know-It-All. The fatuous Weisenheimer World masquerading as Hero. He is a man the audience believes automatically - the moment he says anything about Medicine, God, Politics, or the stupidity of all opposition. Just as Semmelweis is a man the audience wants to turn over to the police the moment *he* starts gabbing.

This is the great casting difficulty in our movie - but a most vital issue. Right is not on the side of the audience and the audience is not on the side of right. This oddity must be underscored.

THE BELL GROWS LOUDER

Semmelweis comes to work on his first day as scientist in the Lying-in Pavilion through February snows. There are two separate pavilions in the hospital for lying-in cases. The Second Pavilion is presided over by Dr. Bartsch - a professor who likes his job a little more than anything else. Dr. Klein commands the First Pavilion.

Semmelweis remembers the day he paced the waiting room full of hope and heard the bell tolling. His wife died here and his child. He has come to avenge them.

He sits down at a desk. His duty is to register the admission of pregnant women. They are from the poor districts of Vienna, from the slums, from the café street corners. They have no money for private obstetrics.

We see Semmelweis surrounded by women come for delivery. They weep. They cry out as if before a firing squad. It is Tuesday and Bartsch's Pavilion Number I is closed. They plead to be entered in Bartsch's. But the Hospital has rules. On alternate days pregnant women seeking free medical service must be entered in Klein's Pavilion. This is the Klein day.

Around Semmelweis' feet, the Klein women moan. They tell him there is no hope for them. All who come to have children in the Klein Pavilion must die. All Vienna knows this. All the basement and tenement brides and the poor girls of the streets know this.

Semmelweis sends for the records. It is true. The percentage of women dying in childbirth from puerperal fever is three times higher in the Klein Pavilion than in the Bartsch Pavilion.

What can this mean? Semmelweis frowns at this curious fact. But he can do nothing. Twenty penniless women, wailing their farewells to life, are admitted on this Tuesday into Klein's childbirth inferno. Others scream and run out and refuse to be coaxed back again by the relatives who brought them in. They prefer to give birth in the streets. Their chances of survival are better.

For this group of twenty, the little bell that goes before the priests tolls nineteen times. Semmelweis hears the priests chanting as they walk slowly, and the bell tolling. He knows the hope and love that die at this sound. He sits at his desk and hurls his mind at the dark.

SCENES OF TERROR AND SMUGNESS

Day after day Semmelweis sits at his registrar's desk in the Klein Pavilion - not a doctor, but a Charon embarking terrified women for the shores of death.

Around him are many doctors. They are a little nervous from their toil in the charnel house. But the mighty Klein commands them. There is no nervousness in the face of this hero. It beams. It knows that a best of all possible worlds lies around it. If you are worried, look at Klein - and peace comes back into your heart. Thus do Prime Ministers and Foreign Secretaries and all High Authorities look when the smells of disaster touch their noses. They look proud and All-Knowing, and the world cheers them.

The mortality rate in the Klein Pavilion has risen to 96%. A hundred mothers come in to have babies. Ninety-six go out as corpses. It is a very bad situation.

But Klein has an answer. He points to London, Paris, Berlin, Rome. It is not much better in those great cities. The pregnant women of the poor die off in all the free hospitals of the world. The percentages vary from thirty percent to fifty, to ninety. It is obvious to Professor Klein and to the world that venerates him and all his colleagues in Edinburgh, London, Paris, Rome, and Berlin, that puerperal fever is a curse of nature. It is a sort of pox that belongs among the divine mysteries. God is restive with his sinful children. Did He not once send a flood? Now he sends puerperal fever. Perhaps because it is easier to transport than water.

Nevertheless, there is a scandal in Vienna. The poor have clung only to one basic right - the right of producing more poor. This has been always the single joy that no monarchs or taxes or hellish laws could rob them of. And this right is now in jeopardy.

Investigations are started. The professors meet, listen to each other speak (using many Latin phrases), and finally figure out the professorial cure for puerperal fever. Close all the lying-in hospitals. Then there will be no hospital statistics to frighten and depress anybody.

Semmelweis does not attend these learned conferences. He sits in the gloomy reception room. His heart is burdened and he hurls his mind into the darkness.

A RAY OF LIGHT

A student stops to talk to the brooding, snarling Charon at his desk. The student says humorously, "I bet you the reason there are fewer deaths in Bartsch's Pavilion than in Klein's is because the work over there is done by midwives - and not by doctors."

The student has a hangover and a grudge. He walks on chuckling at his mot.

But Semmelweis is on his feet, staring at something he cannot see. But it is there. And it is not a joke. It is a Fact, a ray of light from God, or from His only child - Genius.

Semmelweis rushes to Pavilion No. 2. He drags out all the record books. It is true. It has been true for fifty years. Always a half, a third as many dead mothers at Bartsch's as at Klein's.

Semmelweis makes his first move. It is more the move of a checker player than a scientist. Skoda and Rokitansky support him. He moves all the midwives from Bartsch's to Klein's. He moves all the doctors from Klein's to Bartsch's. Bartsch and Klein are amused at this childish game.

The move is an overwhelming success. Semmelweis has moved Death from one space to another. The doctors are Death. Two weeks after the doctors have taken over Bartsch's Pavilion, its mortality rate has doubled. The mortality rate in the Klein Pavilion, where the midwives now deliver babies, has been cut in half.

LIGHT BEATS ON DISASTER

Why do doctors carry death - and not midwives? Why are men, nobly trained in medicine and surgery, villains of the darkest hue - and ignorant midwives medical heroines?

Semmelweis puts these questions to Klein. The Professor with the beard is outraged. Says Klein, these are not questions. They are insults. They impugn. They defy authority.

Semmelweis, Master Surgeon and question-asker, is fired.

LIGHT DIMS AND THE WORLD TRIUMPHS

Semmelweis has lost his badge. He is no longer the official Charon. He has no other standing in the Klein Pavilion now but busybody.

And he is a daily busybody at the Pavilion of the 96%. He sits at the bedsides of the dying women. This is now his love affair. He loves these agonized ones who try to bring life into the world - and die trying. His heart bursts with a hope for them. He would take their fever away. He would open their eyes and let them see the new face of a child of which they had been dreaming so long. He would place life at their breasts to feed.

Such is his desire. Not his own dead but all the dead torment him. Not his own lost hope, but all lost hope aches in his heart.

All day the priests in their vestments march with the viaticum. The attendant in front of them tolls his bell. Semmelweis, lover of life, hears only the tongue of death. He sits and weeps beside the dying ones, snarls over them when they are dead, not at them, but at Death. He is the poet who has found a Cross from which to look on the world. It is not yet a big Cross, but it will enlarge.

THE CROSS GROWS BIGGER

How does it happen that Semmelweis suddenly looks into tomorrow, suddenly looks on the truth - a flash, a tittle, a finger of it? The Camera will have to explain this. The Camera will come close to his face as he sits at a bedside and holds the hand of a dying mother. It will see his eyes widen, see a stare come into them and register a grimace as of terror that fills his face.

Sitting at the bedside of the poor dead ones, Semmelweis knows suddenly why women die of puerperal fever. Women in Rome,

London, Berlin, Paris, Edinburgh, Boston, New York. With what he knows in this moment of light, Semmelweis can save a million lives a year in Europe alone.

Skoda and Rokitansky hear the news. It is so simple and Semmelweis speaks so violently that the thing is hard to understand. But they manage to figure out what he is saying. He wants wash bowls placed beside all the lying-in beds. He wants all the doctors to wash their hands - before delivering babies. This is the great Semmelweis discovery - that there is dirt on the hands of authority that needs washing off.

Skoda and Rokitansky abet this mad plot. The wash-stands are installed, the orders given to the doctors. The results are astonishing. In one week the Klein mortality rate drops to 70% - a twenty per cent fall.

But Professor Klein is outraged once more. The Devil is loose again. He summons this laundryman of a scientist, this washerwoman savant Semmelweis, into his office. He demands to know - why does he want doctors to wash their hands? What in God's name does Semmelweis think is on their hands? Are doctors evil people? Does he think scientists are witches?

Semmelweis replies a little wildly. He has not the facts of tomorrow's Pasteur. He cannot name the thing. But it is there - on the hands of doctors. He has seen it kill.

"Why do you want theories now?" he cries at Klein. "Look at the facts. Facts are enough for the time being. Fewer women are being killed by doctors with washed hands."

The thing drives Professor Klein out of his head. How does a priest feel if he hears God called dirty? How does a patriot feel if he hears his land slandered? How does a citizen feel if he listens to criticism of his reason? Klein is all these things. He rises up like a trinity. No priest, no patriot, no citizen was ever more righteous. He calls for the dismissal of Semmelweis from the hospital.

Hospital directors, physicians, surgeons, journalists and believers in authority, make an army around Professor Klein. They sustain him. They chant his praises. He is defending his Time. He is saving authority from an enemy.

Semmelweis, who had almost saved a million women a year, is thrown out of the hospital. His Godfathers Skoda and Rokitansky can do nothing. Scandal shakes the pillars of medicine. Not the scandal of a numskull slayer of poor women, named Professor Klein - and named all the obstetricians of Europe and America, great and small. But the scandal of a man who dares question Professor Klein, dares challenge today - who dares ask a few men to wash their hands and save a million lives.

HIDEAWAY IN LAUGHTER

Disgraced, derided, Semmelweis leaves medicine, leaves Vienna - city of science. He is a little mad. The worried Godfathers send a friend to look after him.

Semmelweis goes gasping to Venice. Here he drinks, paddles around in gondolas, laughs in bagnios and sings at the top of his voice. He plays pagan in Venice. He is never still, rarely sober. He falls in love with Art. Art is noble and serene and has triumphed over the Kleins. He rhapsodizes over paintings and sunsets, over women and barcarolles.

He is trying to put out of his mind the memory of a light that was in it, and out of his ears the tolling of a bell. But this bell rings through all his revelries. It wakens him in the bagnios. Drunk, he hears it. It comes through kisses and sounds out of emptied wine bottles. And it pulls him back to Vienna - and the death beds.

MELODRAMA OF A FACT

Semmelweis arrives in Vienna to find that his best friend, Dr. Kolletschka, is dead. Kolletschka was Professor of Anatomy and dear to him. He had died in the night as a result of infection through a finger wound. He had been dissecting a corpse.

Semmelweis weeps. He weeps - but he investigates. No one else is investigating the death of the estimable Kolletschka. But Semmelweis has genius. Genius is a quality that knows nothing but works as if it knows. This is the way answers are found - by not knowing them. And Semmelweis finds an answer. He investigates not Kolletschka, but the cadaver on which he operated. He finds the same death in the cadaver as in his friend. He finds that pericarditis, peritonitis, and meningitis can come from the exudations of a corpse. It is all theory, for he has no microscope to identify the villains. Nor has he enough chemical learning to make a scientific case of it. But he has light without words, logic and the gift for truth. And he proclaims his discovery.

Up to the moment of Semmelweis' proclamation, corpses were considered to be objects thoroughly done with living. Semmelweis proclaims that corpses are alive - with death.

Thus the plot is solved - for Semmelweis. He has an answer now for the mighty Klein. He gives the answer.

"The fingers of the medical students soiled by recent dissections carry death dealing cadaveric particles into the genital organs of women in childbirth - and cause their deaths."

He speaks again,

"Disinfect the hands of the students. Every mother will then be saved."

The great Professor Klein is outraged for a third time. In fact, he is more outraged this time than ever. He summons his cohorts about him. They are also outraged. Why? A man has not only questioned authority but answered it. Toppled it. Outwitted it. Disproved it. Made it suddenly seem little as a match flicker in an abyss. There are thus two lines of action. Either Authority capitulates. Or it gets rid of this man.

It gets rid of the man. Semmelweis is ordered out of Pavilion Number 1. There is no room for a busybody charlatan in the sacred death chambers of science.

Skoda and the beer drinker, Rokitansky, intercede. They have enough power to effect compromises. Through their efforts Semmelweis is permitted to experiment in Bartsch's Pavilion Number 2.

The "charlatan" orders the doctors brought again from Klein's to Bartsch's. The midwives are moved once more from Bartsch's to Klein's. But Semmelweis is doing something more than playing checkers this time. He is taking his place now beside Pasteur, Lister, Koch, Banning, Ehrlich, and all the great of medical history.

Naturally nobody is aware of this. The little world of Authority around Semmelweis scowls as he toils - and busies itself organizing a lynching mob.

In two weeks, with doctors delivering the babies, the death rate doubles in Bartsch's. Semmelweis bides his time. Up goes the death rate - thirty per cent, fifty per cent, seventy-five per cent. Now is the moment for Truth. Semmelweis gives his epic order. "Every medical student who has touched a corpse must wash his hands thoroughly in an antiseptic chlorine solution before undertaking the examination of obstetrical cases."

Such is the order. It is put into operation. And Semmelweis watches - and gloats. The tolling of the bell subsides. In a month of handwashing in chlorine water, the mortality rate falls from 70% to 12%.

But Semmelweis is not content. The bell must stop - forever. He insists on more thorough and longer washings. And the bell stops! For the first time in history the mortality figures in Semmelweis' wards are lowered to those of the best maternity wards of modern science - two-tenths of one per cent!

VICTORY!

And does the world rejoice? Does medicine raise its head proudly to the light? Do the Professors of Europe and America join hands in hosannahs?

No. Here, where our movie should end, it begins. Here where truth smacks the world, error alone triumphs.

Semmelweis has completed his love affair. He has brought hope and life to the bedsides of birth. Nobody rejoices. Nobody sings. Instead, a roar of laughter rises from all the professors in Berlin,

Paris, Rome, Boston. Edinburgh, and New York who hear of the goings-on of this charlatan.

How can they laugh? How can these pontifical fools pontificate? Are there not facts? Is not truth evidence?

But what are facts and truth to the unyielding and ferocious stupidity of the world? Science in all its centers asserts itself as wiser than Semmelweis, more All-Knowing. It kills off one million, five, ten million mothers in order to make its statement of contempt for Semmelweis. But what are ten million mothers beside the triumph of Authority? A hill of beans.

Everybody is for the magnificent Professor Klein. This is no mystery and no Devil's work. The world is Klein - yesterday, today, and tomorrow. The world is never Semmelweis. It will stumble forward, our world, out of exhaustion, out of the proddings of disaster. It will never move forward honorably or gracefully.

Supported by communications from great men all over the world, Professor Klein storms into Board of Directors meetings. Skoda, Rokitansky and a few others oppose the righteous beard and the thundering communications. But they are the immemorial disciples. They have power only to beat their bosoms - and turn their heads from the crucifixion.

Science from all over the world stands firmly behind Professor Klein. Blaming doctors for infection is like blaming politicians for economic distress or blaming rich people for the woes of poverty. It is not to be contemplated. The medical students stand firmly behind Professor Klein. They cry they are bored with those "filthy washings."

And imagine who else stands behind Professor Klein? The Press, of course, but who else? The government, naturally, but who else? The mothers. The howling, frightened pregnant ones. The poor sufferers whom Semmelweis loved, for whom he toiled, snarled, wept and won. His loved ones - the people. His dream girl - humanity. These join Professor Klein in the denunciation of Semmelweis. They call him a fool, a busybody, a crazy man. They defend the doctors with beards. Doctors are clean people. How can anyone dare fly in the face of enlightened Authority like that Semmelweis! Semmelweis, if the truth were only known, is the only dirty one!

Thus the common people - the Audience. The pack at the heels of Authority. The black hearts who go to the movies to hear how white they are. The fierce echo that echoes only ignorance, that repeats like a parrot the screeches of Authority. That dies rather than surrender its hatred of poets, Christs and Semmelweises.

TWO CAMERAS FOR THIS SCENE

There is a meeting of the Academy of Sciences in Vienna, foremost city of medical learning. All the Big Wigs assemble. Skoda, valiant but no longer laughing, reports to the meeting the absolutely conclusive results supporting the theory of Semmelweis. He has verified the theory by the "experimental infection from exudations of corpses of a certain number of animals." The animals infected died - like Dr. Kolletschka. What does this prove? It proves that Skoda is a fool and had better watch his step.

Another Semmelweis friend, Dr. Hebra, speaks to the august Society. "Semmelweis' discovery presents so great an interest for the future of Surgery and Obstetrics that I ask for the immediate naming of a Commission to examine with complete impartiality the results he has obtained."

This is an excellent movie scene. It is full of action. The scientists scream. Five Big Wigs knock Skoda to the floor. Eight more of them beat up Dr. Hebra with their fists.

The government is shocked. Vienna has been disgraced - by Semmelweis. It forbids the appointment of any such Commission. It orders Semmelweis - the alien - to quit Vienna.

The Press exults. The Professors breathe with relief. The women return to Klein's Pavilion Number 1 to die. Nobody minds this. Authority has been vindicated. Semmelweis, the charlatan, the anarch, the undesirable question-asker, is back in Budapest, where he came from. He lies weeping in bed, beating the walls with his fists. He has seen God - and is paying for the privilege.

THE FIDDLES TUNE UP

Now our movie must move faster. Its points are in the bag. What we do now is sock away at a finale. And what a finale! You can take any finish you want - even Calvary. I take Semmelweis in Budapest.

Outside his window he hears music and shouting. Hungary has troubles. It is demanding freedom from the Austrian tyrant. Semmelweis gets up. He joins the mobs screaming, "Down with the Austrians." He knows an Austrian named Klein.

The screaming revives him. War comes. Men fight for freedom. They fight against Croats, against Russians and against Austrians. Semmelweis goes almost mad laughing at this. Can Freedom be fought for? And when Freedom is won - what is free? Does the little bell of human wickedness stop tolling?

Hungary fights and loses and Semmelweis falls down a flight of stairs and breaks an arm and a leg. He is laid up in splints. He becomes silent. He speaks to no one. He lies staring at a wall.

Skoda sends the friend who went with Semmelweis to Venice. They speak of Venice. No word of the 96 per cent or of the chlorine water. Or of the two tenths of one per cent. No whisper of the truth that lies like an oak tree seed in Semmelweis' brain.

Skoda gets him a job under famous Professor Birly, head of St. Rochus Hospital in Budapest. Birly loves beer, pastry, and sensible attitudes. He soothes Semmelweis. What does it all matter - life, death, wars for freedom, puerperal fevers, genius, stupidity? It is all alike. Eat, work, amuse yourself - and be a human being. That is the best.

And Semmelweis agrees. He learns to dance like a faun. He is at all the Balls. At thirty he learns to ride a horse like a master. He rides in all the parks. Society people meet and adore him. This dancing, riding, bubbling, handsome young man! What a fellow to have around to make the day cheerful! What jokes, what cynicism, what wit! "Come and meet Dr. Semmelweis tonight at our party. You'll adore him!

But the dancing and adorable Semmelweis, the gay blade doctor, is only playing a joke. He is quite mad but nobody smells this out, not even Professor Birly. For at night he hides in his room, like a criminal engaged on a crime, and he writes his book. "Etiology of Puerperal Fever." It is all going into a book - the oak seed burgeoning in his head. They may deride and hate a man - Semmelweis looks furtively out of his window. But a book can outlive even Professor Klein - and Authority.

While composing he writes also letters to the Medical Academies of the world. He submits his findings and posts the letters secretly at night. No letters come back from the world. The Medical Academies have no time for cranks.

DANSE MACABRE

Birly dies. Semmelweis, the gay horseback rider, is made head of St. Rochus Hospital.

He arrives, bows, is installed. Authority shakes him by the hand. Presto! Semmelweis is Klein. Students salute him. He has only to grow a pointed beard and chuckle. All-Knowingly.

And at this very moment Semmelweis explodes. The oak seed is thriving in his head.

He issues an Open Letter to All Professors of Obstetrics. It begins,

"Assassins! So I call all those who have defied the rules prescribed to combat puerperal fever. Against those I stand as one should stand against a band of criminals!"

Now Budapest is shocked, the same as was Vienna. Good God, that old nonsense again - about saving a million mothers! And Semmelweis seemed so sane, so gay and witty. What a sad thing! The society folk, the counts and barons and fine ladies are sincerely hurt.

In Paris at a conclave of the world's greatest scientists in July 1858, held at the Academy of Medicine, the most celebrated obstetrician of his time - the great Professor Dubois - rises and proclaims. Semmelweis is an ass. His theories are nonsense. They have been proved worthless. Some minor statistics juggled by a charlatan. Vienna, itself, has abandoned him and cast him out. Let us be sensible men and ignore Semmelweis and his vaporings and get down to business.

And what is the business of this conclave of the world's greatest scientists? The business is to study the menace of puerperal fever - to find out how God can be induced to withdraw it from the better hospitals.

In the streets of Budapest you can now see Semmelweis. He is putting up posters on the walls. "Fathers, the doctors are killing your wives when they go to the hospitals to have children. Don't let them. Demand that the doctors wash their hands."

The head of a hospital cannot go around pasting up stickers on a wall like a small boy on Halloween. The doctors shake their heads sadly at poor Semmy's monomania. And he is removed.

People step aside as Semmelweis passes in the street. His head is big with an oak seed growing. This makes it difficult for him to walk. He takes to tottering, to standing still, to screaming at the sky. And to laughing suddenly when people look at him. He is a spectacle for Budapest.

Screams come from his room. The authorities call and discover nobody in bothering Semmelweis. He is alone. He is howling at phantoms.

Do you remember Cyrano under the oak tree in the convent garden, mortally wounded and drawing his sword for the last time - to fight the shadows around him?

Here is another Cyrano. He fights Klein and a hundred great men. He fights a hundred thousand. He fights a whole world that has trampled truth. He charges down the stairs of his rooming house, haggard and pursuing phantoms.

The good people of Budapest stare at a madman howling.

History looks back and smiles tenderly at a man of wisdom pleading.

CROWN OF BACTERIA

It is a spring afternoon in Budapest, 1856. A man is running through the street. That crazy Semmelweis again!

He runs to a building, runs inside, runs into a room full of doctors. It is the anatomical amphitheater of the Medical Faculty.

A cadaver ready for demonstration lies on the marble slab under a bright light. Semmelweis knocks over doctors and runs to it. He seizes a scalpel from a student. He cuts his own finger with it. Then he plunges his bleeding finger and the scalpel into the liquescent and oozing interior of a dead man.

This is what Kolletschka did and died - proving that there was death in corpses. Semmelweis wants to prove it over again - the theory of the cadaveric particles.

He holds up his bescummed and bleeding hand. His head is too mad with truth to talk. But his hand will speak for him. His hand will rot. His body will rot. His eyes will go blind. The world can then look on a great tube of pus called Semmelweis and know the truth.

Skoda comes to Budapest. He takes Semmelweis from his bed, full of fever already, full of pus. He rides the case of lymphangitis and peritonitis back to Vienna. Semmelweis waves his putrescence in the air. He cries only the word, "Look! Look!"

He is put in an insane asylum in Vienna. Here he demonstrates the truth for three weeks with his dying.

But the world looks on Semmelweis dying and sees no truth. It is conscious only of a horrid smell.

Semmelweis dies - and they open the windows.

They said - even his friends - that Semmelweis died a madman. He screamed with pain and something worse. Nobody could understand him. Therefore, he was mad. They did not see that the last action of Semmelweis was full of courage and clarity. They did not see that his desperation was a cry of love, that his pain, his reek and his death were a plea for truth. There is sometimes nothing else one can do for the truth - but die for it.

They did not see that the only madness involved was the madness of the world that buried Ignatz Philip Semmelweis, and millions of helpless women - rather than pause to wash its hands.

STORY CONFERENCE

Having gone to all the trouble of making up this scenario about Semmelweis, I owe myself a little reward - one daydream, at least. Not of the scenario being put on the screen and becoming an overwhelming film classic and being hailed by all the movie critics as better even than the last film classic - whatever that was.

Such a daydream does not allure me. I am partial to a hundred childish fantasies of power - among them, for instance, a certain fantasy about critics. In this happy reverie I am able to undress my adverse critics at will by the exercise of a magic power newly come to me. When they go out as critics, no matter how bundled up they are, they always end up nude, if I wish it. I am fond of the picture of naked critics, ablush like the rose, fleeing down the aisles of First Nights or Movie Premières, or bolting, thus divested, out of literary salons where they have come to nibble at me and the hors d'oeuvres.

But among all my fantasies is none of writing and directing a movie that becomes the most famous movie of the week - or even month. I know why this fantasy is missing. It is because my mind balks at the partner in this daydream - the Audience. I have never fancied the pleasures that come from its applause and approval.

My daydream about my Semmelweis movie is no more than a small, realistic one involving the Story Conference that might take place after I have arrived in Hollywood, read the scenario to the studio head and sold it. It is now ready to go into production. Then comes the Story Conference, the purpose of which is to keep all the fine things in the scenario and, at the same time, make them completely different.

This daydream is the scene in which Plato, the Producer, and Glaucon, the Director and staunch friend of Plato, and several valiant and anonymous Platonists who are on the producer payroll, all assemble for "Conference on Semmelweis." I am, as usual, without cohort in their midst.

THE THEORY OF THE HEEL

The conference is on. Plato has shut off all but two of his telephones. He presides behind a desk large enough to play ping-pong on. His silver carafe is at hand, his three boxes of pills stand ready, the photographs of his wife and children smile up at him, as do a number of Trophy Cups, Award Statues, and Mysterious Diplomas.

"A marvelous piece of work," says Producer Plato, beaming on me, "and I feel sure we are going to get one of the finest pictures out of it this studio has ever made."

The valiant Platonists nod in unison. Hope is everywhere, except in my bosom.

"But," continues Plato, "there are a few little points we have to lick first. Nothing difficult. I'm sure we can lick 'em."

"Licking a story" is the phrase that is innocently used in Hollywood to describe the difficulties of turning ideas into lollypops for the Audience. For instance, if you have a story in which a character, full of psychotic quirks, sees no sense in becoming a soldier and fighting for democracy, this character is known as a heel. And if in your story this nasty figure ends up the head of a large, thriving business which he has managed to acquire because his business rival was off in the Solomon Islands fighting for Uncle Sam - then this story has to be "licked." The Story Conference, full of grave faces, assembles. The perspiring composer of the story is summoned and allowed to sit in a chair where everybody can see him easily and frown on him. And Plato, the Producer, walks up and down in a deep silence as if he were communing with a Spirit Guide.

Finally Plato speaks, his face alight.

"I think I've got it licked," he says. "Yes, sir. It solves everything."

The Platonists continue to sit frowning, for it is their business never to stop thinking - in silence.

Continues Producer Plato.

"This fellow, this heel. By the way, that's the worst heel I ever saw in a picture. This heel is just about to *get* the business. But what happens? I'll tell you. He catches pneumonia. And dies in his bed -

still a heel. He doesn't reform, change his point of view. Or anything obvious. But he dies! He pays for his bad character. And we have a scene in which his rival comes back from the fighting in the jungle. The rival hasn't even been wounded. He comes to this heel's bedside - and we play a death scene between the hero and the heel. Full of irony. The whole thing is not only good -it's artistic. The man who stayed at home *died.* The hero who went to fight comes back and *he's* the one who wins the business. It's perfect!"

"I think that's it," says Glaucon solemnly.

A sigh of awe goes up from all the Platonists. It is obvious even to the author that the story has been licked.

Very well, here's my Story Conference on the Semmelweis scenario.

AT GRIPS WITH PLATO

"The thing that needs licking in this Semmelweis story," says my Plato, "is a sort of lie that's in it. You've got the Public and the Authorities playing the villain. I think we can make the whole thing more understandable by underlining the fact that Semmelweis is actually his own worst enemy. It's his own character that defeats him. You say yourself that he was insolent, snarling, hot-headed - in fact, a thorough heel. That is, looked at from the psychological point of view. And that's why he doesn't put his discovery over - because there's a rotten spot in him."

"That," I answer calmly, "is hogwash. Semmelweis doesn't put his discovery over because there's a rotten spot in the world. Because Audiences are idiots and Authorities are all swindlers."

"Now hold it," says Glaucon, "We'll never lick this story with that kind of talk. I think, personally, that Plato has put his finger on its whole weakness. It's the heel in Semmelweis that defeats him. And defeats his own greatness. I buy that, absolutely. What's more, it improves the picture. We can get a great psychological document out of it - a sort of Jekyll and Hyde affair."

"Yes," says Plato moodily, "it's the sort of thing Dostoievsky would have written. The study of a heel - a great heel, mind you."

"Let's talk about Oliver Wendell Holmes," I say. "You'll admit that Oliver Wendell was no heel."

"What has he got to do with it?" Plato demands. "Please let's not waste time on any sophistries. We're talking about Semmelweis."

"No," I say, "we're talking about who is the villain - Semmelweis or the world. And that's where Oliver Wendell comes in - very logically."

I remove a little packet of notes from my coat pocket, consult them unhurriedly, and then continue,

"Dr. Oliver Wendell Holmes presented his 'Essay on Puerperal Fever' to the world in 1844. He was thirty-four years old. He was probably the most charming man in Boston. He had a honeyed tongue. He was socially as graceful as a Chinese diplomat. And he wrote that puerperal fever was caused by infection from dirty-handed doctors. He came to his discovery through pure logic and the study of case histories. It was the same conclusion that Semmelweis came to by experiment and medical genius."

I turn to another page of my notes.

"'Death and the physician enter the chamber of the innocent patient, hand in hand' is what Oliver Wendell wrote in 1844," I continue.

"Then Semmelweis didn't discover it first," Plato looks at me indignantly.

"The truth was discovered by many men in different parts of the world," I answered. "By Dr. Charles White of Manchester, England, in 1773. By Dr. Alexander Gordon of Aberdeen, Scotland in 1795. And by others. In each and every case the truth was angrily discarded by the world and its Authorities. The notes are all here. But let's stick to Oliver Wendell of whom we know one salient fact, to wit - he was no heel."

"Do you suggest we put Dr. Holmes into the movie?" Glaucon asks a little sarcastically. "A sort of flashback and montage affair. Very confusing to the story line, I say."

"I suggest only that we put him into this argument," I answer, and continue from my notes. "Oliver Wendell Holmes' paper, superbly, scientifically and soothingly written, was violently repudiated by the obstetrical Authorities of America. All of them. Its epochal humanitarian discovery was treated as if it were the babblings of a porch climber."

Plato, in my daydream, does nothing more than scowl. I continue speaking.

"Holmes' 'Essay on Puerperal Fever,' identifying it and naming its causes and its cure, was again presented to the profession of Medicine in 1855. And again in 1906. It was denounced, and Oliver Wendell with it. Two of America's leading professors of obstetrics voiced the general argument. They were Drs. Charles Meigs and Hugh Hodge. They declared Oliver Wendell's discovery to be 'the jejune and fizzenless vaporings of a sophomore writer.'"

"I wish," says Plato, "that you would stick to Semmelweis and our picture and not go bouncing off into history. We are going to photograph a movie script and not a Public Library."

I continue inexorably.

"Holmes, in republishing his repudiated essay, grew more and more polite. He called nobody 'Assassin!' He sweetened his eloquence. Listen to this. 'I do entreat those who hold the keys of life and death to listen to me this once. I ask no personal favor, but I beg to be heard in behalf of the women whose lives are at stake....It is as a lesson, not a reproach, that I call up the memory of these irreparable errors and wrongs.'

"Here," I smile at Plato, "was no heel with a rotten spot. But Authority refused to capitulate to Oliver Wendell's honeyed tongue any more than to Semmelweis' outcries. Women continued to die in droves - millions of them succumbing to childbed fever right on into the twentieth century, due to infection by doctors. Murder by Authority never let up. And not until 1933 did the New York Academy of Medicine appoint a Committee to inquire into maternal mortality in this city. The Commission 'discovered' the truth that Semmelweis and Holmes had offered the world almost a hundred years ago. Dr. Benjamin Watson, present director of Sloane Hospital for Women in New York City, writes that the Commission's report was given 'none too warm a reception from some of the profession.' In 1933, my good Plato! Nevertheless, truth finally triumphed. After a hundred years of murder and stupidity, it burst upon an astonished profession."

"What is your point, exactly?" Plato scowls at me.

"Only that you are a thumping jackass," I answer, "and that you haven't a leg to stand on in your defense of the world. Your theory that Semmelweis defeated himself by his own faults of personality is knocked cold by the case of Dr. Oliver Wendell Holmes."

Plato is silent. What can he say? How can he lick this unlickable story? How can he turn Philip Semmelweis' Cross into a lollypop?

But he is a wily Plato and he smiles at me. Despite it is my daydream and not his - he sees through me.

"Why do you want this story made this way?" he asks. "Is it because you hate doctors?"

"Not at all," I answer. "In my mind the story has actually nothing to do with doctors."

"I thought not," says the wily Plato. "It has to do with priests and politicians, Congressmen, Foreign Secretaries, village barbers, university professors, clerks, amusement seekers and honest folk generally. Am I not right?"

"You are entirely right," I answer.

"It is all these you hate, says Plato. "May I ask why?"

"Their minds only," I protest, "their triumphant clichés, their mania to protect their ignorance, their God damn' snaffles, blinders, and surcingles."

And in my daydream a miserable honesty compels me. I have to reveal a thing that will expose me as someone with a mission and not a scenario writer at all.

"I wrote the Semmelweis movie," I say, "in order to dramatize the backwardness and stupidity of the world. Semmelweis is only an accident that I use. The truth is I am writing a book about anti-Semitism and there is a villain I want to expose who is vastly greater than any anti-Semite. I am aware of a character more disturbing by ten light years than any of the sick and abortive creatures I have described as anti-Semites. This is the character of the world itself. Utter, blank, wooden-headed indifference to all truth, is the world's deepest quality. There lies its rotten spot. The Bible says that it was the Devil who entered Eden as a snake and tempted man with knowledge. This section of the Bible must have been written by the Devil himself. What the snake brought Adam and Eve was ignorance. He handed them an apple full of worms. And their descendants are still chewing on it, on actually the same apple."

"I never imagined for a moment," says Plato, "that your Semmelweis movie had anything to do with anti-Semitism - or I would not have wasted my time discussing it. As a matter of fact, despite your rude talk about the world, I still see no relation between them."

Would that I could be silent - but my dream has turned entirely against me now.

"Here is the relation," I answer. "If a world would not save mothers, imagine its incalculable indifference to saving Jews. It is in the world of these indifferent ones that anti-Semitism flourishes. Anti-Semitism and everything foul. It is these Nice People who make all horror and wretchedness possible - by their unfunctioning Niceness. By their fierce pride in the little they know. By their abominable laziness. They are the neutrals - the myriads of neutrals - in the war between reason and unreason. To me these sleepy, dopey, primping and evasive onlookers are the true scoundrels. They are the stillborn of the world. They are the vast army of social fetuses that clog the highways, the theaters, the street cars and the halls of lawmaking. If I am looking for the villain responsible for the murder of three million Jews, I must, as an honest man, not single out a few anti-Semites. I must attack a world from pole to pole."

"You have come to the wrong place for such activity," the wily Plato smiles at me. "Hollywood is not Armageddon. Here we do not seek to make truth triumph by the dubious business of killing off all its enemies. Whom would we sell pictures to, in such a case? To corpses? If you want to fight the world you must not be naive enough to ask the world to line up on your side. You've got to go it alone. And here's your movie. Take it with you. I don't think we can waste any more time on it."

"That's right," says Glaucon. "We've got the story of Thomas Paine to lick."

"Yes," says another of the payroll Hellenists, "we haven't licked the story about Kropotkin, the Russian hero, yet either."

"Very true," sighs Plato. "We've got a lot of stuff to lick. And we're way behind schedule."

Plato walks out of the conference with his arm around me and whispers to me in a very friendly voice, "Think it over. Gable, Boyer and Cooper have all read the script. They're all crazy to play Semmelweis."

Thus ends my daydream. I am almost sorry I started it. For like all daydreams about Hollywood, its ending is not entirely satisfactory. In fact, I have a feeling that it is Plato's daydream, and not mine. For it is Plato who triumphs in it, Plato who ushers me and Semmelweis out of his sumptuous door.

LOVE AFFAIR

What a town that was - Hollywood! (1925). It never slept. It had the look and sound of an aeroplane propeller - skimpy and powerful. You can fall in love with a city on sight. I fell in love with Hollywood the first night I spent in it.

I came home at 8 a.m. (to the Rajah's Palace in which the Mankeiwiczes lived), having seen innumerable fist fights - one excellent one between a husband and a most irritating wife; having made up a movie plot for which I was to receive a King's ransom; having promised to abandon this King's ransom and join up in an enterprise, unnamed, with my two hosts - the brothers Selznick, who were dressed in white turtle neck sweaters and who spent most of the night battling with swanky hostesses alarmed by their proletarian appearance; having been in an automobile accident - our car demolished a lamp post while evading a motorcycle policeman (no one was scratched or stopped talking); having heard all the bosses of Hollywood denounced by everyone around me as so many swine and imbeciles (in those days I always looked on a man who presumed to pay me money for my services as my immediate and outstanding enemy); having seen the dawn fill the hills with misty circus wagons and tipsy halos; and having so fascinated a troop of seven listeners with recitations from Gibbon's history of the last Roman emperors that they followed me to the Rajah's Palace and sat on the steps as I completed the story of Claudius and his pigeons - by which time it was nine o'clock and time for everyone to go the studios and make movies. Having survived this night, I went off to my own place of employment, and the enchantments of the city continued.

Within an hour I was deep in intrigue against certain studio satraps, and had learned to dictate to a stenographer. My name was on a door, dinner invitations poured in over my telephone, and an admirer of my books lay on the office couch drunk and sobbing that he was going to commit suicide because he had been ruined by Hollywood. (We gave this unhappy man a party that night and took him to the seashore in a roaring rain and waved him good-bye as he swam out to drown. He was back on my office couch the next morning complaining that the tide had washed him back ashore to a fate worse than death - Hollywood.)

I saw Richelieu and Pochahontas and streets full of pirates, and enamel-faced beauties in red and purple evening gowns; carpenters and Wizards and Russian Dukes, Poets and mud-caked Jungle Explorers, Moguls, Geniuses, Pharaohs, and the Lady of Shalott - all pouring out of a cornucopia and hurling themselves into the manufacture of the world's greatest toy - the movies.

So avid, so full of liveliness and mystery was this town that I had not time to contemplate it. I could only make comparisons. I remembered certain nights I had spent in Jim Colisimo's café in Chicago. There at 4 a.m. the leading burglars, yeggs, and vice purveyors of the city would assemble, with their loved ones, and the loot of the day's work would be divided between sweethearts and fences. Wine would flow, music play, and the occasional scream of a beauty smacked in the nose would arise.

I remembered the storming of the Wittelbacher Palais in Munich by the Sparticusts led by Dr. Max Levine, Professor of Zoology, and Erik Muhsam, the red-bearded poet, and the gaudy events that marked their brief reign in Bavaria. I remembered all the hangings and gun battles I had seen, and all the Coasts of Bohemia on which I had played. And none of these memories was as fine and thrilling as the fact of Hollywood.

Here in this city engaged in making a toy that was already sweeping the world clean of Mah Jong sets, yoyo sticks, and lonely evenings, was everything and everybody - great thinkers, mighty swindlers, phantasts astride dreams as spavined as Rosinante, artists falling down stairs, poets screaming for help (I saw one catch fire in a fireplace seven feet high), millionaires who had not yet had time for a shave; here was a new-born aristocracy that had leaped seemingly out of nowhere - and over it all a promise of fame and riches unparalleled in the history of *belles lettres.*

I have written many stories about Hollywood and made much fun of its clap-trap splendors. I have criticized its whirligig castrations of the Arts, its triumphs over sanity, and its coronation of buncombe. But in nearly all I have written there has been a lie of omission. I neglected to say that all these things I loved. How can you help doting on a town so daft, so dizzy, so sizzling; a town tumbling with the alarms and delights of a fairy tale book?

I am older, and Hollywood is older, but I never enter it - even with a touch of lumbago - but what I hear again its calliopes playing and see behind its now conventionalized façades all the happy skullduggeries and zany glamour of our mutual youth. It is the only place on earth where an adult can play pirates and Indians; where an artist can sell his soul (nobody will buy it any place else for a plugged nickel); where an idiot can make a fortune and a genius lose his shirt - in a twinkling; where the travails and insanities of the world run always second; If God sent another Flood, I promise you that Hollywood would photograph it, dub it for sound, and market it at a great profit as a work of art. And rewrite it also a little and put a happy finish on it so it would get by at the Box Office.

ANOTHER LIE OF OMISSION

In all that has been written about Hollywood - and no town in my time has been so garlanded with print - there has always been a lie of omission - much greater than the one to which I have confessed. This is the lie of its unspoken significance.

Hollywood is a town, an industry, an empire of toy-making, invented by Jews, dominated by Jews, and made to flourish like unto the land of Solomon - by Jews, and a few embattled Irishmen. Such is its truth, and if you wish to look for its deep meanings, it is into this truth you must look.

This truth has appeared only in the furtive communiqués of our anti-Semites. I have read many of these mimeographed or badly printed "attacks," listing all the stock holders, producers, and power wielders of Hollywood who were Jews. Such brochures have been handed me by indignant movie satraps (Jewish ones) as evidence of the dastardly tactics of the anti-Semites. For there is nothing that disturbs Hollywood as much as this fact - that it is a town made and dominated by Jews. Not by Jewishness, God knows, but by a swarm of chameleon-like Semites who have taken on all the colors of California but one - its Christianity.

I have sat at dinner tables surrounded by a score of the great toy-makers - men renowned in the farthest reaches of the earth - and, though they were nearly all Jews, I have never heard the word "Jew" spoken. This does not mean that the leaders of Hollywood hide their Jewishness, or are indifferent to Jewish problems and Jewish charities. The contrary is true. No group of Jews in the world is more philanthropic toward Jewish causes than these great ones of movieland. They hide their Jewishness only from the cinema. It is only as toy-makers that they are fearful of being identified as Jews.

I propose to look into this situation for it is truly a remarkable one. In an industry controlled by Jews, there are, for instance, practically no Jewish actors or actresses. Those who have slipped under the studio guard have altered their names to un-Semitic sound. And the characters they play on the screen are the furthest removed from the Jew possible - Italian gangsters, French scientists, Mexican potentates, or effervescent Pierrots. Their Jewishness is made to disappear from the audience as adroitly as the yellow handkerchief that vanishes under the magician's wand. Excepting always the comedians and the musicians - the tune-makers and tune-players. (The Jew, like the hunchback, is permitted always the part of jester and troubadour in all the courts - even those run by the Jews.)

There are also comparatively few Jewish movie directors - and those who do flourish are known, not as Jews, but as Germans (ex ones), Russians, or more generally, as eccentrics. The reason for this is that the directors are in direct contact with the horde of non-Semitic actors performing daily on the sound stages - and even from these hirelings the Jewish satraps would like to keep the fact of Jewish domination at least half hidden. There is also the belief among the satraps that Gentile directors will aid in giving a generally non-Jewish glow to their product.

In the background are Jews a-plenty who write, produce, sit in final judgment on the product, market it and reap the top rewards. But, as in the synagogues where no Jew is allowed to light the candles on Friday nights - and this task is relegated to a "Shabbes goy" - so it is in the studios. The Shabbes goy plays the picture - and, as far as possible, makes it.

There is, in this campaign to un-Judaize the movies, always the hazard of Jewish names that appear with disturbing frequency in the writing and producing credits. The procedure is to keep the credits short, ignore the whole matter and hope for the best.

How is it that men so bold in their personal Jewishness should be so fretful toward keeping any Semitic color from their product; and how is it that the movies themselves - the most un-Jewish of all modern manifestations, the most unrelated to Jewish culture and heritage - should have been created and perfected by Jews?

The movie chieftains have an answer to the first query. (It is not my answer.) They desire that their product be known as un-Jewish in order that it might sell more easily and have a wider appeal. This, they say, is only sanity, to refrain from advertising a world product with a label distasteful to the world.

The second query is a matter of history I will unravel later.

MY MISSION TO HOLLYWOOD

My "betrayal" of the secret of Jewish domination of Hollywood will be most eagerly embraced by our anti-Semites, who will study these pages and quote me with glee on their mimeographs. This is what I hope. They are not very bright - our anti-Semites, not much brighter than our Jews who cringe before their infantilism and illogic.

They play a game with Jews and the Jews abide by the rules. The anti-Semite finds out by studying the fears of the Jews what it is he does not like to hear said - and says it. He attacks where he smells weakness. He runs where he smells strength. I do not betray the Jew when I summon forth his greatness. I only depress his enemy.

Many Jews are fearful of Jews becoming too prominent. They argue that this happened in Germany and inspired the Germans to murder all the Jews - in order to "win" back their country. This is nonsense of a most pathetic sort. The prominence of the Jews in Germany kept them safe for almost a century - and held off like a flashing sword the German instinct for murder and brutality. Anti-Semitism has never thrived on the strength of Jews, but on their weakness. The massacres launched by the Germans are proof only that not Jewish strength nor even the entire weight of the world's humanity could keep in check any longer the need for murder that is at the bottom of the German soul.

Yet many Jews continue to advance the opposite argument. They argue that the fame of Jews for their financial or cultural achievements is a dangerous factor, that people get angry when too much Jewish genius and success flaunt themselves. This is a profoundly sad and silly argument.

There is nothing wrong with making fools angry. It is better than making them happy. There is nothing wrong in the flourishing of Jewish talent. Obviously it makes for anger and obviously there is a sort of danger in it. But it is an anger of which Jews may be proud and a danger that can be fought more easily than any of the other threats in which they walk.

It can be fought with more genius and more success. And this is the great battle open to the Jew- that he continue contributing to the culture and excitement of the world until he contribute so much that his contributions can no longer be called Jewish; until, in self-defense, the world embrace these contributions as its own and without the mark of "alienism" on them.

This is a look far off but it is the only land of promise on the horizon. Not in the "education" of the world, nor in its medication - its ridding itself of its sickly Jew complex - does the salvation of the Jew lie. It lies in his own activity, in his continued knocking on the door; a louder and louder knocking, a knocking of talent and inexhaustible human liveliness that must finally drown the sick protests of the door-keeper - and cry "Open Sesame" to the door. Hollywood, disguised by a hundred thousand Shabbes goys, is, nevertheless, such a knocking.

A TROT OVER QUICKSANDS

Make up your mind, as the sailor said to the girl, are you loving Hollywood or hating it, flinging rocks or roses? I have made up my mind - but as the girl said to the sailor, it'll bear a bit of discussing.

The Jews of Hollywood, in submitting to the attitude of the anti-Semite that Jewishness is a foul and indefensible thing, have played Machiavelli - and triumphed. They have also played turncoat - and lost. I hold that their winnings are a nickel greater than their losses - but I would examine the matter.

The greatest single Jewish phenomenon in our country in the last twenty years has been the almost complete disappearance of the Jew from American fiction, stage, radio, and movies. Were the Jews a totally extinct race surviving only as a few Passover cups and saucers in the Metropolitan Museum, they could have hardly less representation in the cultural and entertainment media of our land. This, I know, is a phenomenon that makes many Jews sigh with delight. But they are the Simple Simons who mistake a broken mirror for oblivion.

When I was young, the stage was full of Jewish dialect comedians, of Jewish family plays; the magazines were full of Potashes and Perlmutters, of tales of Jewish struggle and comedy. There were popular songs about Jews, sung in accent - "Don't do dot dance, I tell you, Sadie." The Jew was a comic, crazily human figure to be encountered everywhere - in song, fiction, and behind the footlights. His foibles were part of the American curriculum. His oddities and his accents were known to all.

Whereupon the two great media of mass entertainment appear - the move and the radio, both dominated by Jews - and the Jew vanishes. He vanishes not only from the screen and the air waves, but he is also out of print and gone from the footlights. No greater kidnapping has ever been witnessed.

But though it seemed to happen in a twinkling, it was a crime long prepared. The various Jewish anti-defamation societies had been toiling a considerable period toward the denouement. Oversensitive Jews, overnervous Jews, Jews frightened at the crude reminders of their own immigrant beginnings, Simple Simon Jews, hoping to blot out all consciousness of Jews in their country by breaking all the mirrors they could - these worked mightily, and are still dizzily employed, in the exorcising of the Jew from literature and the stage. The movies and the radio suddenly won the battle for them - chiefly the movies - for here there were mainly Jewish potentates to influence; potentates as full of Simple Simonism, as any of the mirror breakers.

The Jew vanished as a *dramatis persona*. The result is typical of the triumphs Jews win when they hurl their fears into battle rather than their valor. One of the most concrete and important reasons for the increase of American anti-Semitism is this vanishing of the Jew. A generation has grown up without having seen or heard of a Jew -

except as a massacre victim or "a world menace."

Instead of being an obvious little fellow full of jokes, chicanery and a bubbling heart, the Jew is an unknown factor. He is a mystery to the "goyim." They see him around them - but his soul is invisible. Only a single spotlight is on him - the German spotlight. The arts that humanize, that make men and ideas familiar to one another, are turned off. The little Jew whom actors and writers once joked, wept, and sang into comradely existence, sits in the dark of censorship - and becomes an ogre, a pariah, an alien.

The movies, the radio, the anti-defamation societies, have managed this divorce of the Jew from all all the arts. They have set an example that has been followed by the magazines and publishing houses. Out with the Jew has been the cry of his Simple Simon "well-wishers," let no uncouth or satiric sight or sound of him be offered. And the broad currents of our national fun-making and of the deep American fellowship with caricature know him no more.

He is safe now, the little Jew. No baggy pants, no oversized derby jammed over his ears, no mispronunciations or waving of hands. The caricature has been wiped out. And with it has gone the open-heartedness, the quick sentimentality, the eagerness for fun; most of all this genius for fun - the half-mad capering of irony and jest that is the oldest of all the Jewish tradition. The first poetry of the Jews, three thousand years ago, was a poetry of irony and jest.

And with the vanishing of the caricature, the original, himself, has become invisible. He is no longer a citizen known through the many arts, but a word to be discussed - a word without human connotations. The arts once ran interference for his alienism. They took the edges off his oddities. They fitted him in, they made him a known part in the many alienisms of the USA. They were his Master of Ceremonies, introducing and explaining him whimsically to his new audience. Now he appears bleakly without introduction or explanation. All the friendly voices are silent. Only the anti-Semites speak and write of Jews, only these offer the caricature and play Master of Ceremonies.

And for this false oblivion and for this dangerous exile, the movies are the most to blame. This is one of the losses achieved by the turncoats of Hollywood - and not an inconsiderable one.

THE MASKED HEROES OF ISRAEL

It is nothing new for the Jews to have heroes who will not speak to them. Nor to have champions preoccupied elsewhere. In times of stress, the Jews usually find themselves standing behind heroes who are as silent as the tomb and looking to champions whose backs are turned to them. The great Jews of the world are not frequently found on any Jewish barricades.

The Jewish kings of Hollywood are part of this tradition. Though they have the hearts of lions, they will not fight as Jews. As anything else, yes. For any other cause, yes. For ideals they never heard of and that mean nothing to them - yes. As Jews - no.

I can tell you this - that two-thirds of the mighty Jews of Hollywood who read these pages will blaze with anger against me. Why? Because I am writing of them as Jews. They will pass the word out that I am an anti-Semite of ugly proportions. And they will pronounce that I have done my best to ruin the cinema industry. (It is not a serious charge, and I will ignore it.) I shall also continue my admiration for the great Jews of Hollywood. And, if I pause here to criticize them for a few paragraphs, it is only to make my ultimate admiration seem that of a sane, rather than infatuated man.

These Jewish heroes of Hollywood put a hundred thousand churches in their movies - and nary a synagogue. They ride to the rescue of every wounded folk in their films, and glorify the valor of all afflicted peoples - except the Jews. For they have a mission. It is to convince the world that their Americanism is untainted by any special consideration for Jews.

It is a mission in excellent standing among most of the great Jews in politics. This high "American" attitude of Hollywood is to be found also in Washington. There we have also magnificent Jews, fully as magnificent as those of Hollywood. And have you heard a single outcry from any of these Jews high in the councils of government, a single chirp of righteousness against the murder of

Europe's three million Semites? Not one. For the Jews of Washington, like those of Hollywood, are not hysterical people. They are a fine, stoical lot - these great Jews. No crimes against their kind can betray them to a public wince of pain or any uncouth demand for Justice. As for a tirade from them against anti-Semitism - the age of Jewish miracle died on Mt. Sinai.

Roman Rolland once wrote: "There are people who have the courage to die for the cause of another who have not the temerity even to speak up for their own."

But should they speak up? Would not their speaking up lessen them? Most certainly it would - in their own eyes. It is a little inconsiderate that we ask of great men that they throw away their greatness - and participate in some potato sack race or anti-Semitic block party run by the Germans. But what kind of greatness is it that can be lost - through the exercise of a little extra courage? The answer, alas, is Jewish greatness. I am one of its admirers, and I make these points only that I may not be accused of blindness.

In Hollywood our Jewish heroes, as do our Washington ones, give alms to three hundred and ninety Jewish organizations who are all busy as beavers distributing free cribs and crutches, etc. These Knights of Charity also give for the support of rabbis and rabbinical schools. For the Kol Nidre, as Heine wrote, will remain, whatever songs they hear, always bumbling in their heads; the Kol Nidre and the Memories of Childhood which are the chief cement of Jewishness.

But to throw their American won greatness into the battle against anti-Semitism - that, do not ask for. To stand up as the great of Hollywood and proclaim in their films against the German murder of their kind - that, too, do not dream about. Their position they have told me is obvious. Though they own them, the movies are not theirs to use willy-nilly for special Jewish pleading. That, they argue even in their synagogues, would be an out and out betrayal of trust. For the American people trust them to be Americans and not Jews. It is a pact understood between the movie fans and the movie makers that there is nothing Jewish about the whole thing.

Do not examine these statements too closely. And forget all the special cinematic pleadings for Chinamen, Greeks, Norwegians, Serbs, Danes, Dutch, French, and Ethiopians that have been flashed on all the screens of the world. Forget, also, the neutrality of the cinema before our entrance into the war. It played with the issues of the rights of man like a monkey with a hot brick. And forget the finickiness of these Jewish heroes toward allowing any hint of the German massacre of Europe's Jews to soil the Americanism of their product.

Ignore and forget and do not argue, for it is unwise and unprofitable to examine heroes. The Jews must be extra cautious in the appraisal of their own. They must be cautious even about cheering them, for the Jewish hero is not always pleased with Jewish cheers.

Forget the many losses and look at the winnings these heroes bring. They are considerable. Twist and squirm though they will, they are actually that - Jewish heroes. And that's a winning.

So shy, so tongue-tied, so masked a hero as the great Jew of Hollywood has seldom appeared in the long history of Abraham's children. He hangs from a Gentile Christmas tree covered with candy crosses. He stands up, beaming, in a red, white, and blue gauze stocking, and when you squeeze his middle he sings, "Onward Christian Soldiers" and "The Wearing of the Green."

But he is hero of Israel, nonetheless. And now that I am done carping at him, let me admire him sanely and with much respect. For he has greatness, and however fantastically and un-Jewishly he uses this greatness, it remains Jewish greatness.

A great Jew - a Jew of success, of talent, of power - is the most potent Jewish propaganda that exists. Whatever tune he whistles, and even though he contort himself so he comes apart at all the seams, the great Jew is always the most powerful weapon against anti-Semitism that Jews are capable of forging. He can turn his back all he wishes - but he points always at the enemies of Jews.

Thus let us take the silence of the great Jews of Washington and Hollywood with good cheer. It is a pity they will not speak, for they could speak so well. And in their silence, others who have the voices of nanny goats and screech owls often pre-empt the podium. It is a pity they will not act or call for action or hurl their greatness at those who hate them. Nevertheless, they are a historical riches, sort of Jewish museum pieces of incalculable value to the Jews. Silent, inactive, and with their backs turned, they exist. And their existence is a tremendous asset. It is a treasure greater than polemics. It offers, also, a strength. For even though they do not battle, these great Jews are, in themselves, victories - to be shared by all Jews.

If I would have them a little different, it is not because I disdain them as they are. Looking on Hollywood and Washington, I know that such Jews - though they seem empty - bring to Jewishness more than they take from it. They have my applause; for it may be that in my obituary it will turn out I was one of them.

MY MISHPOCHA FINDS A NEW CALIPH

The Jews I knew in New York, were, as I wrote, as "unracial" as myself. They were all artists and Americans, and seemingly a thousand years removed from the synagogues. It was usually only twenty years, but a Jew travels swiftly when he heads away from Jewishness.

In Hollywood I found quite another tribe of them. My first impression was that all my uncles and cousins had gone West. They were of the tribe of my family and they were unmistakably Jews. No lily-waving nonsense about them. They talked like my uncles, hollered like them, knew as little about art and literature as the dumbest of them - and were, on the whole, a warm and familiar lot to me. That they were all Pharaohs of a new empire startled me a bit. And that they were in a position to tell me what to write and how to write it, wrung a loud yell out of me. For I knew that, like my uncles, these were gentlemen only a few pages removed from illiteracy - and as unfit to offer me directions as so many scarecrows.

And here I was wrong as the Devil. For I was not in the presence of scarecrows and illiterates, but in the midst of a great historic current -

the current of Jewish genius that had, for two thousand years, specialized in the business for which it had come to Hollywood.

THE TWO FACES OF THE JEW

I have extolled the anarchic genius of the Jews and made no mention yet of another spirit which, like a stepbrother has come to roost in their souls. It was a spirit given them by the world, handed them by abuse and exile - the spirit of servility.

Centuries of adversity served to bring Elijah low. His genius remained in the crevices of the Jewish soul, but it grew another face - the face of the unwanted one. Servility became the manners of anarchy. The Jews of Roman, French, Spanish and German Europe were no longer in any position to challenge kings and proclaim the divine rights of the individual. They were not even in the position of asserting themselves as individuals. In most of the lands they came to they were denied the rights of citizenship and the privilege of participating in the industries and military pursuits of these nations. They were thus forced to invent activities which would not compete with the existing deeds and labors of their hosts. They were forced to create a world out of their limbo.

This they did. They became peddlers, journeymen ready to fill in all shortages, hobo bankers ready to loan money where none existed. They sought out all the lowlier forms of toil for which only slaves might compete. And they became, also, scholars, translators, diplomats. They could serve the world only as the lowliest or the highest. The great in-between norms of existence were denied them.

Thus again were a handful of the Jews brought face to face with kings, for to no one else could they talk and no one else could they serve - if they were men of talent. And thus they grew the face of the servant of kings - brilliant and servile. They became Wazirs, physicians, jesters, accountants, and even friends of kings and royal courts. They forged large human rights out of their own talents. But these were rights they could not share with any other Jews. The other Jews, the great masses of them, remained locked away behind the economic boycott of their hosts.

It is of these king-serving and court-serving Jews I write now - for they are the ancestors of Hollywood. These cinema uncles of mine came of that gaudy servant line that had for twenty centuries, served the courts of the world by bringing them spices, jewels, fineries, and faraway wonders. The trade routes had been their chief homeland. They were the Jewish peddlers with a touch of genius in their pack. Denied traffic in the commodities of the people, they had wandered off to uncompetitive activities. From Persia, India, China, Africa, and the mysterious islands of the seas they came, bringing luxuries and diversions. They were to become a shrewd and adventurous tribe, who studied the world and knew by instinct the whims of the masters they served. They were the forerunners of the modern showmen.

For who are the kings and tyrants of Democracy? Where lies the royal favor and the great profit for adventurers in a Democracy? The people are the kings, and in the people lie all favor and profit.

This the ancient tribe of king-serving and luxury-bringing Jews had already found out in America - long before Hollywood. They had reached for the possession of the theaters and amusement parks. These were naturally theirs, for were they not long trained and adept in the business of catering to masters? People, and not royal courts, were the new masters. But the instinct of adventure, the instinct to please and the gift for knowing and abiding by the whims of masters were as serviceable in a Democracy as in the Abbasside Caliphate - if you knew how to please and serve.

My uncles, having found a new monarch, mightier than any they had ever delighted in the past, hurled themselves into the business of serving him with an avidity that frightened off nearly all competition. They knew the simple trick of how to win favor and gold out of bringing ornaments to masters. You brought them ornaments they liked. You did not sit, pale, and truculent, in an artist's attic, fashioning ornaments they did not like.

Yet there was the violence of the Jew behind the creation of the cinema. He was servant to the new royalty - the public of a Democracy, this uncle of mine - but in his obsequious genius roared an ego undiluted since Elijah. He was a Jewish servant, than which there is no more hilarious and rambunctious flunkey in the world. The servility of the Jew was a mask that reality imposed on him. But under the mask there has remained the gift for loving oneself above one's master. In this fact lies the paradox of a servile Hollywood run by the world's most startling collection of egoists.

VALE, THE GAUDY PEDDLER!

So we see how so un-Jewish a matter as the cinema came to be created by Jews. The movies are as un-Jewish as the Persian shawls, Hindu tiaras and Chinese silks brought by the adventurous Jews of the Middle Ages to the courts of Europe. The Jew who makes them is not an Elijah with a mission but a peddler with a customer.

His timidity and truckling are the virtues of the peddler. It is folly to inveigh against them. And that the great Jews of Hollywood bow to the dictates of the Jew haters is only part cowardice. It is also the mark of consistency. For the Jew haters are part of the Public, and the servility of Hollywood makes no distinctions in its master. The Public is an All-Master and not to be offended even in his lowest moments of irration. He is the King-Customer and the peddler knows only one attitude toward him - to woo him with sweets.

I say farewell to Hollywood now as philosopher. The things it has taught me are spread through this book. And the things that I would teach it are not for its cameras or its conferences. It is an unfair exchange. But I doubt if Hollywood feels the loser for it. I wonder, also, how much wisdom there is in the advices I have poured into its celluloid ear. I can see it looking back at me with its always happy and harassed grin, and replying with great sanity that the world is not to be fought by a peddler. A belligerent peddler would only find himself and all his wares kicked down the steps.

I let the reply stand. Better, perhaps, that the Hollywood peddler continue to bring fineries in silence. And better, perhaps, that he continue to outfit the folly and stupidity of his master with glamour. Hairshirts do not belong in a peddler's pack, nor ashes to wear on the head. Nor nightmares. For these commodities we should not look to peddlers but to unsavory gentlemen howling in the wildernesses.

When I return to Hollywood to make movies - not the one about Semmelweis - I shall be of a softer mind about all these matters. Then it will come to me ironically, as it has always when I enter its golden doors, that Hollywood, rather than Elijah, holds the only possible hope for tomorrow. Its function is to supply the dream of goodness missing from the reality of the world. Who knows but what I am wrong about the whole thing - and Plato is right? Who knows but that this is the only goodness possible - the dream of it, the pretense of it, the photograph of it? Who knows but that Plato solved the bestiality of man in the only way it was solvable - by singing falsely to it, by showing it movies? Perhaps I am too Old Testament. I can see the safer logic of the Greeks - virtue is a lie to dangle fetchingly over the beast head as the only way of quieting it.

A man as clever as I am can solace himself easily, if he so desires. In Hollywood, where the intellectual climate is as soothing as its balloon-like pay checks, I shall find it not too difficult to forget most of the matters that agitate me now. And if I raise my nose out of movie-making to recall them for a moment, it will be to ask this philosophic question: Why protest too much against Jews succeeding - as anything - even liars? They peddle out of Hollywood the greatest fabrication of history - that the world is a sweet place and full of sweet people (who don't mind killing Jews, mothers, children, honor, reason and tomorrow). But it is a pleasant dish to set before the king.

And of an evening I shall ask the palm tree: Which is the final truth - the fact or the lie? Who is the better man, Elijah or the peddler? Who is the finer hero - the servant or the anarch? The palm tree, in the yard of the peddler, will answer me pleasantly.

"TRUMPET IN THE DUST"

Looking back in my book I find a volume of unsaid things. Most of these, on examination, I have decided to leave unsaid - in the interests of clarity. But there is one omission which glares and needs repairing. There is a phase of the Germans I have skipped over without even a hint of its existence.

I was surprised to notice its absence, for it is the only phase of the Germans that is usually written about by two-thirds of our writers. It is the good Germans. I do not mean the goodness in Germans - I have had my say on that - but the Germans of actual and total virtue. The truth is that I either forgot they existed, or more likely, forgot they were Germans.

This is a curious thing to forget, for nearly all the Germans in my memory and nearly all whom I know today belong to this fringe of virtue that ornaments the headsman's block of Middle Europe. I hasten to include them in my book for they belong in it - along with the few bad Jews of whom I have hinted.

I have not been deaf to the fact that, in the midst of German brutality, there have been German voices raised courageously in behalf of human honor - and even of Jews. Who are these voices and how does gallantry speak out of a pigsty, and are they really Germans who raise these voices? I know the answers to these questions and am pleased to make amends for my oversight by giving them in full.

Yes, they are Germans, not half-breeds, nor Jewish "tainted" Teutons, nor a special tribe of Intelligentsia. They are Germans who have fled their nation, as virgins might flee a debauch. And there are Germans who have not fled and who have no voice but who give high testimony by their deaths in concentration camps. And there are the usual eunuchs of virtue - the "good" Germans who toss a little at night. Their decencies are not strong enough to override their urge for conformity. In a land of brutes they are unable to bear the anti-social stigma of asserting themselves as human beings.

But I do not hold this against them - too much. I have always disliked people, writers particularly, who asked of others that they be heroes. I do not ask them to be heroes - but I suspect these 'possum-playing human beings of Germany. I suspect that if you examine any one of them carefully you will find he is no soul in torment, but a coin with two sides. He can offer either side as coin of the realm. He can cash in on his virtues and his evils at separate counters. And if he suffers a little when he is a man of wickedness because of the secret proddings of his goodness, you may be sure that he suffers also when is he is a man of goodness - from the secret proddings of his need for villainy. He is the German murderer with a convenient conscience, with a capacity for rue, as well as sadistic glee. I know this Hans and Fritz well and know well his chief function. It is not moral, but political. He is the little mask that Germany puts on when things go bad for it. And he is an obliging mask. He will throw away, sincerely, all his expressions of wickedness and arrange his face in all the honest expressions of goodness. He was one of those who helped murder three million Jews. And he will be one of those who will mourn this deed and denounce it.

"When the Devil was sick, the Devil a Saint would be -
When the Devil got well the devil a Saint was he."

But how many truly good Germans are there then - if you discount the Teuton of two faces? Is it a number that challenges the murder-character of Germanism? I have not interviewed all the Germans in Germany - no more than have those ambivalent Americans who are so eager to show their own humanity by finding a large measure of it in those who have committed murder. I wonder why their sympathies go so quickly to the culprit in danger of punishment instead of to the victim dead and outraged. And I wonder why the agony of three million murdered Jews is less a matter for humanitarian concern than the inconvenience that may (only may, mind you) be imposed on their murderers.

No, I have not interviewed all the Germans, nor heard all their voices. But the voice is not the only identity of the soul. It is, in fact, its most dubious one. There are more certain identities - the deed, for instance. This identity I have heard, and it speaks loudly. Beside it the voice of the good German - the German of unquestionable human virtue - is no more than the whisper of a lost child; a tiny German orphan who sits beside a dark road and has no home.

As I said, much has been written about this virtuous German figure

- dramas, novels, movies, essays, panegyrics - and he is everywhere embraced. I, too, embrace him but not as a symbol of Germany - yesterday's, today's, or tomorrow's Germany. He is symbol of nothing but his eternal unfitness to be a German and live in Germany. When the war is done and German brutality slapped into quiet, this good German will go back to his home again - the roadside.

CINDERELLA IN AN OPERA HAT

Of the German orphans I knew, the one I liked most was George Grosz, the painter. I met him the first week in 1919 when I had just arrived as a correspondent in Berlin. It was a meeting of import, and I will recount it fully, for out of it came much knowledge.

I was riding to Berlin on the first of January from Rotterdam on a train as crowded as a New York subway express during the rush hour. It was the first rusty and battered train to bring the outside world into the four-year island of German militarism. I felt as excited as Spencer and Gillan when they headed for the unknown bush country of Australia. The Germans, then as now, had this quality - they could make you feel more like an anthropologist than a journalist when you went calling on them.

I had squeezed myself onto the rear platform where some fifty passengers stood congealed and coated with cinders. It was cold, and we rode standing on each other's feet all night. When we had been riding thus for an hour I noticed that the man into whose ribs I was wedged was oddly troubled. He was holding a cardboard box such as opera hats come in and was desperately concentrated on keeping it from being crushed by the joggling jam on the platform.

He was a tall, dark-haired man, with bright gray eyes and an expression of courtesy which no discomfort could apparently alter. He wore a black overcoat with velvet lapels, such as I had never seen in Chicago, and a high wing-collar that seemed certain to choke or stab him to death before the journey was done.

The spectacle of this beleaguered passenger so concerned over a hat box - and so indifferent to the horrors of our travel - grew on me.

I decided, finally, that the hat box was full of bombs - hence his tenderness with it - and that this fellow into whom I was morticed was some Hohenzollern addict hastening to Berlin to blow up the Allied Commission already there. I caught his eye and began to explore the matter casually.

"It doesn't look as if you're going to get that home in one piece." I nodded at the box.

"Oh, yes, I will get it home in safety," he said.

"Frightful ride."

"Very bad."

"Why don't you put it on top of your head? It might save it."

"I have thought of that. But I am afraid the wind would blow it away."

"What's in it?" This very casually.

A pause. The bright gray eyes, practically on the end of my nose, looked intently at me. The train lurched on.

"Forgive my curiosity," I resumed. "I'm an American correspondent assigned to cover Germany. And this is the first question I've asked any German."

"In that case, I am honored to inform you what is in the box. It is a hat."

"Thank you." I became silent. I was not to be outwitted by the first German terrorist I had met on my new assignment. The hat box holder continued with disarming friendliness.

"I went to The Hague to buy it. I was demobilized last week, and I had a very difficult time getting a visa for Holland. Things are still very complicated, not so? But I managed finally - and got to the Hague yesterday. I was lucky to find the hat."

"There are no hats in Berlin?"

"Not like this."

"What kind of a hat is it?"

"It is an opera hat."

"You went to The Hague only to buy an opera hat?"

"Oh, yes."

"It's a curious world."

"Would you care to see it?" He was looking at me eagerly.

"Yes, I'd love to."

He opened the box. I looked inside. It held a tall silk opera hat, such as comedians wear after mussing them up a little. He lifted the hat out carefully, and I noticed there were no bombs in the box.

In this bleak, windy night on the train platform, Dr. Karl Dohman looked on his new possession bought in The Hague and there was love in his eyes. I was confused. As a reader of Krafft-Ebing, I though vaguely, "A hat fetishist. Funny I should meet one right off the bat." I considered it perhaps worthy of my first cabled story to Chicago that the first German I should speak to in Germany should turn out to be a case history.

I never wrote such a story, for I was wrong about the whole thing. Dr. Dohman was a young surgeon, highly educated, the owner of an Iron Cross; and the purchase of the silk topper was a political whim. He desired to walk down Unter den Linden in an opera hat for reasons I shall explain later. He was, also, a poet of some renown. The next evening when I sat in his rooms he read me from his printed work.

"As she sleeps, the moonlight falls on her neck and lengthens it out like a piece of rubber pipe."

Later when we were leaving a café, he said, "I would like you to meet a friend of mine. He is an artist. But much more than that, I assure you. He is an important part of Germany for you to know, as a correspondent. I mean, you will like him."

It was after two and we woke Grosz up by kicking on his studio door for a half hour. A sharp-featured, slightly reddish-faced young man finally peered out.

"Forgive me," he said. "What time is it? Oh, it is you. It is an honor. Come inside, please."

I was impressed by the formality of the tone and words. He might have been a diplomat admitting a colleague into a great conference, instead of an artist with a hangover, rudely roused from sleep.

When he had learned who I was he bowed to me and continued in the same precise and elegant tones.

"A very great honor, indeed. I am delighted. It is lucky Dr. Dohman brought you. Because you are the first American I have seen. How is Chicago, do you care to tell me?"

"Thriving," I said. "Getting taller."

"And the jazz and the advertising business, they are also all right?"

"Yes, getting along fine."

"Very good," said Grosz. "I am glad to hear that. I have never been to Chicago. Or even to America. Although I tell the story sometimes to my intimate friends that I am born there and abducted at the age of six months. You know how it is, among artists or - what shall I say - men with thoughts. I have made some interesting pictures of your city. Do you happen to know the Chicago Beach Hotel?"

"Very well."

Grosz looked triumphantly at Dr. Dohman and said softly to him, "He is a fellow after my own heart. I thank you for bringing him."

He held up one of his scratchy lined, exuberant drawings.

"Here it is," he said. "The Chicago Beach Hotel. Notice the sign, please. And now," he continued, "it is my honor to offer you something to buy. No, no, not pictures. A book. The greatest book in the world. I will get it for you. Kindly be seated. It is under my bed. Are you, as an American, interested in buying such a book?"

"I'd like to see it."

"You will imagine it is, perhaps, very expensive. But I assure you not. It is - what shall I say - a bargain. Only $50,000. If you have not the money, your newspaper will be glad to supply it, I am sure."

He was down on hands and knees hauling something out from under the bed. It was a book two feet square with wooden covers.

"The name of this book is 'The Book of Dada,' like the Koran. or the Bible, you understand. Something simple."

I looked through its pages. It was a sort of glorified and cockeyed scrapbook, with thousands of pictures, newspaper headlines, and things pasted in it. There were bits of cork, feathers, coins, beer bottle labels, pebbles, pieces of lace, and around these and other diverse objects was pasted an eruption of advertisements and illustrations all cut carefully down to their outlines. There were stoves, minarets, chimneys, horses, soldiers, bedsteads, parrots, cannon, liquor ads, and every other kind of ad, and in and around these cutouts and objects a fanfare of German, French, Swedish, and English newspaper headlines. The pasting job had been done with fanatic care and on each of the eruptive pages were exuberantly drawn scrolls connecting the curious rabble of clippings. The scrolls were full of angels, bleeding hearts, clasped hands, and there appeared as a running motif a large fat face with shrewd eyes sucking on a piece of candy. I looked for a half hour at the clippings, headlines, and cherubic ornamentation and said nothing.

"It is very cheap at $50,000," Grosz sighed. "I can tell you that Dr. Dohman and five of the greatest minds in Germany assisted in the making of this book. You may ask him what he thinks."

I was surprised to hear Dohman, whom I had considered a completely sane fellow up to this point, say quietly, "A book like this is worth maybe a million dollars."

"Exactly," said Grosz.

"What makes you think that?" I asked coldly.

"Because," Grosz answered, "this book is the world. Everything in the world is in this book. If you study it you can become the wisest man on earth - without going to school."

"Yes," Dohman corroborated. "All knowledge, all truth is in it. When I was on furlough last year, I spent my entire week in Berlin doing nothing but looking at this book."

"I'll wire my paper about it," I said, "and see if they want to pay $50,000 for it."

"Very good," said Grosz.

My editor was already screaming across the Atlantic at me for my profligacy because of a two hundred dollar loss in a poker game with the Mayor of Hull and some English heroes who had all looked like honest gentlemen.

"Very fine," Grosz beamed. "Now that we are finished with business - how shall I say - concluded our undertaking- we will have a drink."

This was my meeting with German orphan number 2. When I went to bed that night it was with the thought that I had come to Lewis Carroll's country.

THE MYSTERY OF GERMAN LAUGHTER

My friendship with Grosz grew quickly, and I was inducted into the true mystery of the opera hat, the Book of Dada, and of German laughter. I had, on the train coming into Berlin, met one of the rarest human specimens in the world - a laughing German. Dr. Dohman was a Dadaist. And Dadaism was a cult of laughter founded by Grosz, and a number of other anarchs. It was an art movement based on a turned stomach and a yell of derision. Its purpose was to wipe out every trace of Germanism from Germany - its dripping poetry, its wattled professorialism, its sarchophagi canvases, its musical opium, its Prussian strut, its obsession with greatness. And above and beyond all these, its brutal manners and national oafishness. It was the helpless effort of Germany's human orphans to deride the future out of crushing them. Of all the things I noted in Germany, this cult of Dadaism was the most important. It was the only German revolution that took place in Germany. The rest were all fakes, as will be all its future revolutions. But Dadaism, small, doomed, and fleeting, was the one little uprising of the ego in strudel-headed Deutschland. It cried out shrilly, comically, and bitterly for the overthrow of the German soul.

The men and women who had undertaken this program gave it many bizarre expressions. Among these was the plan of making German stupidity self-conscious by imitating it - with an extra fillip. Hence, Dr. Dohman's hat. Hence Grosz' pompous and elegant ways of speech. Dohman and hundreds of others swarmed through Berlin, out-acting and out-pomping the witless Prussians, caricaturing them in restaurants and theaters.

I remember the famous Dada Concert of the Arts given in the largest hall in Berlin. It was advertised with the dignity of a Wagner festival. The tickets were priced as at a championship fight. Full dress was demanded. Special boxes were decorated for high army officers.

And all Berlin came - all the high-born, high-collared, and highly spiritual ones. They had paid large sums for their tickets and been assured that they were to witness a veritable congress of German culture. The first "number" on the stage was a poetry contest. Grosz was master of ceremonies for the evening. He announced in the longest German words I had ever heard that the Dadaists were going to stage not only a poetry contest, but a simultaneous poetry contest. Twelve of the most distinguished poets of the Fatherland and one hotel porter were going to read simultaneously their thirteen poems - the winner to receive an award of five thousands marks.

The thirteen poets lined up, Grosz fired a gun in the air, and they began declaiming simultaneously their thirteen different poems.

The second number was a race between a virgin of twenty-five at a sewing machine and a poet, weighing 125 pounds, at a typewriter. Again Grosz fired the starter's gun, and the typewriter and sewing machine started off. The poet, said Grosz, had won because the virgin had stabbed her finger with the needle. The third number was a Modern Concert. Five large posters, each with a single music note drawn on it, were placed on the backs of five chairs and the audience was invited to drink in the beauty of sound with its eyes.

There were other numbers - but they became inaudible. The audience rioted. Shots were fired and the Noske soldiers sent for. The last I recall of the Concert of all the Arts was the entrance of a hundred pre-Stormtroopers from General Noske's garrison - and the shrill voices of Grosz and Dohman calling out from the stage the two slogans of the evening, "Art Is In Danger," and "Take Your Foot Out of the Butter Before It's Too Late."

A number of heads were broken, but there were no fatalities. The Dadaists scattered to their various ateliers and Berlin seethed for a week over the insult.

"We may yet succeed," said Dr. Dohman to me the next evening, "in making the Germans ashamed to be fools."

But the truth of the Dada movement lay more in Grosz than in Dohman or any of the others. The truth lay in Grosz' drawings - the ten thousand fabulous black and white pictures which established him as the greatest caricaturist Europe had ever known. But he was more than caricaturist. Grosz was the German revolution, the brief, wild answer of the orphans at the roadside.

I brought a photographer to Grosz' studio a week later. He photographed hundreds of Grosz' black and white pictures. The pictures enchanted me. I knew at the time the work of Felicien Rops and the daft Austrian Alfred Kubin. But beside Grosz, these two Satanists and convention rippers seemed a pair of aldermen.

The works of George Grosz were the single-handed answer to a nation and a national psychology. They were Nietzsche turned into a skyrocket of ink. No more ruthless lines have even been put to paper. A draughtsmanship of invective, a world that looked like a smashed strawberry box, a courage that raised caricature to a religion, filled the pictures. Not an artist or even a revolutionist was behind these drawings, but a surgeon at work on Germany, an unfrightened surgeon carving away at the greatest cancerous area ever seen on a modern operating table.

Looking at this Germany drawn, carved, hacked, sprinkled on paper by Grosz, you beheld lust and murder, murder and lust. You saw a desperate, retching criminal clawing at life with his fat neck dripping and his little pig eyes unaware. Always unaware. The Four Horsemen of the Apocalypse were prettier and more lovable than the Germans Grosz drew. The scratchy lines, the half lopsided, battered exteriors of buildings, streets, furniture and faces seemed to scream as in some Devil's Confessional. They screamed their Germanism.

I met the other orphans, one by one. Poets, publishers, journalists, professors - there was a Professor of Mathematics who wore a black cloak and walked the streets of Berlin after midnight playing a cornet till dawn; physicians, lawyers, businessmen, were among them. And also, scores on scores of people who were neither artist nor professional, but the ill-shod, untutored, hungering disciples of something that did not exist in Germany.

The German orphan long ago gave up his brief revolution through laughter. Ridicule, he discovered, is never a match for the ridiculous. But he still exists, in and out of Germany. And he is a pariah more pathetic than his friend, the Jew. He must roam the strange streets of the world - the German freak who is not a German; the two per cent of humanity trapped under German hair cuts and behind German wing collars.

I know them well and embrace them all. They are fine fellows and fine women, but when I look at them I do not see Germany. I see only those whom the Germans call always criminals.

The German underground of today (in our last war year) is the descendant of these Dadaists. The German humanists who speak or merely dream in silence of a world rid of German brutality are the inheritors of Dada- the Indian Rope Trick cult by which the little orphan of Germany once sought to make it disappear.

These good Germans - the egoistic believers in life - continue to fight for the cause of human honor. They die for truth. But why honor warriors by giving them the name of their enemy - Germany? Germany does not produce them. It merely throws them out, cripples, crushes and hounds them to the ends of the earth.

These good Germans represent no German current, no German party and no German future. They are the brothers of talent, and not the sons of Germany. There have never been enough of them to clean even a patch on the German face.

MY TANTE'S MAGIC UMBRELLA

There is another matter that has been omitted from my book, but this omission is a deliberate one. In what I have written thus far of Jews I have made no effort to defend them against the charges that assail their name. I have, more likely, in the eyes of many Jews, attributed to them nearly all the faults of which the anti-Semites accuse them - that they are a sharp, subtle, and boastful lot; that they are an egoistic lot who do not fit in with the herd instincts of other peoples - (this sort of generalization reminds me of a saying by Ted Cook, author of Cook's Cuckoos, to wit, "The narrower the mind, the broader the statement"); and that, view them through any colored glasses, you will find them (the Jews) standing out in a community like flies in a milk pail or raisins in a cake.

It is the habit of Jewish apologists to deny all this. But I am not a Jewish apologist, and have never understood the technique of apology. When I am dead and present myself to my Maker, I may, if I am properly spoken to, make my first apology. I will apologize for having been a human being.

I see nothing else for Jews to apologize for than this. But it is an apology they need not make to other human beings.

When I read the semi-scientific and semi-apologetic explanations for the Jews (they are not a race, but a group of seven vanished uncles from Palestine....tyranny and boycott are responsible for their nose blowing...the feet of the Jew, according to the latest anthropological findings, are exactly the same as the feet of the inhabitants of upper Silesia); when I read this touching, apologetic twaddle, I am reminded of what my Tante Chasha once said to me on this general subject.

I was six years old and she was forty and we had both been ejected from a theater for denouncing one of the actors on the stage. This actor, a policeman, had walked on the stage and accused another actor of having stolen a diamond bracelet from the heroine. Both my aunt and I had seen the crime committed under our very noses - we were in the first row, balcony - by another man. I was unable to contain myself when the handcuffs were put on the innocent actor, and yelled loudly that a miscarriage of justice was taking place. I pointed to the real rogue, smirking to one side of the stage, and cried that there stood the man who had stolen the diamond bracelet. I demanded his arrest.

Ushers arrived to silence me and when one of them tried to clap his hand over my screaming mouth, my Tante Chasha hit him over the head with an umbrella.

"He's a bright boy," she roared - she was a large and easily offended woman - "and he's got a right to complain if he don't like the way this bit of offal of a show is going (I am translating from the Yiddish). He's got an absolute right."

My Tante and I were rushed up the aisle, her umbrella swinging like Porthos' cudgel.

In the lobby we were met by the theater manager, a short fat impresario who belonged to the same circle of poker players as my aunt - it was a Yiddish theater.

"Mrs. Swernofsky," this manager looked at her full of hurt, "I am really surprised at your behaving yourself like this....I am afraid, Mrs. Swernofsky, I must ask you to apologize."

My Tante, who was a genius at cursing, stood looking at him, to my surprise, without a word. Then, gripping the remains of her umbrella, she swung it through the air and cracked him over the head with it. The manager groaned and staggered. My Tante seized my hand and whisked me out of the lobby. On the street she gave me a sunny smile.

"Remember what I tell you," she said. "That's the right way to apologize."

A PHILOSOPHY OF WOUNDS AND HALOS

The Jewish apologists are avidly and pathetically intent on stating the case for the Jew by contradicting his enemies. They do not even pause to study the accusations of these enemies. They feel only that anything an anti-Semite says must be contradicted and disproved - and they rush forward with statements that Jews love their mothers, are full of patriotism, sweetness and solid human charm.

These denials, contradictions and affirmations are a preposterous waste of time. Jewish diplomacy has been wasting its time in this fashion for almost twenty centuries, offering alibis and mitigating circumstances - for what? Is there anything of which a Jew can be guilty that could match the unsavory and contemptible antics of his accusers? Apologies to whom? To that judge with blood-caked hands who sits leering from his bench? To that enfeebled and chaotic brain that calls itself an anti-Semite? Or to that smug and highty-tighty bystander, World Opinion - a gentleman who hasn't been able to find his buttocks with both hands since he was given an alphabet to play with?

You would think that the Jews would wake up to this one fact about themselves - that their defensive position is the chief delight and arsenal of the anti-Semite. But never comes such awakening. There have been some who have opened their eyes. Heinrich Heine woke up one day and filled the world with a burst of bitter laughter. This "greatest of their poets" announced that, whatever the Jew was, the spectacle of the monstrosities who call themselves Germans setting themselves up as his judges and superiors was one which must set the Devil and all his friends to laughing.

But Heine is only a Jew - not a Jewish spokesman. The Jewish spokesmen are usually a little too stunned with calamity to make epigrams. Their very egoism bids them look to themselves for answers, rather than to their enemies. And they answer, scientifically, vaingloriously, despairingly. That they are arguing with lunacy, that they are titillating sadists, that they manage only to inflame their accusers by revealing their wounds - never daunts their propaganda.

And in this struggle to disprove the anti-Semite by presenting themselves as a noble, worthy, and even wondrous people, the Jews fall into a trap that leaves their enemies cackling. For even these have enough cunning to punch holes in such contentions. The mere fact that the Jews are to be found on this earth is enough to deny their cries that they are noble or remotely wondrous. No people known to history is that - not even the Americans.

There are two very unwise things to do in the world. One is to proclaim the fact that you are in distress - and expect your plight to bring Samaritans rushing to your side. An occasional Samaritan will arrive - but accompanied always by three hooligan sadists intent on the sport of increasing your misery. The other is the business of advertising your virtues. The "Jewish propaganda machine" is more or less devoted to both schemes, and the results continue, century in and out, to be the same. In a world that admires only victors, the Jews have persisted in advertising themselves as victims only. This the Jews are not. I am not writing of those murdered but those alive. No man alive is a victim. It is not only stupid but dangerous to pronounce himself one.

And no man alive is a good man. In such pronouncements lie further stupidity and danger. Whenever a man parades his virtues I always look over his shoulder at his follies and evils. I know that virtue is always a minority, and I dislike to be taken in by any durbars it stages. And if a man grows too loud with his claims to piety and goodness, it is my human impulse to bring him to my own measure by examining studiously his many failings.

Such, to a large degree, is the effect of the Virtue-Apologist propaganda of the Jews. The bystander - not necessarily an anti-Semite - on hearing the overpraise attached to the name Jew, ignores it a little irritably and bethinks himself at once of Jews he knows he wouldn't be found dead with.

My own attitude toward the Jews is that they need no defense - and that defending them is the major disservice I can do them. They are and have always been children of the world - and they look to me as good as the rest of their playmates. And, now and then, a little better.

If there is anything special in the Jewish make-up, it lies in the ancient and still undissipated egoism of the Jew. Here is the quirk of which the anti-Semites make always a great noise. I wish only that the accusations of egoism were as true as they proclaim them to be. The echo of Elijah is all too faint in the Jewish spirit. I wish also that many other of the accusations were true - that Jews are dangerous, that they are a world menace (to the Germans), that they cannot be assimilated by Nordic peoples (Is this really a charge or a complaint?). I wish too that there were complete truth in the accusation that the Jews are an implacable barrier to the philosophy of rampant nationalism.

There is only one truth in all these charges. No Jew, were he given a Swastika to wear on his sleeve, could exist in the Hell made by the Germans. Not even a bad Jew. There is enough of Elijah left in him to make of him the eternal Underground against tyranny.

It behooves every Jew to embrace this truth in the charges of his enemy with gratitude and a grin.

A YALE SCHOLAR

I have read many books dealing with the "truths" of the Jew's place in the world. Our scientists and scholars have been unusually busy of late measuring Jewish noses, occiputs and thigh bones; investigating Jewish migrations and European demonology; discussing the Jew's vanishing culture and interest in God (and seeing in this a fine hope for his future well-being); or dealing more soberly than yesterday with the great murder mystery - "Who Killed Christ - the Jews or the Romans?" (Or the Germans?)

All these professorial books, whether they are tender or cold, whether they accuse or disprove, strike me as part of the great library of evasion the world has piled up on the subject of the Jew. I read - and marvel that so many honorable and learned minds should continue to seek solution and explanation of "the ancient Jewish problem" by blindfolding themselves with the word Jew. Not in the Jew, but in thyself, good professor, lies the peritonitis.

Of the many professors, I select one to look at here. He has no particular importance, nor does he make his points with literary distinction. He is an ordinary scientist writing in an ordinary way - which is why I select him. His opinions have the value of being typical of the borderline of anti-Semitism where most of the blindfolded sages lurk.

He is Raymond Kennedy, Professor of Sociology at Yale University. As sociologist, he has studied the "Jewish problem" and discovered that it exists. He writes (in "Jews in a Gentile World," published by The Macmillan Company, New York) that among the student body at Yale there is a pronounced aversion to Jews.

This is not particularly news. I have never been to Yale (in any capacity), but I have heard tales that indicate that anti-Semitism is one of the *sub rosa* courses of that institution. If a Yale college boy cannot row, swim, jump, run, or get the hang of the arts and sciences, he can, nonetheless, achieve great distinction (and win a sort of social Y) by prowling the campus and snubbing Jews. I understand also, that the best Yale anti-Semites are secretly made into a team each year, and sent to Harvard University to compete with the best Jew-haters in its halls of learning. I am told that in thirty-five years of this series, the Yale contingent has never won a contest, due to the fact that one or two Jews always manage to sneak on the Yale team.

Hearsay being my only witness on college anti-Semitism, I must skip over Professor Kennedy's remarks concerning it. Yale college boys are apparently too proud to eat with Jews, says the Professor, and the Jewish students are too nervous to foist themselves on their Gentile college chums. For all I know, it may be the other way around - at least I have often found it so in areas off the campus.

From his Yale springboard, Professor Kennedy vaults into wider fields. He writes that in the United States as a whole there is a similarly definite feeling that Jews are given "to avarice, cunning, sharp dealing, clannishness, crudity of manners, and internationalism." (The Professor's politics may be glimpsed in his climactic criminal word "internationalism.")

Dr. Kennedy then offers the theory, first reassuring everybody that he is writing as a scientist, and not as a man of bias (like the professors who wrote of Semmelweis) that the American Jews are a caste, God help them, and present caste problems similar to that of the Negro.

Comparing Jews to Negroes is a rather recent scientific hobby and a step up for both the Jew and the Negro in the professorial debates. Is was not so long ago that Negroes were being compared chiefly to anthropoid apes, and Jews to demons hatched under gibbous moons. How much more valid and entertaining it would be to compare a white trash Alabama coon-hater with a white trash New England Jew hater! What is it they have in common? What, if any, political, psychiatric, and glandular maladjustments belong to both these citizens?

But back to Dr. Kennedy. "The caste," he defines, "is a strictly hereditary group. Those born into it can never rise out of it into a higher caste....It seems likely that a major proportion of (American) non-Jews regard the status of the (Jewish) group as fixed and immutable. Other nationalities are encouraged and expected to move rapidly toward assimilation - but the Jews, even though they may adopt the outward aspects of American culture, are supposed to remain a group apart."

I pause to underline the phrase "even though they may adopt." There's a picture for you of the Semite reluctantly and infrequently shedding his Chassidic curls and his phylacteries, and stepping gingerly into a theater for a look at Errol Flynn.

It is careful work - being a professor. Observe Prof. Kennedy, building up, phrase by phrase, his anti-Jewish vocabulary. This is extra, over and above his labor as an observer of the American scene - or beneath it, if you like. Thus:

"They (the Jews) are certainly discouraged from mingling freely with Gentile fellow-citizens," he continues. "We even find the term 'passing' used to indicate the process by which Jews conceal their ancestry, and, often changing their names, disappear into the mass of Gentile society. The parallel with the Negro case is obvious. With all this, however, the Jews are not so completely shut off from assimilation as the Negroes." (Sorry, Sambo, but this is a mighty keen professor, and he ought to know.) "At the very least, being white, they can 'pass' easily....The hereditary out-group allocation of the Jews is not so strictly enforced as that of the other racial minorities (Negroes), still they encounter barriers which other white immigrant groups do not face. They occupy an intermediate quasi-caste position."

Here the Professor seems to have frightened himself into promoting the Jews from the ordinary low-down "caste" to an "intermediate quasi-caste," which shows you that, scientist though he is, his heart is in the right place.

One is not a professor for nothing. In addition to a generous heart, Prof. Kennedy is given to fair-mindedness. He now examines, as I have urged my readers to do, the anti-Semite cranium. I quote:

"The success of Jews in business or the professions is not generally praised, rather it is regarded as a threat. They are not said to have 'made a success' of the clothing business and cinema industry, they have 'got control' of them. Usually this claim is accompanied by the assertion that whenever they do gain control they squeeze Gentiles out by their clannishness and unethical business dealings....Bright Jewish students are not given full credit for intellectual superiority, but their Gentile fellows attribute their success to almost inhuman concentration on study."

This last is a rather pathetic piece of inside Yale information, and offers a startling picture of how study is regarded by the Gentile sons of Old Eli.

But I have allotted Mr. Kennedy's prose sufficient space in my book. Enough that he goes on to chide our country for this state of affairs, and to point out, not very electrically, that there is a discrepancy between our claim to democratic ideals and our practice of them. I too think there are many things wrong with our democracy. One of them is Raymond Kennedy of Yale.

MY THESIS ON THE PROFESSOR

First for the Professor's "facts." Sociological facts, such as Dr. Kennedy deals in, have the merit (to me) of not being at all "scientific." They can be examined as the opinions of a human being and not as the indisputable markings on a test tube.

The first obvious thing about the Professor's facts is that he believes them. I assure you that no doubt, wonder or debate intrude on the Kennedy prose. He is a man of certainty, which is as it should be, for it is the duty of professors to live always in a world of facts. That is why in retrospect they usually look so homeless.

The second obvious thing is that Kennedy has not got hold of his facts by mere book reading. He achieved them also out of his own observations. This is an interesting point. What are observations? Are they something we make outside our own beliefs? Or are they data we gather to make our own notions stand up? A little of both, perhaps, with a tendency more one way than the other, depending on who observes. An artist, for instance, will find out only things he does not know. A professor, very often, will discover only things he does know.

I do not challenge the Professor's "facts." I am certain that he has personally noted numerous cases of antipathy to Jews, his own University providing him with an ideal place for research. That there are industrial heads, school heads, society heads, and dunderheads, of all kinds, who boycott the Jew and refuse to let him "pass" is a fact a sociologist aged seven can find out with a minimum of inquiry - particularly if he resides in New Haven.

But Professor Kennedy is not satisfied with his facts as facts, nor even with his observations as observations. He enlarges them into an All-Over Fact - a bird's-eye observation of the United States. And, thus, he succeeds in presenting the facts, not as they are, but as they would be in an ideal anti-Semite country.

For the Professor's facts do not apply to the USA. They apply to its anti-Semites. The Jew is a caste figure only in the eye of the anti-Semite, which eye the professor appears scientifically to have borrowed. If he will return the eye to where it belongs, he will see quite reasonably that the only thing the American Jew cannot "pass" into is American anti-Semitism. Into everything else American, including even college football, he "passes" with celerity and grace.

As a Jew, I am a better authority on this than is the Professor. Not only have I my own "passing" as a bit of data, but I have a covey of relatives and friends (all hereditary Jews) who have also "passed." With few exceptions they have neither changed their names, bobbed their noses, nor pulled in what Semitic horns they have - yet they are all in the "open class" of American society. They have all passed into restaurants and drawing rooms where Professor Kennedy would be frowned on for his provincialism - and probably not invited again.

These data Jews of mine have met with evidences now and then of anti-Semitism. They have, on occasions, been barred from hotels, occasionally been refused a job, or received a social snub for their Jewishness. But this does not make them a caste. It is quite the other way around. It is a caste that snubs them - a minority caste such as the Professor defines: a caste that cannot rise but must remain trapped in its anti-Semitic psychic pigmentation - which is that of the disordered liver, come Hell or high water. It is not, however, a hereditary caste, but an illness open to all. You can catch it in the subway just as easily as at Yale - and less expensively.

To declare, professorially, that this caste group of anti-Semites is the USA, to announce that these alienated gentry have conquered the Republic and succeeded in turning it into the ideal anti-Semitic state (without recourse to a single pogrom), is to strike your democratic colors a little too eagerly. But I may be unjust in this statement. It is, perhaps, not his colors the professor strikes, but his intelligence.

My thesis, if read by Dr. Kennedy, will very likely bewilder him. For he is obviously a man a bit more sensitive than his background, old Eli. If he sees the Jew as half pariah he is somewhat inconvenienced by this "fact." He even calls, albeit dulcetly, for some remedy or other - "more assimilation and greater tolerance." This mutter of "out, out, damned fact" may ring even as a bold cry in the professor's own set, and one which raises a number of faculty eyebrows. And he may, accordingly, feel that he is a veritable knight in armor battling for a prettier world. My criticism will thus seem to him ungracious and ill-founded.

But I must point out that if you examine Dr. Kennedy's battling carefully you find something odd about it. You find that he does not battle to right a wrong, but devotes all his energies to making the wrong seem triumphant. He does not merely write with dissatisfaction of what he thinks is unjust. Rather he finds a curious professorial satisfaction in exaggerating the injustice.

True, this may be due to the fact that he is (obviously) no writer, but a school-teacher. And it may be therefore that he lacks all those tricks of mathematics and poesy which, employed in a considered way to create a desired effect, go to make up the business of the writer. Not knowing this business, one is apt to achieve the opposite of what one intends.

But, lamebrain or no, the Professor practices a sort of Black Magic. Whatever his conscious intentions, he affirms the battle (against anti-Semitism) lost that has not gone beyond a skirmish. And in crying these dark tidings, he helps, whether he desires it or not (I am not his analyst) to lose the battle, so far as he, all his readers, and good old Yale are concerned.

But this is not the chief crime of the Professor. Dr. Kennedy is presumably a gentleman trained in the art of reason, and dedicated to the training of others in that art. It is this training and dedication he betrays (and there is his larger crime) when he offers as the fruits of scholarship what is no more than an avid discussion of the oddities of the Jew. Not censuring these oddities, mind you, and not even saying definitely that these "caste" oddities exist. Merely enumerating them, like some gossip repeating eagerly all the details of a nasty scandal - and concluding his recitation with the pious regret that it's a pity there's so much scandal around.

Such is the ghost of scholarship - all shadowy, gaseous and unsavory - that is wafted toward us from the old halls of Yale. Unsavory, threadbare ghost of scholarship! I never went to school, but I humbly offer these assignments to the dean, or superintendent or president, or whoever is in charge. Why doesn't Prof. Kennedy go on to his true research - to the examination of the prejudiced ones in whom he himself announces lies the whole truth? Why doesn't this eager Jew investigator investigate the college boys who call the Jew names? For instance, here is a theme for Kennedy's sociology class: What is it in the Yale student that flinches at the Jew, and out of what psychic disturbance does our Yale man fetch his anti-Semitic attitudes? Or, if the Professor finds such public query embarrassing and contrary to the traditions of the Alma Mater, here's another more private theme: What's wrong with Professor Kennedy? What makes him prefer to see the USA as if it were a land of happy anti-Semites and writhing caste-suffering Jews?

Not Kennedy nor any of the professors speak of the nightmare that begins where their contributions stop. Their faces are turned toward truth. They announce its presence and then a silence falls. Their voices stop where the voice of science should begin. Observing these front ranks of education in all the ages looming always on the threshold of battle - silent, blind, inert and renowned - I wonder whether the human mind has ears or eyes at all, or any other weapon against ignorance than complacency.

And it is studying such scholars as Professor Kennedy, and similar good souls with their brains in a gunny sack, that I understand better the disasters of civilization than in looking on the rabble ranks of anti-Semitism. My brother, the anti-Semite, runs amok blowing smoke out of his nose and making a noise like the King of Beasts. But, good God, look at his keeper.

ENVOI TO THE PROFESSOR ON FLYPAPER

I am in fact not much worried about the brother amok. I am certain that the anti-Semites are no match for the Jews, and that their way is a hard one. The victories they win are illusions, and the illnesses that come to foam on their lips end by inconveniencing them more than they do the Jews - in the United States, not Europe. Although it is yet to be seen who lost more in Europe, the Jews or the Germans.

But these others, these professors, bystanders and amiable ones - this mass of good people through whose goodness a little worm is always crawling - they are the gentry who make the future grim. And not for Jews alone. They are the proof that history will not change, that however tender the heart of man may become, his brain remains an instrument for outraging the truth under his nose and the very decency in his soul.

It is not the Semmelweises alone that Authority crucifies, but every truth that calls for light. The pogrom against Jews (and discoverers) is a minor thing. The battle against reason is the real show. And if you read this some day far distant from the autumn in which I write - and if around you there rages another and greater destruction than distinguished my time - credit my bones with having understood the two chief ingredients of human thought. They are poison and folly.

VILLAINY AS A POLITICAL PLATFORM

The great political success of anti-Semitism demonstrated by the Germans (and not yet by their American imitators) is not a new thing. Anti-Semitism has been for the last fifteen centuries one of the handy forces at the disposal of every political scoundrel in Christendom. It has served to cement a hundred thrones and erect a thousand cathedrals.

The scoundrel - prince or priest or adventurer - has known always that it is easier to win followers through their deep talent for hate than their (biologically) recent capacity for love. He has known that hatred is the magic for victory, if you can control it. Hatred strengthens people and solidifies them - behind you, if you are lucky. When we hate someone, we feel the courage necessary for their slaying. If we happen to hate someone weak and unarmed against us, this does not lessen our sense of courage. In fact, it increases it. Not only the Germans, but scores of nations have shouted themselves to battle by first "triumphing" over the Jews.

Hatred is also a great political deflector. It has served leaders well as a vital change of subject. Alter the enemy from a confusing economic system and its confusing ills to something as simple and easy to lay low as a Jew, and you have restored security around you.

A thousand years of Christianity, 700 to 1700, are based almost entirely on hatred. The Religion of Love triumphed most swiftly when it could be used to harass and outrage the weak and the helpless.

All these matters and explanations have become a cliché - a sort of cliché of disaster. We frown at the monomania of people who bring such matters up for examination. They are there, always have been there, and will remain there - so why examine them? There is no reason, if reason connotes remedy. Such investigations as this are as powerless as the wind blowing at a mountain base. The absurdity and monstrousness of the human mind have survived books of this sort by the thousands and hundreds of thousands - have, in fact, battened on them.

Yet not to write them would be to deny tomorrow. They are the prayers of sanity.

LAST ARE THE LEADERS

Leaders are easy to indict. History holds hardly more than a few hundred men responsible for the catastrophes that have warped the earth since Attila. I am no historian (as I have said) and the misdeeds of a few overpublicized scoundrels have failed to impress or deflect me. I have wondered always when I read of public villains where their Public came from, out of what caverns it arose. How easy moral progress would be if we had only to chop off a few chieftain heads to attain it!

The psychology of human misbehavior is too vast a topic for discussion, as I stated at the start of this book. It has not yet been even indexed. Any minor poet can sing all the virtues of man - in a thin volume. But the moment you set yourself to reporting his villainies, you are lost in the infinite.

I pick out, therefore, for my final essay only a little evil, the evil that makes men into political apes, that induces them to follow leaders whose unreason and viciousness gleam on their faces like birthmarks. I have a theory that enables me to understand these followers (and their leaders). It may not be a new theory, for there are so many theorists in the world today that novelty has become a mathematical impossibility, but it is one I have not read, which makes it new to me.

MY POLITICAL STETHOSCOPE

My theory is based on the meaning of egoism. I have used the word egoism often in this book, and meant by it the creative force that has urged man to assert and improve himself. This is still my definition of the word, but I am concerned now with the disease of uncreative egoism. The legs can run but they can also rot.

God knows what the Ego is - and so do I. The Ego is a ferocity for identification that exists in all of us. Deeper than our lusts and all our other good and bad hungers, is this obsession we have to be Some One. It is not of fame necessarily we dream, but of a special identity, of existence as an individual. We clamor to acquire a meaning, to participate, however, humbly, in the world of ideas and events; to hold opinions that will make us significant, and place us, like the greatest of philosophers, jowl to jowl with all the truths. We struggle to lift ourselves out of a herd-loneliness that eternally engulfs us.

The Ego is the whip on our brain. It cries constantly, "Think, think. Find a thought." It urges, "Come to life. Achieve a special color, a distinctive inner face." On all the herd of humans this whip plies endlessly. There is no man so low but feels its sting. It flails away at dummies and geniuses alike, for it is no special goad designed to make men celebrated. It is a universal and eternal whip handed to the species to turn its children into men. And each man wields it according to his strength.

I can understand how our Maker must have deemed it a brilliant device for the evolution of our species from herd to individuals.

"The ego," He very likely said to His angels, "will make every human creature a little discontented with himself. He will always want to be more than bones, flesh, and organs. He will want to have Intellectual Identity, which is a desire lacking in all the other fauna."

But our Maker, who fashioned so excellently the whip, was a little less attentive to the construction of the winged horses of the brain that were supposed to leap everlastingly forward under its urging

And yet I may be entirely wrong in thinking that our Maker had anything at all to do with fashioning the mind of man. For every other bit of His handiwork, from the smallest gnat to the largest constellation, has in it sanity and perfection. Of all the productions of the universe, the human mind alone is given (almost entirely) to lunacy and distortion. It is a crippled thing as faltering as the chugs of the first automobile. It is as clumsy as the paw of a stranded lobster. Indeed, its very existence is dubious, and there are whole eras where this mind is no more than a fog in which the race wanders like a homeless old beggar.

ROGUES IN RAGS

Rogues are usually creatures whose egos are greater than their minds. And often they have no minds at all but a resounding whip in them to drive this nothingness forward. The disproportion between whip and wits is the measure of their villainy.

The population of rogues varies. At times there seems to be only a handful of them about, and we grin at them from our superior roosts and say to each other, "Look at these imbeciles strutting around and pretending they are full of wisdom and genius." We are amused by their daft antics to achieve individuality, and we watch them walk through snow in their bare feet, or discourse from soap boxes on subjects that are total mysteries to them, or invent perpetual motion machines or peddle proclamations heralding the end of the world. We call them "nuts," and find their silliness a little picturesque.

On this topic I wrote in my unfinished epic poem:

"No egoism that I know
Puts on such florid airs, or wags
So powerful a tongue, or so
Admires itself and preens and brags
As does Stupidity aglow
And wrapped in intellectual rags."

But at times the population of "nuts" rises alarmingly. The spurring of ego in empty skulls becomes an epidemic and creates not a handful of street corner caperers but a political constituency. Out of the ranks of the gutter misfits comes then the Praetorian Guard for folly. And to find amusement in this we need a vantage point not in our world.

POLITICAL PORTRAIT I: THE ANTI-SEMITIC GOON

He is the true bottom of the litter - the creature with a windswept cranium; old chasm-brain, the golem. He stands on the outskirts - any outskirts. Wherever there is an organized group of human beings, on its outskirts stands our golem, known to the trade of troublemaking as The Goon.

He would like to join the party, but two things prevent association with his fellows. One is the contempt they have for him. He is too ignorant, too pre-historic to invite into human environs. Even the wardheelers and the neighborhood statesmen running for dog-catcher will usually have none of him. There is a cavernous sound to his babble that depresses even the boys in the poolroom and the flop houses. No wit or culture are expected in these elemental circles, nor niceties of manner nor eagle feathers in your hat. Here are the poor or the wrestlers with poverty, and to intrude in their conclaves you need a minimum of credentials. But one you need. You have to give off the aura of a semi-rational human being. The poor are prone to confusions but they are leery of freaks.

The Goon remains a fringe figure among them. They do not like the gleam in his eye. They know that it is dangerous for a stupid man to have a gleaming eye. And they toss him out of their bar-rooms and bingo games.

This is one of his sorrows - the suspicion and contempt of his fellows. Sorrow number two is the Goon's ego. There is a whip plying his empty skull and filling him with a discontent like a toothache. He is too dumb to make the grade of errand boy, yet he would be the boss. He would be top dog, this bottom of the litter.

There are no openings for him in the world of rationality. All the sane and semi-sane slogans of society are too involved for his hollow noggin. And too unpromising. Spelling these out, he can move forward from the fringe to the seats at the back of the hall reserved for stutterers; and this is not movement enough. Our Goon who has not sufficient brain to qualify as a human being dreams of being a superman.

Thus he stands on the fringe, glowering, snorting, and full of an impatient misery. He is the ancient and immemorial recruit for unreason. Let a backward cry go up within earshot and he is there. Let the slogans be brash and meaningless enough and he will embrace them with a manly shout. For where there is no sense there is no competition, and no superior minds around pushing him to a back seat. The senseless slogan is a great leveler. It reduces all its apostles to a mental equality. There can be no nuances to zero.

Anti-Semitism is a slogan made to order for this golem. If he yell, "Kill all the Jews!" loudly enough he comes into existence, instantly, as a leading philosopher. The promotion is a delirious one. He achieves overnight the status of a menace and a dangerous "thinker." He who could not think up ten words to which any human being would listen, has got his mouth on four syllables now that place him in the limelight as if he had been coached by Aladdin.

Does the Goon who cries "Death to all Jews!" hate them? Does he dream of a world purified by the extermination of Jews? Does he believe that "Jews are ruining civilization," that "Jews are throttling the American spirit?"

The Goon understands these matters about as much as a turtle in a mud bank. The words Civilization, American, Christianity, Purity, Spirit, Economics, and Jew are not containers of ideas for him. They are word-rattles with which to make angry and ego satisfying sounds. He knows no civilization, good or bad; and he knows no Jews and hates no Jews. He has a score to settle with life - or with God. For something gave him a whip and a full set of harness - and no horses to drive. And he will win the race astride a phantom - if he has to kill all the actual horses on the track.

And so our Goon, turned anti-Semite, flourishes. Leaders use him. They hope, in our land, to move him forward a fraction, to induce him to vary his cry to "Down with Democracy!" But the Goon is reluctant here. He prefers Jewish indignation to Irish police clubs. As anti-Semite he is enemy of the humanities, a much safer and more rewarding thing to be than enemy of government. To boot, the cry of "Down with Democracy!" is a little too complicated for him, and there is the competition of better minds around this slogan. He will stick to the Jews. "Down with the Jew" is an island of unreason on which the Goon is a match for all comers. Where the ring rules call for clogged nasal ducts, a slap-happy expression and rubber legs, the

Goon is champ.

I bow to the Goon and his basement headquarters. So cockeyed a masquerade as these spike-haired imbeciles parading as "thinkers," "patriots," "tomorrow's world," brings a grin to me. I do not consider them dangerous or even important - in my country. They are dangerous and important in a land that wishes to use them. We have a handful of Goon-users in the USA but no more than that. A few of our statesmen flirt with the voting strength of the Goons, and a few more like the Goon for himself alone. He is a dramatic and picturesque expression of their own more sickly anti-Semitism. We have a few lawmakers and literateurs who haunt his side.

I leave this strutting cypher, this golem-soul, empty as a drum, and making as loud a noise on a few street corners. He is the vanguard of the pogrom. He not only can commit murder but infect a land with murder. He is able to reduce the soul of a land to his own measure. This he has done in Germany and Romania. Three million murdered Jews have given the European Goon a sense of glamour and prowess. When civilization is killed he struts his little hour as King of the nightmare. He is a great man in Germany, this Goon. He is still a Goon in the USA.

POLITICAL PORTRAIT II: MAN WITH A NOWHERE TICKET

This is not the Goon in disguise - not quite. He is a slightly more elegant fellow. The Goon has to count on his fingers, but this one can run a cash register. He is Little Business, Little America, and Little Casino. His clothes are pressed, and the gleam in his eye is offset by the toothpick in his mouth. He can read, too; nothing very complicated, but enough to distinguish a newspaper from a tomato can label. He has some trouble, though, with the crossword puzzle.

There is a certain stir of intellect in this Lord of Littleness that gives him an in-between status - more than a cypher and less than a figure. He knows how to say "hello" like a big shot when he is introduced to somebody in a saloon or on a Pullman train.

Yet with all his charms and accomplishments, something bothers this near gentleman in the almost white collar. There is an unrest in his toothpick chewing. The world is too large and too impersonal for him. His talents cannot embrace it, and his personality cannot say "hello" to it like a big shot; nor even like a little shot. He is a white collar castaway. The Goon clamors fiercely for identity. Little Casino, his half-educated brother, only sighs for it.

He comes home at night with his brow puckered. His day has been full of matters beyond him, discussions he could not follow, books he could not read, institutions too complex for his understanding. He takes to bed with him in the dark a vision of the vastness and confusion of the things outside him. The vision of great things does not inspire him. It frightens him and fills his soul with a loneliness. He has a mind, a wife, a business - yet he is part of nothing. He has a country, but this country is like a rich uncle far away. He has a God, but He is another rich uncle even further away. Lying in his dark bed, he feels the loneliness that comes with little thoughts and little spirit.

For people who suffer from littleness there is an ancient relief - intolerance. Good people, made desperate by loneliness, look hopefully to the Pandora Box in their natures. They do not tear its lid off as does the Goon. They open it cautiously. Allies emerge.

There is little for his feeble talent to love, but much for his hidden powers to hate. He arms himself with these powers. And he is suddenly not lonely, or powerless. He has found a more satisfactory personality - one that can hold its head up - with intolerance.

"Keep moving," cries the ego, and this Little Casino, unable to move forward an inch as a man of wallflower virtue, stands in his tracks and looks about him. He sees everywhere people as lonely and immobilized as himself. And everywhere are organizations in which people can pool their littleness - and come out wearing secret badges and carrying fiery crosses.

And so our little Casino comes home another night with the pucker gone from his brow. He is no longer worried about books that are Greek to him, and a vast, impersonal world that looms like a closed gate over his head. He has come home from a meeting at which it was decided that the trouble with everything was the Jews. Speeches were made that proved the Jews to be an ominous and corrupting force. What they threaten, and how, and what and how they corrupt were matters avoided by the orators. Nobody noticed the omission. What all the Little Casinos at the meeting noticed was that a glow of purpose and comradeship filled their lonely spirits. A significance arose in them like a benediction. From being nobodies, with no understanding of the vast events around them, they emerged from the meeting as secret Knights pledged to the overthrow of a great dragon. They had passwords and a mission, and the night in which they walked was no longer full of mysteries painfully beyond them.

At this meeting all the Little Casinos pledged themselves to wage war, *sub rosa*, against Jews. Their first orders were to snub Jews and not admit them into the equality of their lives. Here was already a happy change for Little Casino. Instead of being an unwanted figure, he had become one who declared somebody else unwanted.

Now our hero whistles as he shaves to go to the movies. The world has improved for him - by the exact ratio with which, in his mind, he lessened it for his brother - the Jew. His virtues left him everybody's butt. His intolerance gives him a butt of his own to play with - the Jew.

A glint comes into his eye. Courage enters his heart. He is part of a new America, an America that knows what it wants - to snub Jews.

And Little Casino, with a sneer for thirteen million Jews uplifting his spirit, walks happily to the neighborhood theater. Passing Mr. Levine's grocery store, he says to his wife. "I don't want you to do any more buying here." "Why?" she asks. "Never mind," says he. "I heard certain things at a meeting the other night." "What meeting?" she asks. "I can't go into that, for certain reasons," he says. "Just take it from me. No trading with Levine." "You mean he's no good?" says his wife. "I mean," he answers, delphically, "that he's a Jew."

And his wife looks at him with wondering eyes. He is a man of unexpected depth.

I am more impressed by Little Casino than by the Goon. He is more American, and he has many high born relatives. The vaster and more complex our land becomes, the larger grows the loneliness that is his breeding ground.

The factories have already become too large for him to feel himself a workman in them. He is demoted from artisan to cog.

The huge stores have taken away from him his sense of kinship with merchandise. He does not shop for needs as much as drift through a movie set looking at other people's wonders. His government is too intricate for his understanding. The Heaven offered him in the churches has lost its fairy tale simplicities. The interpretations of the Bible have become as difficult to follow as lectures on Kant and Hegel. There will soon be nowhere for his say, and nothing open for his personal, human imprint. When this time comes, Little Casino will erupt with secret badges and underworld passwords.

He is already the most numerous of the anti-Semites. He will become the most powerful. He will break no heads and order no pogroms. But he will make laws, or try to make them. He can, if the buildings grow too tall and the winds become too faraway, alter America without a street fight.

POLITICAL PORTRAIT III: THE LOON

Long before there were Goons and Little Casinos, this grimacer, fly-catcher and jockey of phantoms sat ogling the world. He is the ancient one who laid nets for leprechauns and fancied griffons were chasing him up chimneys. Lunatic is his name, but his callings are varied. Among them anti-Semitism has been always a prominent one.

The lunatic's place on the Jew hating front is one of importance. For he is the sick brother of talent. He can write, sing, hurl rodomontades and wag a silver tongue. He becomes often the "brain" behind the Kill-All-The-Jews cause; and he is invariably its troubadour.

That he is mad (medically mad) is as obvious as if he signed his pamphlets "Schizophrenia" or "Dementia Praecox." There is hardly one of these troubadours of hate whose work does not qualify him at a glance for the booby hatch. His symptoms are more prominent in his screeds than his Jews. Yet he thrives unchallenged and is rarely called for by the ambulance.

This is due to the fact that the detection of lunatics has presented difficulties in all the eras of history. The eras themselves were so full of mania that it is almost like straining a point to pronounce any of their spokesmen as suffering from a special incoherence. Our own day offers as subtle a problem. It is so full of half-mad philosophies that it is nearly impossible to identify lunatics by their speech. People who seem to be raving like the veriest Ophelias turn out to be uttering only widespread social ideas. It takes rather a far gone lunatic to give tongue to fantasies that are not to be found on the political slates of one party or another. If he only keeps from going to work in baby clothes or bringing his soap bubble pipe to Congress or pushing people off bridges, he has an excellent chance of escaping detection. And even if he commit these and similar suspicious acts, he may find himself, as often as not, on the shoulders of admirers rather than behind the bars of a booby hatch.

Along with his accomplishments as a troubadour, the lunatic who enters public life has another quality that causes him to stand out for admiration. Unlike the Goon and Little Casino, he is not a transparent creature. There is a mood about him that provokes wonder. His words are sidelong and pregnant, his arguments full of silent spaces. He is not one ready to babble everything on his mind. Thus among the babblers, he stands out as a man full of mystery. His admirers are ready to vote him a character - full of deep secrets.

This is true. Our troubadour actually knows things nobody else knows - that there are little green men three inches tall chasing him; that the Communists are building a tunnel under the Pacific Ocean from Vladivostok directly to his house for the purpose of capturing him; that his own mother and father are plotting to hang him for wetting his bed as a child. If he can edit these and kindred convictions into fears less absurd, he can achieve much distinction as a Knight against the forces of Judaism; and does. For he is a creature fully equipped with authentic terrors. These enable him to see deeper into the "menace" of the Jew than people not as endangered as himself. And when you read of "a new and horrible plot by the Jews to undermine the American Republic," you can be sure that our literary knight has been busy again - with a few *errata.* For "Jews," read "little green men three inches tall." For "American Republic," read "Joseph McGillicuddy, recently under observation at Bellevue for sulking seven days in a manhole."

Until our time, this singer of boogiemen has been a creature too involved for labeling. As troubadour he was (as he still is) of great help to all Causes that must avoid logic in their sales campaigns. Become out of hand, he was called merely lunatic when caught, and small attention was given to his wheres and whyfors once he had been chained securely to the floor.

Our own age is kinder to the lunatic, if to no one else, and has turned some of its best scientific thought upon him - with many interesting results. The Freudians, in particular, have done much to clarify what once seemed only a Devil's howl in the world. They have revealed that the virulent Jew hatred of our pamphlet writers (as of many of their panting readers) is based on a variety of factors.

Sexual impotence, for example, can set a man to dreaming of killing Jews, as can homosexuality. In the first case he finds in murder the proof of virility denied him in amour. In the second case he dreams of stabbing Jews because a knife looks (to him) like a phallus. He is also revealed as a creature stunned by early constipation, which may sound a comical explanation of lunacy but is nonetheless a true and wise one. For the Freudians have demonstrated that our infantile resistances are signs of our aversions. Having made ourselves bilious and liverish by the withholding of our functions, we mature amid poisons. Grown, we find it convenient to transfer our hatred of parents to Jews.

There is also the discovery that the fanatic who bashes Jews on the head is actually trying to kill his own father (for having loved his mother and thus kept her from his embraces). It is to the Freudians, also, that we owe the discovery that the creature who venerates Dictators is often sublimating a desire to bed with his own father. He substitutes the worship of Authority for his homosexual father love, and in obeying supinely the edicts of a Dictator finds a shadowy version of the pleasures for which he actually longs.

These are a few of the motives that set our furtive Knight to strafing Jews; from which it can be seen that his anti-Semitism is, in reality, a sort of cure for his lunacy. At least it is better (for him) than marrying his mother, seducing his father, or slaying both.

Our new science is also at work on other, less troublesome, cures. It is, indeed, possible that the psychoanalysts might remove anti-Semitism from the world altogether, if there were enough of these fascinating doctors to go around - say one to every anti-Semite. And who knows but that the time may come when half the world will be lying on couches reciting its dreams and early pot-troubles to the other half, sitting wisely and attentively in the analyst's chair.

But until this millennium arrives, we must continue to cope with Schizophrenia in its printing press cellars.

The Loon, adding his dark lyric to the cause of anti-Semitism, is a creature whose importance (as of most poets) is dependent entirely on the numbers of his readers - and their readiness for his message. When the Goons and Little Casinos multiply, the Loon grows in stature. His standing in our time is already phenomenal. Given a larger stage, his song may rise, his greatness enter history.

POLITICAL PORTRAIT IV: NAPOLEONS IN SHADOW

Goon, Loon, and Little Casino make the anti-Semitic underworld of the USA. Around them hover the many fellow-travelers of anti-Semitism - a nimbus of sly killers, bird-brained dowagers, crippled libidos and cockeyed professors. Lump them all together, and they look like a practical joke. But joke they are not. For in addition to their boobishness and their psychoses, the anti-Semites possess another quality that raises them out of their clown category. They have numbers; and where there are numbers there are politicians.

There is no cause so low, no slogan so vile but it will find leaders to champion it. And not necessarily leaders without brains, not necessarily leaders as oafish as the rag-tag they command. For in our

Democracy there are men of talent and wit ready to pretend unreason if it will get them anywhere. There are always egoists ready to shelve their honor and sanity for the sake of shining with any sort of leadership.

These beggars of politics who go pawing the city dumps in quest of riches are all of a piece, and as obvious as a paper hat. They are the raucous egos who lack the patience or talent to angle among the sane for their admirers. They come haunting the sand-box of the aberrated. Some of them, to be sure, are as goony and loony as their followers, and are not to be distinguished by sound or look from the ninnies and invalids who caper in their ranks. But many more of them are cynical rogues who devote themselves deliberately to the traffic in human passions. They set themselves shrewdly to aggravating the prejudice around them for no other reason than that it is easier to lead people who have lost their heads than those who have kept them.

Only a single motive animates these sub-politicians. They are (in our land as yet) too frowzy a tribe to dream of victory, or to offer themselves to the full light of day. They yearn for acclaim. That the acclaim rises in basements, hideaways, bar-rooms and on secret stages, does not lessen it for their fame-hungry ears. For they are heroes too crude and avid to boggle at the foulness of their admirers. They are like half demented actors to whom all applause is meritorious; and, like actors, they have only one criterion for an audience - its existence.

There is no arguing with these unscrupulous day-dreamers, nor enlightening them. If killing Jews (or grand-mothers) is the road to power, they will take it and be proud of their progress. They do not care that their activities are capable of changing a fair country into a foul land. The land will not be foul to them if they sit high in it. And these begrimed and conscienceless egoists already sit in many of the high places of our country. They are in our Congress, in our Bureaus and behind editorial desks. They are forming Parties, bombinating over air waves and sending out loony literature. True, numbers of them have been sent to jail. But even these are happy in their careers. It is no come-down for an anti-Semitic leader to turn jail bird. Their followers do not even notice it.

Men of probity who listen to the prattle of these leaders are more inclined to chuckle than protest. For they are - these shadowy bidders for greatness - such obvious hag born charlatans, that it seems folly to denounce them. Their platform of anti-Semitism is compounded of such blistering noises that rebuttal smacks of childishness. And they make hay during the period of our indifference.

In our Republic, the hooligan parades of anti-Semites have not yet come down our Main Streets. They shuttle back and forth in their alleys and half alleys. Whether they will remain there, and whether the greatness of our gutter Napoleons will remain a matter celebrated only by Goons, Loons and Little Casinos, is one of the questions our dismal tomorrow will answer.

DIALOGUE BETWEEN THE AUTHOR AND HIS CONSCIENCE

We (my Conscience, and I, the author) sit together in my room and watch the winter come. The wind outside is sharp, the trees are tattered and there is evening in the morning sky.

I turn from the window to a log fire burning and sigh for a difficult task behind me. I am all for calling it a day. But Conscience - the little Demon that sits ever on a man's shoulder - speaks to me.

CONSCIENCE: Do you really think you are through with this book?

AUTHOR: Yes. An author can say only so much. If he says more he adds nothing but his ambition to his project.

CONSCIENCE: But there is so much more to be said.

AUTHOR: If I have any disciples, they will say it.

CONSCIENCE: Do you not intend to go over what you have written, however, and correct its inconsistencies?

AUTHOR: No. That would be an underhanded thing to do.

CONSCIENCE: What if readers lose faith in your ideas because they find contradictions?

AUTHOR: The Bible is a mass of contradictions. Spinoza points out a hundred major ones. I have noted as many more in it. Yet the Scriptures have survived for thirty centuries.

CONSCIENCE: They might last longer without the inconsistencies.

AUTHOR: I shall be delighted to be read only as far the year 4,944.

CONSCIENCE: It is a pity. All that research in Biblical history - unused! And that scholarly essay on the innocence of the Jews in the death of Christ - unwritten!

AUTHOR: Sensible omissions, particularly regarding Christ. I have decided that this is not a matter for scholarship, but accusation. Who dares raise such a question today? What kind of theologians are these who, instead of concerning themselves with the punishment of hordes of living Germans for murdering millions of Jews, are still concerned with punishing the sixtieth generation of Jews for the torture and death of one man whom the Jews neither tortured nor killed?

We are silent, and I am hopeful that the voice is done. But as I arrange my manuscript for transport, the Little Demon speaks again.

CONSCIENCE: Well, what about Palestine and the efforts of the Jews to build for themselves a nation in that land?

AUTHOR: They are admirable efforts, and the solution of the European Jewish problem may well lie in their success.

CONSCIENCE: If that is what you think, your silence on the subject will seem curious.

AUTHOR: The Palestinian situation is basically a problem between Jew and Jew. I have avoided it because I am of two minds about it. I would be glad to see a nation of Jews under a Jewish flag, and I am sure that such a nation would perform valorously and importantly on the world stage. Yet I have no impulse to contribute anything of myself to its existence. And if it did come into being, however attractive that being was, I would look on it with foreign eyes. I could no more feel myself part of it than of any other country beyond the USA. I wish for its existence, and recognize the great values it would have for all the Jews of the world. But when I contemplate a Jewish state I become something I have never been before - an exile. It is, perhaps, better that such as I be exiles from Palestine than that millions of Jews remains exiled from life. My silence is not an argument against a Palestinian homeland but an honesty toward the dreams of others.

CONSCIENCE: (moodily) I wonder if that is all true.

AUTHOR: Whatever is true, there is one solid fact. In the face of Britain's political aims, Palestine does not need abstracted champions like myself. It needs heroes with the smell of its soil in their noses; heroes with the word Jew stamped in their souls, and not hanging on them like a tag. I am pleased to know that Palestine is already teeming with such George Washingtons and Patrick Henrys.

CONSCIENCE: But you have reservations.

AUTHOR: A few historical doubts. The Jews have been always wretched politicians and ridiculous diplomats. They are too active minded for agreement on anything and too untrained in social chicanery. They began (with Moses) by arguing nose to nose with God when He was actually in their midst. The Jews lost Jerusalem to the Romans, after a magnificent resistance, by stopping to argue whether it was correct to fight on the Sabbath. Getting wind of this controversy, which had tied up all the captains and priests and half the soldiery, the Romans attacked and breached the undefended walls. This partiality for debate is still one of the high charms of the Jew. I feel certain that if he established his new Kingdom amid the orange groves of Palestine, a new and mighty Jewish Prophet would arise to decry again the vanities of state and the sins of glory. These are my reservations. They are entirely naive.

CONSCIENCE: Having glorified the mission of the Jews as anarchs, perhaps you are looking forward to this new Prophet of negation?

AUTHOR: He would fascinate me more than the new kingdom of David and Solomon.

I reach for the little cardboard box into which to put my book, but the creature on my shoulder halts me. It is not yet done, though I am doubly done.

CONSCIENCE: Would it not be wise to go over what you have written and temper some of it - remove a little of its shout here and there?

AUTHOR: No. It is unnecessary. There is nothing that subsides as quickly as a shout in print. If I seem a bit loud today, my voice will grow more modest tomorrow, without the altering of a comma. I have held always to the line that the wisest thing a writer can do is be himself and trust to God that the people he offends are those he doesn't like.

CONSCIENCE: (craftily) Then you have no regrets?

AUTHOR: Yes, I have regrets - but helpless ones. I regret having had to write about so much stupidity, cruelty and coarseness. In my next book I hope to use my talents for the examination of sun and air and the many delights of living. Nevertheless, my book has a charm for me, like that of a small battle won or, at least, fought without disquiet. I suspect that some criticism will rise on its appearance. But my heart will remain full of triumph. For my mission was to write of Jews with love and of their enemies with hatred. This I have done.

CONSCIENCE: If it should turn out, after your book is published, that it was unfinished - then you will, perhaps, write a sequel.

AUTHOR: Most certainly. I still have pencils left, and a fraction of youth - and a new day is coming.

CONSCIENCE: A better one?

AUTHOR: No. Merely a day with new problems.

CONSCIENCE: Will anti-Semitism be one of them?

AUTHOR: Yes. It will always be one of the new problems. And I shall write of it, perhaps, with more wisdom. For my mind in this book was sometimes darkened and disturbed by the massacre of the Jews. I could not always see clearly when I looked into the psychology of this massacre. I could see chiefly the mists of murder, like the emanations of a swamp, moving through the heads of the killers. There is, perhaps, more to see.

CONSCIENCE: You are perhaps apologizing for the Germans?

AUTHOR: For my inability to damn them with all the resources of my mind.

CONSCIENCE: Then this is farewell.

AUTHOR: Yes. Until tomorrow.

CONSCIENCE: If you are without hope, why this promise of tomorrow?

AUTHOR: Without hope! Have you also misunderstood my violence and pessimism? They are the finest kind of hope. They arm me against a thousand tomorrows. The future is an enemy, marching. But I go out to meet it - with a cutlass in my hand. Adieu!